The Culture of Experience

Philosophical Essays
in the American Grain

Simon Rodia's Towers in Watts, Los Angeles, California.

The Culture of Experience

Philosophical Essays in the American Grain

John J. McDermott
Texas A & M University

WAVELAND
PRESS, INC.
Prospect Heights, Illinois

1) Philosophy, Americanism
2) Experience
3) National Characteristics, American
4) United States — Civilization -- 20th century

We are grateful to the following publishers and journals for permission to utilize earlier versions of these essays, either in whole or in part.

Charles Scribners Sons for "To Be Human Is To Humanize—A Radically Empirical Aesthetic," 1968.

The University of Notre Dame Press for "The Community of Experience and Religious Metaphors," 1968.

Soundings for "Nature Nostalgia and the City: An American Dilemma" and "Space, Time and Touch: Philosophical Dimensions of Urban Consciousness," 1972, 1974.

Williams and Wilkins, Co., for "Feeling as Insight: The Affective Dimension of Social Diagnosis," 1973.

"Deprivation and Celebration: Suggestions for an Aesthetic Ecology" in *New Essays in Phenomenology*, ed., James M. Edie (Chicago, Quadrangle Books, 1969) Reprinted by permission of Quadrangle Books—New York Times, Copyright © 1969.

Illustrations by Alan Stacell; photograph by Seymour Rosen.

For information about this book, write or call:

Waveland Press, Inc.
P.O. Box 400
Prospect Heights, Illinois 60070
(312) 634-0081

Printed in the United States of America

For
DAVID McDERMOTT
1955–
Our Third Born
—Nature Without Nostalgia,
Affection Without Sentimentality

Real culture lives by sympathies and admirations,
Not by dislikes and disdains: under all misleading
Wrappings it pounces unerringly upon the human core.
—William James

Preface

The following essays constitute an effort to comment on contemporary culture from a philosophical vantage point, traceable in the main to the American philosophical tradition. Although this tradition is chary of ideology and bristles with internal dissent, we view it as having a tensile thread of continuity, ranging from John Winthrop, through the thought of Jonathan Edwards, Ralph Waldo Emerson, and on to its philosophical high point in the work of William James, Charles Peirce, Josiah Royce, John Dewey, and George Herbert Mead. While the language utilized in this tradition changes from a religious to a psychological to a philosophical ambience, the focus is consistent throughout, that the task of inquiry is to elucidate and ameliorate the fabric and import of *experience*. Taking experience to mean nothing less than what we do and what is done to us, as well as the "way" in which these transactions proceed, we note that only in the American philosophical tradition is this the *primary* concern. This tradition acts for us as an interpretive touchstone, and it is in such a spirit that the subtitle of this book, *Philosophical Essays in the American Grain* attempts not only to invoke the title of a collection of essays by William Carlos Williams but also to symbolize the reinvigoration of efforts to integrate the philosophical and literary versions of the originating characteristics of American experience.

Many of the problems under consideration in these essays have an immediacy to them, and all of them have the ring of twentieth-century culture. It is hoped that these themes and problems are not simply "transient excitations," to use a phrase of John Dewey. To the contrary, we believe that despite the immediacy of their themes, both experientially and in their formulation, the following essays reflect an attempt to address long-standing activities of human life, too often bypassed by contemporary philosophy. In methodological terms, an effort has been made in these essays to wed a diagnosis of actual situations to a philosophical language which most approximates the way in which we "have," that is, undergo our experiences. On behalf of this approach, I have tried to avoid professional jargon and in-house philosophical terms known only to initiates. Of course, the fact that these essays are philosophical in perspective and in evaluation, and the fact they draw heavily on philosophical sources, means that our language, at times, will involve the precision, the metaphors, and the technical detail common to philosophical inquiry. Stressed also will be the implicit philosophical significance of much of the non-philosophical literature cited.

Two further stylistic characteristics are relevant to a reading of these essays. First, I do not regard the world as inhabited or interpreted solely by the male species. I have attempted to demasculinize my prose in the most recent essays, that is, the fourth and fifth, and tried as well to retroactively change those essays written earlier, wherever stylistically feasible. Sheila Rowbotham writes of "Woman's Consciousness, Man's World," a depressing but accurate description of our language, if not our politics. In the absence of a totally adequate linguistic resolution of this sensitive and important problem, I affirm here that my references to the human condition refer always to male and female, women and men, boys and girls.

A second stylistic characteristic is also of importance. With the exception of occasional personal anecdotes or distinctively personal opinions, as for example, those which appear in this Preface, the working pronoun on these essays is "we." This decision results not from modesty, false or otherwise, but rather from the conviction that I write on behalf of the ongoing legacy of reflection and wisdom, lamentably too often bypassed because it is publicly unsung. If we live profoundly, we are taught by everyone, especially by children, by students, and by those without public intellectual portfolio. Who is to sort out my idea from yours? Is it not more genuine and fruitful to work on behalf of a community of inquiry, such that these essays take as their task the relating of otherwise disciplinarily isolated wisdom to our common needs? If, then, few of the ideas in this book are uniquely mine, nonetheless I take responsibility for the shaping, contrasts, emphases, and judgments which provide its personal quality.

An additional dimension of the following essays is that they are interdisciplinary in approach and scope. As a term, "inter-disciplinary" covers a host of interpretive and educational strategies, often having political implications. During the last decade, the interdisciplinary approach to inquiry and curriculum was *de rigeur*. In the present time, it has fallen prey to the American penchant for obsolescence. Despite a few years' sojourn as director of interdisciplinary studies for one thousand students, I was never very clear just what "interdisciplinary" meant for most users of that word. It often became a canopy for any educational innovation, however bizarre, unwieldy or diluted. Many advocates of the interdisciplinary approach seemed to hold that if representatives from different disciplines discussed a common topic, each within their own denotation of the problem, this was interdisciplinary education. Still others held that if several persons discussed their own interests, by discipline and within a common century or epoch, then this was interdisciplinary education. For the most part, these approaches and others similar were shallow and rescued only by an intrepid and broadly educated teacher. Actually, little interdisciplinary inquiry took place beyond the new and often flamboyant titles given to the courses and seminars in a standard college

catalogue. Similarly, interdisciplinary publications also prom-
ised more than they delivered. In our judgment, the core of interdisciplinary studies is not to
be found primarily from the side of the academic disciplines.
Rather, we need a shift in the designations of problems to be
analyzed. Granted, that the academic disciplines have their own
methodology, language, and history. On the other hand, they
have exercised too much influence on the nature of the topics of
inquiry, such that we very often have under consideration
problems created by the parameters and language of the
discipline in contrast to those generated by our own personal
and collective experience. We find this to be true even of the
more creative and important recent curricula additions, such as
black studies, urban studies, women's studies, and programs
devoted to ecology and film. What is of note here is that these
areas of inquiry, clearly interdisciplinary and long overdue, are
soon treated as traditional disciplines with the attendant organi-
zational, political, and theoretical aspirations. Correspondingly,
their experiential roots and distinctive patterns of articulation
often become lost.

Relative to the distinctive intentions of the present volume,
philosophers should certainly maintain the methods, purviews,
and requisite language of their discipline, but they should not
confine themselves to problems already structured and labeled
as philosophical problems. The human condition is itself
problematic, and philosophical wisdom, no matter its technical
origin, is relevant and welcome. Furthermore, for philosophers
who choose to go this route of an interdisciplinary approach,
there is a proviso, namely, that they steep themselves in the
extant versions of the problems in question, so as not to proceed
from on high, thereby falling prey to an all-too-frequent and
noxious by-product of philosophical writing.

In addition to their proceeding from the generalized interpretive backdrop of the American philosophical tradition and their
attempt to abide by a genuinely interdisciplinary approach, the
essays in this volume have one further strand in common.
Throughout, these essays observe an underlying assumption that

the development of "aesthetic sensibility" is a primary concern of our time and is as central to our ameliorative efforts as are the more commonly accepted political, sociological, economic, and psychological diagnoses and strategies. Referentially, aesthetic sensibility does not denote exclusive or even necessary relationship to the world of art. In this, we follow the lead of John Dewey, for whom all experiencing is potentially aesthetic. In our terms, aesthetic sensibility refers to how we and others *feel our situation* and *feel about our situation.* We contend that much is to be learned by the evaluation of our experiences in terms of the inchoate, the anaesthetic, the aesthetic, and the consummatory, each a Deweyan perspective. This commitment to the importance of aesthetic sensibility contexts our versions of such themes as deprivation, celebration, alienation, repression, nature nostalgia, nature space, nature time, urban space, urban time, and technological artifact. Further, it is our belief that the development of aesthetic sensibility should become central to all of our evaluations and judgments, especially those which pertain to our adopted strategies for social and political change. In effect, this assertion points in the direction of a new cultural pedagogy, that is, a new common source for our personal expectations, sensibilities, and evaluations. The following essays are probes in that direction, with cities, schools, the arts, and community acting in turn as the fulcrum for our inquiry.

I trust that the reader of these essays will not make too much of the en route opinions and judgments of the author, although opinions and judgments of author and reader are inevitable. No, my intention in publishing these collected essays is wider and yet more modest than bringing personal commentary to public view. William James once wrote: "It is, the reader will see, the reinstatement of the vague and inarticulate to its proper place in our mental life which I am so anxious to press on the attention." In my terms, I wish to press upon the reader the hidden complexity of what are seemingly obvious conditions and environs of human life. I wish especially to convey that this complexity is most often traceable to our affective responses to situations, responses which too often are missed or underplayed

in many cultural analyses. Finally, whatever be the relative
merit of these essays, it is not incidental to my intention that
they be read as trying to illustrate anew the significance of
speculative philosophy, even when brought to bear upon the
commonplace. Or perhaps I should say it differently, namely,
that it is precisely philosophical speculation which best reveals
the radical implicitness and potentiality of the commonplace. In
his essay on "The American Scholar," does not Emerson have it
right?

So there is no fact, no event, in our private history, which
shall not sooner or later, lose its adhesive, inert form and
astonish us by soaring from our body into the empyrean.

Then again, you may prefer a more recent voice, that of Alan
Wheelis, from his gentle and provocative book, *On Not Knowing
How to Live.*

The objective mode is not for me, the detached voice rings
false. I must work from the formlessness of my own life,
speak in my own voice, however faltering and unsure. What
I seek is not to be found in my past, is not to be found at all
but achieved, but must be achieved, if at all, from the
debris and clutter of a flawed and limping life. I admonish
myself: Give up this longing for a past of brave adventure
from which to work. Heroic experience is hearsay, is not
your own. Don't just stand there in lamentation before the
junk-heap of memory, the fears and evasions, the missed
opportunities, the cautious advances. Wade in. Pick up the
pieces. Don't expect to *find* anything of value. This is ore,
not metal. Expect only to come upon something—slingshot,
love letter, rusted foil, ancient condom, broken knight from
a chess set—from which with effort and courage something
of beauty might be made.

Yes, the world is not so much found as it is made, *Homo faber.*
Philosophy has been too preoccupied with the eyes, with vision.

Return the hands to philosophy; to touch is to be touched. Extraordinary simply means "out of the ordinary." And so it is, for we can make a world out of the ordinary. Do not await salvation while the parade passes by. Surprise and mystery lurk in our experiencing the obvious, the ordinary. Salvation may be illusory, but salving experiences can occur day by day.

JOHN J. McDERMOTT

Preface
(1987)

William James wrote that "experience grows by its edges." I find myself under obligation to scour these essays, originally published more than a decade ago, so as to see if they have lost their "edge." Certainly some erosion has taken place as is inevitable in a culture as mercurial as ours and one that instantiates obsolescence far more than it reveres the past. To be sure, the thought of Herbert Marcuse and Norman O. Brown is no longer at stage center, nor is painting and sculpture any longer the primary focus for symbolic articulation of our human situation.

Yet, in the main, by far, the concerns of these essays are still viable and in need of constant reflection and reiteration. American culture is still enormously complex, featuring a powerful dialectic between mission and energy on the one hand and alienation and anomie on the other hand. The spectre of AIDS, the periodic flashing of teenage suicides, the startling increase in substance abuse, our inability to purge our inner cities of poverty and violence, the extraordinary secondary school drop-out rate, which has now penetrated children of the middle class, and our continued ineptness with regard to fashioning an equitable economic and social national community, all point to the need for a continuing philosophical diagnosis of our culture. Nonetheless, the up-beat thrust of these essays is still relevant. Emersonian in outlook, I take seriously the belief that, as a people, we Americans have not lost our faith in the doctrine of possibility. Historically, the purpose of the jeremiad in America was not merely to "bemoan our outcast fate" on behalf of collective guilt. The twin prong of the jeremiad was to evoke a resolve for efforts at amelioration, stated cyptically but powerfully in the oft-repeated phrase of Robert Kennedy in the year before his lamented assassination, "We can do better!"

If one or two of these essays now has more of an historical character than a contemporary bite, most of the others are even more germane and on the mark than when they were written. This is true of those essays which confront one of the most serious problems of our time, the inability to ameliorate the social pathology that afflicts our urban proletariat. Of even more direct anticipation is the essay "Feeling as Insight: The Affective Dimension in Social Diagnosis." Written twenty years ago, this essay probes the irreducible necessity of understanding the affective life in any and all therapeutic transactions, a position which is now a central theme in the public conflict raging in the field of medicine as to the proper balance between the utilization of high technology and awareness of the subtleties of patient care, especially as experienced from the side of the "victim."

I believe it to be salutary that the essay as literary genre is once again thriving and receiving critical favor and respect, for, in my judgment, a series of stochastic probes is often more effective as a way to jolt the reflective imagination of the reader, which is a primary task of the writer, particularly those of us with philosophical intent. Consequently, it is my hope that this republication of *The Culture of Experience: Philosophical Essays in the American Grain* will reach a new audience, a new generation as promulgated under the generous publishing aegis of Waveland Press.

Foreword

In response to the perennial charge that Americans disparage thought and do not appreciate ideas "for their own sake," Dewey once pointed out that, on the contrary, thought is so highly prized in America that it is accorded the honor of being put to work. And, of course, by work Dewey meant actual thinking and the central role played by ideas in the articulation, the elucidation and the appraisal of human experience. McDermott's essays fit nicely into this pattern. They are not to be seen as a commentary about American philosophy, but rather as a living exhibition of philosophical ideas at work in the actual task of expressing and understanding the cultural fabric of American life. Therefore McDermott's interpretations must not be fitted into some simple scheme about the American mind of the sort represented by those who believe that the story of American philosophy can be told in terms of a struggle between "science and sentiment." Simplistic alternatives of this sort not only misunderstand the substance of the American philosophical tradition but also cast suspicion on the perceptiveness, not of philosophers, but of the "intellectual historians" who resort to this sort of interpretation. By contrast, McDermott is on a different track. He is making clear, to be sure in his own idiom, what we can learn from America's original thinkers in their open-minded approach to philosophical ideas, an approach which was quite free from the need to pay lip-service to any professional philosophical establishment.

McDermott's aim is to focus attention on long standing activities of human life often ignored by philosophers and to interpret these activities in the light of basic ideas derivative from the writings of James, Peirce, Royce, Dewey and others. In a perceptive, imaginative and, at times, prophetic way, McDermott leads us to grasp the fundamental importance of the American conception of experience developed in its breadth and fullness for beginning a new world and not merely for transplanting the culture of an old one. He wants us to appreciate the creative features of American culture, the interweaving of reflection and action, the valuation of time and ideals in the transformation of reality, and, above all, the importance of keeping all of our thinking in contact with the entire culture, not only its problems but its aspirations as well.

Although he draws heavily on the ideas of Dewey, especially in his concern for developing an esthetic sensibility—*feeling* and *feeling about* our situation—one suspects that it is really James who is McDermott's philosopher. James emphasized the vague, the fringe, the penumbra of primary experience and he was concerned that these features not be left out of account by excessive conceptualization. He insisted on the "maybe's" or the possibilities in existence and stressed freedom, energy and the power of belief for resolving human problems and improving the state of society. These concerns have a strong attraction for McDermott in his own attempts to rejuvenate the esthetic dimension of life through the celebration of the things of ordinary experience, to explore the possibility of a renewed faith in human community, and to overcome an incipient cynicism through a new attitude of amelioration in the face of recent self-criticism and present misadventures.

If one were to ask whether there is for McDermott any one idea which stands out as a central and unifying force in these essays, the answer is yes—the idea of radical empiricism or the primacy of connections, relations, growth and development. The reader cannot fail to be impressed by McDermott's underlining of the resources in James' conception for dealing with such problems as alienation and repression, and especially James' anticipation of the need to recover the centrality of the body for man's experience long before the claims of Brown and Marcuse. James was fond of saying that life is found in the transitions and the novelties; McDermott follows in his tracks and looks for a renewal of culture in an integration of experience made possible only when men are sensitive to the *connections* between experiences, facts and activities—jazz, urban consciousness, painting, the environment, poverty, alienation and human frailty—and cease to view them as so many separate subject matters for academic study.

The importance attached to the thought and spirit of James must not be allowed to overshadow the signal use which McDermott makes of Dewey's *Art as Experience*. He finds there ideas essential for understanding present dilemmas in culture and for reconstructing affective values which grow out of actual experience and are in no need of imposition from without. McDermott has some perceptive things to say about the city and the meaning of urban consciousness. His claim is that modern, urban man has been "seduced" by nature in that he lives by metaphors, expectancies and nostalgia about nature which are rooted in an exaggerated estimate of its importance for his forbears. We have not succeeded in "mythologizing" the city and its virtues as we have the rural scene, so that the urban dweller is less at home in his surroundings than he should be. McDermott is troubled lest a misguided affection for nature lead to failure to celebrate the experiences and values at the center of urban life.

The striking fact about these essays is that they stand as a pungent illustration of Dewey's point about the recovery of philosophy: philosophy is recovered when philosophers do not confine themselves solely to the problems of philosophers, but reach out instead to direct philosophical analysis and insight to the problems of men. At a time of some disorientation and not a little insecurity in the American consciousness, it is of considerable moment that McDermott has chosen to focus attention on

the cultural situation as of primary importance among these
problems. His candor and muscular style are bound to be
provocative and to help stimulate that exchange of ideas which
has always been a hallmark of philosophical thinking in
America.

John E. Smith
Clark Professor of Philosophy
Yale University

Acknowledgments

Versions of these essays have been offered as public lectures at many universities and conferences. Countless people from those occasions have given suggestions, criticisms, and support, for all of which I am grateful. Although they may find much disagreement with the entire book, I was encouraged by a positive response to one or more of these essays by Harvey Cox, Robert Pollock, John Cage, Gerard Deledalle, Roland Delattre, and Philip Rieff. I appreciate earlier editorial support of my work by Sallie Te Selle, Roger Bulger, James Edie and Joseph Cunneen.

I have been helped by the affectionate concern shown for this project by Peter T. Manicas, Patrick Hill, Robert Walsh, Edmund Leites, David Sprintzen, Arthur Lothstein, Alan Rosenberg, Robert Atwan, and Marise McDermott. An early and helpful reading of the manuscript by Milton Munitz facilitated its acceptance. I am especially thankful to my new friends, C. Lee Miller and Donald A. McQuade, for their perceptive editorial suggestions throughout the preparation of this book. My brother, Robert A. McDermott, was of decisive assistance in the early stages of the manuscript, and he remains my most understanding reader and critic.

Of the almost twenty-five years I have been teaching, more than twenty years have been concentrated at Queens College of the City University of New York. During that time, I have taught a course each semester entitled "Culture and the Aesthetic Experience," Philosophy 10. In this book of essays, there is much I have learned from the more than three thousand students, most of them extraordinary persons, who have taken that course. I thank them.

I am especially grateful to John E. Smith, Clark Professor at Yale University for writing a perceptive and generous foreword to these essays.

Virginia P. McDermott compiled the index and prepared the final copy of the manuscript, providing as always a rare blend of technical skill, firm criticism and personal encouragement. More to the point, if in my own life I am ever able to move from the rhetoric of aesthetic sensibility to the experience of genuine affection, it has been her doing.

In the preparation of this reissue, I am grateful to my Research Assistant, Patricia Bond. Proofreading of the original edition was performed by Lori Berger and James Campbell. The illustrations are the work of my colleague at Texas A&M University, the artist Alan Stacell, to whom I offer my appreciation.

Colleagues too numerous to mention have sustained interest in these essays and been encouraging in the preparation of this second edition. In this regard Donald McQuade has been especially gracious and helpful. I am also indebted to four decades of student participation in my work, especially, those from Queens College, C.U.N.Y., S.U.N.Y. at Stony Brook and Texas A&M University. My arrangements with Waveland Press trace to the collegial thoughtfulness of Konnie Kolenda. Finally, I am deeply appreciative of the willingness of Mr. Thomas Curtin of Waveland Press to rescue this book from the fate of comparative oblivion. In the context of the market economy syndrome in contemporary American publishing, few editors are so bold to make decisions on the "edge."

John J. McDermott
College Station, Texas

Contents

Contents

INTRODUCTION

An American Notion of Experience

I

... new Philosophy calls all in doubt,
The Element of fire is quite put out;
The Sun is lost, and the earth, and no man's wit
Can well direct him where to look for it.
And freely men confess that this world's spent,
When in the Planets, and the Firmament
They seek so many new; then see that this
Is crumbled out again to his Atomies.
'Til all in pieces, all coherence gone;
All just supply, and all Relation:
Prince, Subject, Father, Son, are things forgot,
For every man alone thinks he hath got
To be a Phenix, and that then can be
None of that kind, of which he is, but he.

—John Donne [1]

The European sixteenth century witnessed a series of major cultural revolutions: the Protestant Reformation, the beginning of Copernicanism, and the utilization of Gutenberg's movable type. For purpose of this essay, still another breakthrough is even more important. In 1507, there accompanied the publication of the *Cosmographiae Introductio* an engraved world map, known as the Waldseemüller map. It made clear that a "fourth" part had been added to Europe, Asia, and Africa as constitutive of the "Island of the Earth." This event signaled the acceptance into European consciousness of a *mundus novus,* and whatever the controversy surrounding the name of this New World, it has been ever since known as America.[2] A full-dress analysis of the origins of American culture [3] would have to confront the significance of the sixteenth-century religious, philosophical, and cultural revolutions, which constituted the inherited consciousness of the American settlers. In this Introduction, we focus simply on the main lines of one crucial outcome of the development of American culture, a distinctive notion of experience.

As an historical backdrop we are given the fact that an articulate and enlightened seventeenth-century generation submitted itself to the rigors of a totally unfamiliar and often hostile environment. In his address to the Philosophical Union of California in 1911, Santayana tells us that:

> As much as in clearing the land and fighting the Indians they were occupied, as they expressed it, in wrestling with the Lord. The country was new, but the race was tired, chastened, and full of solemn memories. It was an old wine in new bottles; and America did not have to wait for its present universities, with their departments of academic philosophy, in order to possess a living philosophy—to have a distinct vision of the universe and definite convictions about human destiny.[4]

The ramifications of this "reflective primitivism," so characteristic of the American seventeenth century, and a factor in the continuing frontier experience, are considerable, for they intensify the effort to force nature to do the bidding of human concern, pose a radically different view of ideation, and point to the introduction of the experimental temper as central to human inquiry, rather than as simply an aid to the codification of a real world. One could say further that the affection for experiential context as the determinant for doctrine yields in the long run an explicit acknowledgment of the primacy of time as the source of intelligibility. Over against the doctrine of obsolescence in which the history of man waits patiently for a paradisiacal *deus ex machina,* the American temper points to a temporalized eschatology in which meaning manifests itself generation by generation and all counts to the end.

It is true that in the American seventeenth century, philosophy was all but nonexistent. Yet, reflection was intense and self-conscious, primarily as a response to a pressing and omnipresent collective experience of a situation that was novel at every turn. And although that period in American history offered no articulation of the notion of experience as such, there was a correspondingly rich awareness of the significance of this situation over against inherited "wisdom." It was a period that dealt with philosophical themes without recourse to a formal philosophical language. In effect, the American seventeenth century realized a broadly based cultural "experience of experience." The most obvious and persistent import of this dialectic between the reflective tradition, as carried by the settlers, and the New World was the dominance of the "experience" over any conceptual anticipation of "how things should be." The original situation had a clarity to it.

> For summer being done, all things stand upon them with a wetherbeaten face; and the whole countrie, full of woods & thickets, represented a wild & savage heiw. If they looked behind them, ther was the mighty ocean which they had passed, and was now as a maine barr & goulfe to separate them from all the civill parts of the world.[5]

Theory broke down here, and "what one *could* build on this continent tended to become the criterion of what one ought to build here." [6] A factor in this development may very well have been the inability of colonial Americans to initially duplicate the English version of cultural proprieties. Thus "the American, 'this new man,' was early conceived in relation to civilized Europe, if not to the savage frontier, as a primitive." [7] The cultural rejection by Europe fostered a sense of inferiority, but at the same time encouraged the colonial man to justify the richness of his own situation, making him open to new resources and ultimately to a different way of evaluating his needs and hopes. In this vein, Charles Sanford states:

> The chosen people of the American colonies increasingly looked upon their mission into the wilderness not merely as the continuation of something old, but as the beginning of something new: they were to usher in the final stage of history. They had inherited a new world in a physical sense, and in order "to vindicate the most rigorous ideal of the Reformation" they felt it necessary in Jonathan Edwards' words, "to begin a new world in a spiritual respect." [8]

The literature of early America—John Smith, the Puritans, and subsequent commentaries on the continuing waves of settlement of "free land"—attests to this re-formation and ultimately reformulation of basic value structures under the press of a new setting. The realization of this new setting was the dominant theme of the second-generation Puritans, of whom Perry Miller said: "Having failed to rivet the eyes of the world upon their city on a hill, they were left alone with America." [9] The stage was set for a long series of transactions between theoretical structures and a primitive but malleable environment.

What is crucial here, from the philosophical side, is that the press of environment as a decisive formulator of thought about the basic structures of the world became the outstanding characteristic of the American temperament. Nineteenth-century pragmatism, so often regarded as the typically American philosophical product, is but a pale reflection of an ingrained attitude affirming the supremacy of experience over thought. It should be emphasized that this sense of the ineptness of a priori and defining concepts for managing experience was not only paramount in the early colonial period but was characteristic of the growth of American culture until the end of the nineteenth century. This is true not only for those who lived at the behest of daily experience but also for those whose responsibility involved an articulation of general responses to the life-situation. The tension between beliefs held and experiences generated by incessantly novel circumstances, often of a physical kind, is a central theme in the thought of John Winthrop, Jonathan Edwards, Horace Bushnell, Emerson, Whitman, and, of course, James and Dewey, to say nothing of the major lines of political literature. For the most part, that tradition of American *thought*, which we now regard as seminal and even patriarchal, clearly sides with experience over reflection as the primary resource in formulating beliefs.

Contemporary America, however, often has grave philosophical doubts about the present viability of this tradition, seeing it as no longer adequate to the complex ideational demands that confront us on every level. There is certainly a legitimate aspect to this contention, particularly if the meaning of experience remains fixed in the romantic metaphors of an earlier American version, or in the narrow formulations of British empiricism. But a careful analysis of the history of the notion of experience in American thought would show previous instances where outworn and sterile terminology was successfully reconstituted.

In a very real sense, each generation is faced with using the method of experience to develop a language that is consonant with the events and potentialities of its own situation.[10] Such a transformation of the meaning of experience was accomplished by American philosophy at the end of the nineteenth century. Not only did this tradition, beginning with Chauncey Wright, effect a total reworking of the properly philosophical meaning of experience, but it also provided an extensive set of metaphors capable of being utilized in the reworking of social and political consciousness. Some of these, as for example Dewey's suggestions about education, have been worked into the fabric of

American life. Others, like James's views on the "Moral Equivalent of War" and Dewey's "Common Faith," have only now been put to the test of relevance. Still others, such as Royce's doctrine of community and James's insight into individual energies within a fully cosmic scheme, can still serve in the future reconstitution of experience along lines consistent with the still active assumptions of the culture.

The point at issue is that the reflective primitivism so deeply imbedded within the culture is primarily an attitude, which more than in any other version of Western culture forces theoretical statements to respond more to the language of events than to its own mode of discourse. What must not be forgotten is the primal fact that the American tradition of which we speak, due to its aversion to any separate mode of discourse, cannot be adequately confronted simply by an epistemological critique of its shortcomings. Historically considered, this tradition was faced with an ever shifting scene, characterized by widespread geographical, political, and spiritual upheavals. These crises were built into the very continuity of the culture, and it was thereby fitting that basic and even fundamental categories of understanding were transformed. Indeed, this transformation had its basis in the willingness of the culture, over a sustained period of time, to listen to the informing character of experience. This was a culture which knew what learning meant and, significantly, was heir to a great tradition of learning. Yet, it was also able to accept the press of experience without necessarily submitting such a transaction to the judgment of a conceptual framework. Although our openness to experience has been well documented in terms of the development of our political institutions, it has not been adequately understood as a broader doctrine of inquiry. Efforts in this latter direction have too often separated the concern for experience from the reflective attitude, thereby failing to realize that in the American context reflection is not necessarily the bearer of traditional intellectual values. What is still needed is an understanding of the tremendous effort within American culture to relocate the role of learning, and even to provide for a different method of generating basic principles—both seen as a function of the method of experience. It has been said that the originality and power which characterized the development of American culture was inseparable from the mobility resulting from its almost continental status and from the ever-present contiguous "free land." Since such a situation no longer holds true, perhaps it would be wise to abandon the attitudes developed in that situation and make a fresh start. We caution, however, that any attempt to redirect American culture has to confront several deeply rooted metaphysical beliefs which are not easily gainsaid by simple shifts in interpretive and diagnostic language. Two of these beliefs are analyzed in detail in subsequent essays in this volume. First, our understanding of nature, seen preeminently as living space and as subject to human fabrication. Second, our understanding of time, undergone as option, rather than as the measure of our entropic situation. Both perspectives, although grounded in early American experience, still claim powerful and direct relevance to the situation in which we now find ourselves.

If nature, and time, as historically undergone, constitute the basic framework through which the qualities of the American tradition developed, their *articulation* constitutes still another aspect of this problem. The full implications of the historical events in American life, worked out within the broad perspective of a reflective primitivism, are not realized until one binds such developments to their subsequent articulation, particularly by philosophy. This is especially true of our leading metaphor: experience. The development in American consciousness from the "experience of experience" to the "notion of experience," and finally with Dewey to the "method of experience," is of crucial importance from both the cultural and philosophical viewpoint. The question, of course, is whether the articulation of these deeply felt cultural traditions maintains the richness and immediacy of the original responses. Second, if such an articulation does keep fidelity with the tradition, can it also show relevance to the more specifically intellectual dimensions of its own mode of discourse? In a word, can American philosophy do philosophy and yet remain within the traditional cultural dispositions of the American cultural past? It would seem that while doing other things, American philosophy must do at least this much if we are to avoid a future characterized by spiritual narrowness or by intellectual irrelevance.

II

American philosophers, young and old, seem scratching where the wool is short.

—William James [11]

Philosophically, the notion of experience traces to Greek thought, especially Aristotle, and it was an important concern of Locke, Hume, and Kant. With William James and John Dewey, however, it takes on heightened significance. James had written of experience as a double-barreled word, figuring as both "thought" and "thing." [12] Dewey also took this position when he wrote:

> Like its congeners, life and history, experience includes what men do and suffer, what they strive for, love, believe and endure, and also how men act and are acted upon, the ways in which they do and suffer, desire and enjoy, see, believe, imagine—in short, processes of experiencing. . . . It is "double-barrelled" in that it recognizes in its primary integrity no division between act and material, subject and object, but contains them both in an unanalyzed totality. "Thing" and "thought," as James says in the same connection, are single-barrelled; they refer to products discriminated by reflection out of primary experience.[13]

The emphasis on primary experience leads James and Dewey to specific philosophical considerations, especially with regard to the importance of relations. As we have discussed these matters in subsequent essays in this volume, we focus here on the more generalized cultural significance of this emphasis on experience. Within the American context, a constant theme emerges, warning us against the intellectualizing of our situation to the extent that we cut ourselves off from the richer and unfettered immediacies of living. Yet, these warnings themselves often take on a highly speculative character and soon become shadows of the very intellectualism they oppose. A fascinating parallel to this problem of "thinking about experience" is found in the brief history of postwar existentialism. In the effort to elucidate the full burden of living in tension between *l'étranger* and *l'homme révolté,* philosophy, omnivorous to the end, blanketed the problem with a host of distinctions and clarifications, worthy of technical philosophy, but hardly of the thrust of the existentialist concern. So too with the method of experience: easy to claim as a touchstone but exceedingly difficult to abide by within the very fabric of inquiry.

It is, therefore, not unimportant that in a general way, the American tradition involves a crucial shift in the method for ascertaining the major focus of inquiry. Because of the preeminence of the experience of nature as open and as subject to reconstruction, the prime analogates for inquiry have centered on life metaphors. From the very outset, the notions of growth, experiment, liberty, and amelioration have characterized inquiry in American life. Not only does this hold for those endeavors traditionally directed to so-called practical concerns, but they equally constituted the very fiber of religious thought. Indeed, more revealing, such concerns are at the center of the American philosophical tradition when it finally emerges in the nineteenth century. With Emerson and again with Dewey, we have a philosophical approach which uses the language of ordinary experience. In a word, the *problematic* assumes the primary role, reserved elsewhere in philosophy for the ineffable, the Good, or the language of being. In such a world view, the most profound recesses of reflection are themselves burdened by the obligation to reconstruct experience so as to aid in the resolution of those difficulties seen to hinder growth. The passion for amelioration of the human plight, so carefully nurtured by the French *philosophes,* becomes almost a total cast of mind within the American tradition. Such a view is clearly put by Dewey when he states that "Philosophy recovers itself when it ceases to be a device for dealing with the problems of philosophers and becomes a method cultivated by philosophers, for dealing with the problems of men." [14] Or again, with James, who tells us that "Knowledge about life is one thing; effective occupation of a place in life, with its dynamic currents passing through your being, is another." [15] Thus, American classical philosophy comprises a highly original effort to maintain a genuinely metaphysical concern within the finite limits of time and nature. This endeavor is most obviously characterized by the refusal to separate the efforts of intellectual life, including those of philosophy, from the burden of confronting concrete problems. In the subsequent essays of the present volume, we have tried to be faithful to that mandate. Following James: "Ideals ought to aim at the *transformation of reality*—no less." [16]

This attempt at amelioration, which burdens the processes of thought, even those of so-called basic research, should not be seen as simply a pragmatic reductionism. Rather than honoring a simple dualism between thought and action, the American bent toward the practical should be viewed from a wider perspective. Both the method of reflection and the method of action are to be seen as conjoined and rotating functionaries of an experimental approach. Neither method is self-contained nor totally reliable but assumes priority relative to the nature of the problem to which it is directed. It is the problem and its resolution, or at least reconstruction on more enhancing terms, that occupies the place of importance in this approach to inquiry. The rotating priority of thought and action covers an important and infrequently analyzed assumption in American life: the contention that experience, as such, has informing, directive, and self-regulating qualities which are ordered and managed as subject to intelligence and as responsible to the burdens of the various contexts in which inquiry finds itself. Experience, as such, is educational. Thought and action are functionaries of the method of experience in a culture which gives to experience qualities and powers usually denied in the larger tradition of Western thought. It is this underlying assumption as to the seminal character of the method of experience for both theory and practice that has to be isolated and reworked in the light of contemporary problems and language. Failure to do this not only results in our falling back into a crippling dualism between practical and speculative activity, on cultural lines, but also, as Dewey warns, denies us the riches of immediate experience in favor of an ever more vacuous conceptual tradition:

> The serious matter is that philosophies have denied that common experience is capable of developing from within itself methods which will secure direction for itself and will create inherent standards of judgment and value. No one knows how many of the evils and deficiencies that are pointed to as reasons for flight from experience are themselves due to the disregard of experience shown by those peculiarly reflective. To waste of time and energy, to disillusionment with life that attends every deviation from concrete experience must be added the tragic failure to realize the value that intelligent search could reveal and mature among the things of ordinary experience.[17]

A brief commentary on this modern jeremiad by Dewey should put the question of the articulation of experience into some perspective. It is clear that Dewey, for one, accepts the assumption about the power of experience which is basic to American life. But he demands also an articulation of this assumption relative to the major problems faced by each generation and subject to the logical structures of the various methodological approaches as embodied in the disciplines of intellectual life.[18] And his major concerns were with the notions of nature, growth, and human transaction with institutional life, often phrased out in the vein sketched here as characteristic language of the American temperament. What Dewey laments is the separation of reflection from the method of experience. In a brilliant statement of the meaning of experience, "congenial to present conditions," Dewey contrasts his position of 1917, with the "orthodox" view. The latter, in general terms, sees experience as blunt and always in need of conceptual formulation before performing any significant cognitive function. Dewey, on the contrary, sees experience as richly informing on its own terms, shot through, as it were, with implicitness and meaning. He offers that in his view "experience in its vital form is experimental" and has as its "salient trait," "connection with a future." For Dewey, experience is not antithetical to thought; he holds that there exists "no conscious experience without inference; reflection is native and constant." [19]

The extraordinary priority given to the notion of experience in American philosophy is not due simply to the work of James and Dewey. Rather, their emphasis is consistent with a wider American cultural setting, especially as it was characterized by an experimental attitude and the absence of an aggressive allegiance to inherited formulations, a priori in origin. We cite some corroborative instances of this judgment. Dewey's colleague and friend, George Herbert Mead, writes in 1930, of this "setting" as follows: "I have indicated what seems to me the important characteristic of American life, the freedom, within certain rigid but wide boundaries, to work out immediate politics and business with no reverential sense of a preexisting social order within which they must take their place and whose values they must preserve." [20] In 1948, the American philosopher and intellectual historian, John Herman Randall, Jr., wrote that American philosophy "adds a new level to the long tradition of Western philosophical thought, because it brings the lessons learned from American experience to all the lessons men had learned before and left for us in the embodied wisdom of the past." [21] Again, in 1963, Randall comments that "American philosophy, come of age by the end of the nineteenth century, could draw on all the different European traditions. That has something to do with the fact that the giants of the last generation could bend them all to the illumination of American experience, in creating a distinctively new and American philosophical attitude and approach." [22] Perhaps the major thrust of this illumination is the place given experience itself. In a somewhat different vein, Paul Tillich, in speaking of the "pragmatic-experimental approach of American theology," can point to the "emphasis on religious experience in the movements of evangelical radicalism which have largely formed the American mind and have made of experience a central concept in all spheres of man's intellectual life." [23]

Although the history of the meaning of the notion of experience in American life has yet to be written, the American mood, even at the outset, more often than not anticipated the later contention of Emerson that "every ingenious and aspiring soul leaves the doctrine behind him in his own experience." [24] The question, of course, is whether this is simply a philosophical correlate to the attitude of ingrained condescension to speculative learning—an attitude so cogently expressed in the commentary on a failure in a colonial Massachusetts iron works, wherein "experience hath outstripped learning here, and the most quick-sighted in the theory of things have been forced to pay pretty roundly to Lady Experience for filling their heads with a little of her active afterwit." [25] Or is Emerson's text to be read rather as an affirmation of the informing richness of experience as such; indeed, of the cognitive thrust in all events, particularly those through which we locate ourselves as persons? Originally biblical in meaning, the experience of the New World viewed the "land" as but the site on which the New Jerusalem was to be founded. Given the press of events, however, the focus of expectation soon shifted, and located around the land itself. In one of his poems, Thoreau calls for a new future by pointing to possibilities hardly credible anywhere else in nineteenth-century Western civilization:

> All things invite this earth's inhabitants
> To rear their lives to an unheard of height
> And meet the expectations of the land.[26]

And closer to our time, Robert Frost, celebrating what he hoped

was a new beginning, significantly repeats the refrain of
Thoreau:

> To the land vaguely realizing westward,
> But still unstoried, artless, unenhanced,
> Such as she was, such as she would become.[27]

The energizing to meet and engage the "expectations of the
land" is but one version of the overreaching dominance of
situation over theory. The assumption that the "land," in time,
will speak to us was a harbinger of our still regnant assumption,
that experience formulates the task of inquiry. The sheerly
conceptual schema is distrusted; concepts serve at the behest of
percepts. Daniel Boorstin describes the significance of this
fundamental attitude in American culture.

> Through the eighteenth and nineteenth centuries—from
> Crevecoeur's notion that America had produced a new
> man, through Jefferson's belief in the wealth, promise, and
> magnificence of the continent, and Turner's faith in a
> frontier-born culture and frontier-nourished institutions—
> runs the refrain that American values spring from the
> circumstances of the New World, that these are the secret of
> the "American Way of Life." This refrain has been both an
> example of our special way of dealing with ideas and an
> encouragement to it. For lack of a better word, we may call
> this a leaning toward implicitness, a tendency to leave ideas
> embodied in experience and a belief that the truth some-
> how arises out of the experience.
> This carries with it a preference for the relevance of ideas
> as against their form and a surprising unconcern for the
> separability of ideas. We have seldom believed that the
> validity of an idea was tested by its capacity for being
> expressed in words. The beliefs that values come out of the
> context and that truth is part of the matrix of experience
> (and hardly separable from it) become themselves part of

the way of American thinking—hence, the formlessness of American thought, its lack of treatises, schools and systems.[28]

At times contemporary reflective thought in America seems to identify itself by locating around a response to what is considered the traditional hostility to the intellectual.[29] Such a response only confronts a by-product of what is actually a long-standing and general cultural effort to rework the nature of thought in terms of its functional role within the total human endeavor. From the Puritans to Dewey, one is offered a series of efforts, alternating in stresses and varying in success, to account for man's most profound difficulties and concerns within the context of ordinary experience. In that tradition, all-embracing systematic truth, whether it be theological, philosophical, or political, was consistently submitted to the broadly based canons of a constantly shifting collective experience. Inevitably these doctrinal stances were broken under the pressure of having to support a more than simply theoretical posture. But there developed a highly sensitive feeling for the riches of experience as a way of reconstructing doctrine rather than as a malleable resource awaiting clarification. The doctrine of an open nature and the perpetual return to the invigoration of frontier language provided a sense of renewal and local horizon which served to constantly galvanize energies. As a consequence, what appear to be more basic questions are often left to fend for themselves in the rush of events. Is it not significant that the major thinkers in the American tradition are recalled more for their attitude and openness to possibility rather than for the specific resolution of the problems they faced? This would seem particularly true of Emerson, James, and Dewey, who, despite their concern with matters philosophical, have a mythic type of existence in the American tradition. Vaguely understood as thinkers, but personally imbedded in the popular consciousness as classic representations of the American mind, they seem to serve in a nostalgic way as the redoubt against the increased complexity of the

modern world. Precisely because of this new role as played out
in contemporary culture, technical thought, especially philosophy, tends to bypass such versions of man's situation.

In failing to recognize that the American tradition in its
emphasis on the method of experience, for purposes of human
inquiry, constitutes a contention of the highest philosophical
priority, contemporary American thought has driven a new
wedge between the role of philosophy and the affairs of human
life. The going assumption often seems to hold that the affection
for experience, so notable in earlier American philosophical
thought, has a naive and propaedeutic ring to it. As such, it
cannot continue as the basis for a response to the increasingly
complex dimensions which manifest themselves as characteristic
of inquiry in our time. If this assumption is basically sound, then
we must conclude that no matter what its verve and boldness in
avoiding systematic thought, the emphasis on experience in
previous American thought, while remaining a cultural deposit
in the wide sense, has only peripheral philosophical significance.
Such a bifurcation, however, falls prey to Dewey's warning that
"philosophy in America will be lost between chewing a historic
cud long since reduced to woody fiber, or an apologetics for lost
causes (lost to natural science), or a scholastic schematic
formalism, unless it can somehow bring to consciousness
America's own needs and its own implicit principle of successful
action." [30]

By way of summary, our position here contends that the
separation of the method of analysis, be it historical or
philosophical in concern, from the basic leaning of the culture,
has two pejorative results. First, widening Dewey's concern,
analysis (particularly so in the academic formulation increasingly characteristic of it) finds itself caught in a circle of
self-sustenance, using the same language for both criticism and
description, with only rare and ineffectual points of contact with
the wider culture. Second, as the culture develops an increased
dependence on intellectual expertise, there is a tendency to
neglect the obligation to conjoin analysis and the reconstruction
of experience. It is, after all, far easier to confront the

interiorized difficulties relative to each discipline, particularly those of the humanities and social sciences, than it is to take full cognizance of actual events, which by their very nature occur as interdisciplinary phenomena. It can be granted that the penchant for experience as the major source for the language of inquiry often leads to a lack of rigor and precision in speculative formulations. Yet such an approach has the important advantage of avoiding the deception that accrues to those who assume that events happen ready-made for analysis within the striated limitations of single disciplines. Openness to experience, with its historical roots in an anthropomorphic view of nature and a sense of frontier as human imaginative horizon, is to be understood as more than an outdated cliché. It should be seen rather as a fundamental attitude through which is strained the tasks of intellect, ever pressed to take account of the novelty that is manifested in the onrush of events. Above all, we should accept the stricture of William James that "Reality, life, experience, concreteness, immediacy, use what word you will, exceeds our logic, overflows and surrounds it." [31] Nonetheless, we do not stand dumb before the messagings of experience, for we are called upon to articulate their communal significance, by virtue of our reflective consideration and formulation. We must strive to institutionalize, socially and politically, the dialectic between the press of experience and the wisdom of reflection.

Let Charles Peirce have the last word. An American philosopher of the first rank and no sentimentalist on these matters, he tells us that "without beating longer round the bush let us come to close quarters. Experience is our only teacher." And "how does this action of experience take place? It takes place by a series of surprises." [32]

NOTES

1. John Donne, "An Anatomy of the World," *The Complete Poetry and Selected Prose* (New York: The Modern Library, 1952), p. 191.
2. Cf. Edmundo O'Gorman, *The Invention of America*

(Bloomington: Indiana University Press, 1961); Antonello
Gerbi, *La Disputa del Nuevo Mundo* (Mexico City: Fondo
de Cultura Económica, 1960); and Samuel Eliot Morison,
The European Discovery of America—The Southern Voyages
(New York: Oxford University Press, 1974), pp. 288-297.

3. For a programmatic statement of work still in progress on
the originating qualities of American culture, cf. John J.
McDermott, *The American Angle of Vision* (New York:
Cross Currents, 1965).

4. George Santayana, "The Genteel Tradition in American
Philosophy," *Winds of Doctrine* (New York: Harper
Torchbooks, 1957), pp. 186-187.

5. William Bradford, *Of Plymouth Plantation,* ed. Harvey
Wish (New York: Capricorn Books, 1962), p. 60.

6. Daniel Boorstin, *The Genius of American Politics* (Chicago:
Phoenix Books, 1953), p. 161.

7. Charles L. Sanford, *The Quest for Paradise—Europe and the
American Moral Imagination* (Urbana: University of Illinois Press, 1961), p. 107.

8. *Ibid.,* p. 97.

9. Perry Miller, *Errand into the Wilderness* (Cambridge:
Harvard University Press, 1956), p. 15.

10. An example of such a clustering of self-awareness is found
in Charles L. Sanford, ed., "The Structure of Experience,"
Quest for America, 1810-1824 (New York: Anchor Books,
1964), pp. 25-114.

11. William James, *The Letters of William James,* vol. II
(Boston: The Atlantic Monthly Press, 1920), p. 235.

12. William James, *Essays in Radical Empiricism* (New York:
Longmans, Green and Co., 1912), p. 10.

13. John Dewey, *Experience and Nature,* 2d ed. (La Salle:
Open Court, 1929), p. 10.

14. John Dewey, "The Need For a Recovery of Philosophy," in
John J. McDermott, ed., *The Philosophy of John Dewey,* vol.
II (New York: G. P. Putnam's Sons, 1973), p. 95.

15. William James, *The Varieties of Religious Experience* (New
York: Longmans, Green and Co., 1902), p. 489.

16. James, *Letters,* II, 270.

17. Dewey, *Experience and Nature,* p. 35.

18. Cf. especially John Dewey, *Logic: The Theory of Inquiry* (New York: Henry Holt and Co., 1938).

19. John Dewey, "The Need For a Recovery of Philosophy," p. 61. In an earlier series of essays, Dewey had argued in great detail that traditional theories of knowledge fell far short of the manifold ways in which experience teaches. Cf. John Dewey, *The Influence of Darwin and Other Essays in Contemporary Thought* (New York: Henry Holt and Co., 1910).

20. George Herbert Mead, "The Philosophies of Royce, James and Dewey in Their American Setting," *Selected Writings,* ed. Andrew Reck (Indianapolis: The Bobbs-Merrill Co., 1964), p. 390.

21. John Herman Randall, Jr., "The Spirit of American Philosophy," *Wellsprings of the American Spirit,* ed. F. Ernest Johnson (New York: Harper and Brothers, 1948), p. 133.

22. John Herman Randall, Jr., *How Philosophy Uses Its Past* (New York: Columbia University Press, 1963), p. 88.

23. Paul Tillich, "The Conquest of Intellectual Provincialism: Europe and America," *Theology of Culture* (New York: Oxford University Press, 1959), p. 164.

24. Ralph Waldo Emerson, "Compensation," *Works* (Boston: Houghton, Mifflin and Co., 1904), I, 95.

25. Cited in Edmund Fuller, *Tinkers and Genius—The Story of the Yankee Inventors* (New York: Hastings House, 1955), p. 34.

26. Henry Thoreau, "Our Country," *Collected Poems,* ed. Carl Bode (Baltimore: The Johns Hopkins Press, 1964), p. 135.

27. Robert Frost, "The Gift Outright," *Selected Poems of Robert Frost* (New York: Holt, Rinehart and Winston, Inc., 1963), p. 300.

28. Daniel Boorstin, "The Place of Thought in American Life," *America and the Image of Europe* (New York: Meridian Books, 1960), pp. 58-59.

29. Morton White, for example, believes "that the current wave

of anti-intellectualism in American thinking has certain affinities with tendencies that have dominated American philosophy from Edwards onwards." *Science and Sentiment in America* (New York: Oxford University Press, 1972), p. 302. Interestingly, White's view of anti-intellectualism pits "raw emotion," "passion," or "sentiment" over against "logic and experience" in the "establishment of reliable belief." For a countervailing view to that of White, cf. William A. Clebsch, *American Religious Thought* (Chicago: The University of Chicago Press, 1973), p. 191, n. 18.

30. Dewey, "The Need for a Recovery of Philosophy," p. 96.
31. William James, *A Pluralistic Universe* (New York: Longmans, Green and Co., 1909), p. 212.
32. Charles Sanders Peirce, *Collected Papers,* eds. Charles Hartshorne and Paul Weiss, vol. V (Cambridge: Harvard University Press, 1934), p. 37 (sec. 50, 51).

CHAPTER ONE

To Be Human Is to Humanize:
A Radically Empirical Aesthetic

> It is . . . the reinstatement of the vague and inarticulate to its
> proper place in our mental life which I am so anxious to
> press on the attention.
>
> —William James [1]

Two themes occupy us in the present essay. First, we contend
that modern art [2] works a revolution in man's view of himself; it
broadens the ways in which he relates to the world and the ways
by which he is informed. Second, we hold that the most fruitful
philosophical statement of the meaning of modern art is to be
found in the thought of William James and John Dewey,
interpreted as a radically empirical philosophy of experience.
From the time of the nineteenth-century impressionists to the
Second World War, these two themes were historically and
imaginatively interwoven. We want to make up for the recent
neglect of these two themes, in order to show the unusual

significance of radical empiricism for contemporary art. We make no effort to develop a complete aesthetic.

The problems we face focus on the relationship of impressionism to the nature of inquiry,[3] the role of philosophy relative to modern art; and the preeminence of a doctrine of relations in a contemporary aesthetic. We shall see that the thought of James and Dewey, so long trapped in the narrow epistemological problems of a pragmatic theory of truth, has extraordinary resiliency when looked at from the viewpoint of a generalized aesthetic. Further, if we are to take seriously the title of this volume, then the possibility of an aesthetic in our technological world poses a challenge of considerable importance for the future.

I. MODERN ART AS AN ATTITUDE

Technique is the very being of all creation.

—Ronald Barthes [4]

It is now a truism to affirm the decisive importance of modern science for the development of philosophical method and philosophical language. The methodology of contemporary science has been especially effective in forcing philosophy to abandon many of its presuppositions and working categories. Less well known is the fact that no corresponding transformation of philosophical language has taken place in response to the drastic changes effected by the artistic activity of the last seventy-five years. The revolution in art is as embracing as that in science, and relative to the life of the person, a more immediate one. We should not underestimate the extension of modern art as a general cultural attitude. Permeating our advertising, decorating our living space, reconstructing our sense of sound, making hybrids of all the classical art forms, modern art is so pervasive an influence that even the most radical departure from the commonplace fails to cause any consternation.[5] Has any culture heretofore found itself nostalgic for objects and experiences a decade or so removed in time but totally obliterated in experienced form? The revolution in primal shapes, colors, and textures wrought by the influence of modern art on industrial design is now so complete an aspect of our living that it would be difficult to single out a set of visual experiences which has not undergone considerable transformation within a single generation. In his essay on "The Man-Made Object," Gillo Dorfles refers to this characteristic as "formal instability." [6] Coupled with the acknowledgment of such restless formal identity is the effort of man to create forms. Surrounded by what he has "made" and aware of his ability to change its character at rapid intervals, modern man takes seriously his role as constitutor of reality. The shift from a denotative to a constitutive response to the world is rooted not only in modern technology but in modern aesthetics as well.

Moreover, the ingrained dependence on the visual and auditory senses is now experienced as inseparable from the sense of touch. The new art forms struggle against the conceptual domination of our traditional patterns of response. The arts of assemblage, kinetic sculpture, and mixed media make the tactile experience central. Modern in theme, these art activities reinvoke the primitive affection for the hands and symbolically restate the case for *Homo faber.*

No longer separated from his world like a spectator from a picture, modern man has slowly acknowledged the presence of an irreducible factor; how he formulates the environment becomes the environment itself.[7] Recently this insight has been stated in cryptic form by Marshall McLuhan as "the medium is the message." [8] We should not, however, be so surprised at this claim, for early in our century the traditional stranglehold on the meaning of nature, exercised through rigid conceptual models, was dramatically broken by the artistic revolution in the use of "media." Subsequently spurred on by the influence of the generic attitude known as "Dada," modern art assaulted the established aesthetic values. In art as in science, the obviousness of common sense was rejected as a resource for creative work. "Nouns," "things," and the consensus of meaning rooted in an "objective" framework were now taken to be but abstractions from a distinctively personalized aesthetic. While the acceptance of this iconoclastic attitude varied widely, the critical and non-conforming edge of Dada as an attitude is still residual in the activity of modern art to this day. Further, in response to these experiences of negation, modern art sets out to formulate new contexts for the articulation of aesthetic values. The most important factor in this development is the new understanding of technique. For the most part located in the very choice of media to be used, technique often becomes the primary locus for the generating of artistic insight. As the medium is shifted, the nature of aesthetic experience and the attendant questions of meaning, participation, and enhancement undergo a like transformation.[9] In these preliminary remarks we insist only that the notion of reality which emerges from this activity is one which affirms a reality whose very being is its process.

With these factors in mind let us return to our initial question. Those sympathetic to the metaphors of process philosophy usually trace the roots of their awareness to the revolution in speculative science and to certain perspectives in recent philosophy, particularly the thought of Bergson and Whitehead. Modern art, on the other hand, despite its being a more directly experienceable phenomenon and despite its having extensive implications for the meaning of inquiry, has not been brought to bear on the basic philosophical issues of our time. The philosophical discipline known as aesthetics continues to deal largely with antique problems, seemingly innocent of the fact that the art-experience of the last half-century has rendered the questions of beauty, truth in the arts, and the search for objective criteria as simply not to the point.[10] If we survey contemporary American philosophical works on aesthetics, it is astonishing to see how little they have to do with our experience of contemporary art—a situation made clear if we were to think of the philosophy of science as still dominated by the problems of classical mechanics. Likewise, in any number of broadly based attempts to deal with the aesthetic dimensions of modern culture, the participation of the contemporary philosopher is at a minimum.[11] Can we offer an analysis of this situation or must we admit to the contention that philosophical discourse and modern art are separated by a linguistic and even experiential gulf too immense to allow for mutual inquiry?

From one side, certain critics and the more articulate artists have become increasingly concerned with a reflective statement of their activities; in a word, have become increasingly philosophical about art.[12] For the most part, however, critics and artists rarely turn to philosophy itself when conducting such inquiries, and seem to boycott even those philosophers who have made an attempt to address themselves to aesthetic concerns. Should we agree with Herbert Read, in his commentary on Naum Gabo?

He is virtually creating a new language, a symbolic language of concrete visual images. This language is necessary because our philosophical inquiries have brought us to a point where the old symbols no longer suffice. Philosophy itself has reached an impasse—an impasse of verbal expression—at which it hands over its task to the poets and painters, the sculptors and other creators of concrete images.[13]

We would argue that Read takes philosophy too literally and condemns us to an unreflective participation in the experience of art and to discourse which signifies sterility of experience. To the contrary, if one is located in a wider philosophical tradition, discourse can have philosophical intention and yet be continuous with the basic attitude and creative direction of contemporary art. Although at times a noble goal, clarity is not the only objective of philosophical discourse. In some instances, particularly those referring to the plastic arts, philosophical discussion of the experiences in question may be illuminating in its *inability* to provide adequate linguistic corollaries as well as in its effort to create new metaphors of articulation. These latter would refer, not to ingrained philosophical language, but to the aesthetic qualities of the artistic experiences. The crucial question has to do with one's expectations of inquiry. To the extent that we seek a final statement, or a methodology able to put the vagaries of experience in fixed categories, the tendency is to push the philosophical enterprise beyond the limits of experience. For some, this is precisely the task of philosophy, namely, to transcend experience. But to those for whom the qualities of our experience are inseparable from their peculiarities in the concrete, such a method is fruitless.

A glance at the ambiguity in the basic attitude toward modern art in philosophical circles will give us some perspective. It will also serve as an introduction to the American philosophy of experience begun by William James and crystallized in the essays on the "live creature" by John Dewey.

It can be said that modern art needs no justification beyond its very presence. Yet when philosophers reflect upon the phenomenon of artistic creation, two distinct viewpoints emerge. The first and more generally accepted perspective sees modern art as a distortion of the "real world." This evaluation arises from a base extrinsic to the creative process itself; it has at its core the claim that the new forms which characterize contemporary art are a function of the widespread dehumanization afflicting our century. For support of this position, not only are we directed to the obvious "distortion" in canvases of Rouault, the surrealists, and expressionist protest art, but we are also asked to respond to the overall presence of dadaistic elements as if they were statements of content rather than an attempt to relocate the aesthetic experience. Recent examples of collage, combine-paintings, pop art, and especially the mysterious versions of assemblage found in the "boxes" of Joseph Cornell seem to sustain the charge that modern art violates our conceptual order and has only a topical significance, of a negative cast.

The major obstacle in the way of this interpretation is its notion of form. Dehumanization in art is taken to be the aberration or distortion of finalized forms, recognized as such by a centuries-old tradition of philosophical and aesthetic sanction. We must acknowledge the depressing truth that twentieth-century man has turned on his brother as never before. And there is no doubt that these circumstances have directly influenced the art of our time, which is said to represent the dark shadow hovering over the human face and the human place. Dehumanization, however, proceeds from still another source. Modern man is also a victim of clarity. Much of our difficulty proceeds from the demand for certitude and an inability to recognize and live with the irreducibility of shadows. Who among us knows the human face, or the nature of man? Have the myriad forms through which man humanizes his environment been approached, let alone exhausted? The departure from the moorings once so clearly recognized and accepted by Western man does not seem to be a fall from grace; it may be a liberation of creative human activity. Dehumanization, then, is often due to the blind defense of traditional versions of human life, now vestigial and no longer able to sustain human needs. Modern art accuses Western culture of sterility and narrow defensiveness. The accusation, often couched as a "manifesto," is at once a rejection of tired forms and a call for a new statement about human creative possibility. The extremes expressed in modern art occur in proportion to the lack of flexibility and imagination characteristic of the cultural attitudes under attack.

If it is folly to think that the old aesthetic values shall return as they were, it is equally true that the new artistic movements are so radical that they preclude any stable, final order. What is at stake seems to be nothing less than reconstruction of the modes and expectations of inquiry, in which we are constantly obligated to fuse the critique of previous forms with an attempt to create new forms.[14] Thomas Hess, writing on the painter Willem de Kooning, supports this interpretation. "The crisis of modern art presupposes that each shape, even a plain oval, be reinvented—or rather, given an autochthonous existence in paint. Nothing could be accepted or received on faith as a welcome heritage."[15]

Here then is the second way to view modern art, as an articulation of modern man's most distinctive activity, the creation of forms. Whether it be due to simple shifting of context, as in the "creation" of the haunted forms of *objet trouvé* or in the more aggressive structuring of totally new environments as brought off by the ever changing styles of assemblage, modern art has made innovation a central theme.[16] It is not difficult to find an acknowledgment of this dimension in the assessment of modern art; indeed, it has become almost a commonplace. The full implications, however, of such an attitude, have not been developed thus far. For the most part, the understanding of innovation has been along the lines of "replacement," an echo of the old metaphysics of objects. The key to the meaning of originality in modern art is not found in a doctrine of the "wholly new" but, rather, in a metaphysics of relations.

Fundamental to this new perspective are two contentions, both of direct philosophical importance: First, the recognition of the inability of nature to act any longer as the objective referent for the creative affairs of men. Rooted in the impressionistic attitude, this development owes much to the modern meaning of symbolism and the acceptance of ambiguity as a persistent dimension in human inquiry. Second, the affirmation that no entity can be experienced in isolation but has to be encountered as a field of relations.[17] Better, the term "entity" should be replaced by "event," that is, a network of relations, historically understood, with a past, present, and future. Furthermore, no matter how these "events" come into being and however diverse their lineage,[18] whenever they become subject to our awareness and touch us in a human way, they become realities of the most direct and intense kind. Citing Thomas Hess once more: "Life as we live it, obviously, is a matter of endless ambiguities and proliferating meanings; transparencies upon transparencies make an image that, while it blurs in superimpositions, takes on the actuality of rocks." [19] Concretion need not be associated with the meaning of "thing," for if we are willing to live with ambiguity, the flow of relations is also concrete and real.

In order to grasp the import of these contentions about nature and relations, we should examine two traditions. One is obvious: the plastic arts from Monet to the present. The other is not so

obvious: the metaphysics of relations as rooted in the philosophy of William James. The remainder of this chapter will have
as its task to show that these traditions, however different in
expression and parallel in historical development, proceed from
a single vision and can be allied to each other as philosophical
metaphor to artistic creation.

II. IMPRESSIONISM AS BREAKTHROUGH: WILLIAM JAMES AND CLAUDE MONET

L'exactitude n'est pas la verité.

—Matisse [20]

The presence of nuance and shading as a function of the
gigantic manifests itself in the impressionistic attitude. Unity is
achieved not by a decisive appeal to an objective referent but,
rather, by a gentle fading into continuous but ever more obscure
edges. It is an attitude whereby all insight is fringed, as if we
were reaching for a horizon with what William James calls an
" 'ever not quite' to all our formulas, and novelty and possibility
for ever leaking in." [21] Writing in the *American Journal of
Psychology* in 1891, G. Stanley Hall evaluates James's *Principles
of Psychology:*

> Passing now to *the work as a whole,* the author might be
> described as an *impressionist* in psychology. His portfolio
> contains sketches old and new, ethical, literary, scientific
> and metaphysical, some exquisite and charming in detail
> and even color, others rough charcoal outlines, but all
> together stimulating and suggestive, and showing great
> industry and versatility. . . . [22]

James's *Principles* is, like an impressionist canvas, a virtuoso
performance, technically proficient and characterized by extraordinary detail. Yet it has an elusive center and its major
theme is the fluidity of consciousness. Further, its concluding
chapter, "Necessary Effects and the Truths of Experience,"

renders the entire effort subject to doubt or at best, in James's judgment at least, renders it a bare hint of the desired statement. James shares, then, in the nineteenth-century breakthrough in sensibility. In an essay on James's aesthetics, Jacques Barzun writes:

> One can begin abstractly by saying that through this book [*The Principles*] James struck a deathblow at Realism. The then prevailing views of the mind were that it copied reality like a photographic plate, that it received and assembled the elements of experience like a machine, that it combined ideas like a chemist. For this "scientist" mind, James substituted one that was a born artist—a wayward, creative mind, impelled by inner wants, fringed with mystery, and capable of infinitely subtle, unrecordable nuances. Dethroning the sophistical Realist, in short, James revealed Impressionism native and dominant.[23]

In but a line, too infrequently noted by commentators, James responds to the call of experience: "It is, in short, the reinstatement of the vague to its proper place in our mental life which I am so anxious to press on the attention." [24] Apparently not satisfied with this phrasing, James is bolder in his *Psychology—Briefer Course:* "It is, the reader will see, the reinstatement of the vague and inarticulate to its proper place in our mental life which I am so anxious to press on the attention." [25] This affection for the "penumbra" of experience is no isolated insight in James. It everywhere sustains his contention that conceptual statements are but truncations of the flow of concrete life. Such insulating cuts in the flow are merely functional and should not prevent us from maintaining a reflective confrontation with those areas of our conscious experience not given to systematic definition.

In a more advanced statement of his views, James tells us: "Our fields of experience have no more definite boundaries than have our fields of view. Both are fringed forever by a *more* that continuously develops and that continuously supersedes them as life proceeds.[26] The experiencing of this fringe yields awareness while defying any conceptual formulation. For James, the crucial area of human activity is found precisely where the conceptual order breaks down, for it is in those conscious but inarticulable environs, wherein we experience religiously, aesthetically, psychedelically, that we are open to demons.[27] Although most often not subject to explanation, the meanings of these situations are intensely personal and, in a way proper to their own modalities, crystal clear.

In 1890, the year of the publication of James's *Principles*, Monet tells us of the struggle he has in painting the "haystack" series.

> I am working terribly hard, struggling with a series of different effects (haystacks), but . . . the sun sets so fast that I cannot follow it. . . . I am beginning to work so slowly that I am desperate, but the more I continue the more I see that a great deal of work is necessary in order to succeed in rendering that which I seek: "Instantaneity," especially the "enveloppe," the same light spreading everywhere, and more than ever I am dissatisfied with the easy things that come in one stroke.[28]

Ambiguity bathes our experience and the one-to-one correspondence between the perceptual act and the objective order is challenged. For Monet, the shift in light was decisive, but there can be a multiplicity of other activities (in James's phrase, "the halo of felt relations" [29]) which challenge the finality of our conceptual view of the universe. The important thrust of the impressionist attitude is to see the object as a locus from which to allow the full range of shades and meanings to show. The vagueness is relative; it depends on how prematurely one cuts off inquiry and attempts to answer the question, What is that? The painter Kandinsky understood this revolution better than most, for it was a decisive factor in transforming his own artistic activity. In 1895, Kandinsky stood before a Monet "haystack" exhibited in Moscow. Of this experience, he writes:

Previously I knew only realistic art.... Suddenly, for the first time, I saw a "picture." That it was a haystack a catalogue informed me. I could not recognize it. This lack of recognition was distressing to me. I also felt that the painter had no right to paint so indistinctly. I had a muffled sense that the object was lacking in this picture, and was overcome with astonishment and perplexity that not only seized but engraved itself indelibly on the memory and quite unexpectedly, again and again hovered before the eyes down to the smallest detail. All of this was unclear to me, and I could not draw the simple consequences from this experience.

But what was absolutely clear to me was the unsuspected power previously hidden from me, of the palette which surpassed all my dreams. Painting took on a fabulous strength and splendor. And at the same time, unconsciously, the object was discredited as an indispensable element of the picture.[30]

The discrediting of the object is no small event in the history of human consciousness. All too often this development is analyzed as the other side of the growth of subjectivism. Such an interpretation is narrow and misguided, for the dispersal of objects does not necessarily throw us back on an introverted self-consciousness, although it does enhance the role of the self in the creative process. By far, the more significant implication has to do with the emergence of relational activity as the focus for meaning. The subject-object duality is no longer to the point, for at both ends these terms are but abstract statements of actually dynamic processes. Pushing further, inquiry moves steadily to an analysis of the interaction between the relational qualities of self-consciousness and the relational qualities of constructed environments. In effect, analysis focuses on "fields" of relationships, rather than on subjects and objects in isolation.[31] From such a viewpoint, the role of "names" undergoes a serious shift. They stand for loci or gathering places of ongoing relational activities, and thereby merely focus attention. In modern art, names of art objects are not to be taken as descriptions of the work. Rather, they merely announce the presence of activity and are bypassed as soon as we tie into the peculiar qualities of such activity. More often than not, such nominal delineations of works of modern art become increasingly less relevant as we broaden our participation. Thus, to speak consistently, there is no single canvas in modern painting; for experienced as an event, the physical environment of such a canvas, the psychic thrust of one's own personal activity at that time, and the myriad historical and cultural factors involved in such aesthetic participation are all irreducible dimensions of the painting. If we can apply such criteria, retrospectively, to traditional works of art, this does not gainsay the fact that such a possibility emerges primarily from the method of modern painting. Among artists, Kandinsky, for one, was aware of the nature of this shift away from the object to the relational event as the real source of meaning. He offers a metaphorical statement of this new philosophical insight.

This isolated line and the isolated fish alike are living beings with forces peculiar to them, though latent. . . . But the voice of these latent forces is faint and limited. It is the environment of the line and the fish that brings about a miracle: the latent forces awaken, the expression becomes radiant, the impression profound. Instead of a low voice, one hears a choir. The latent forces have become dynamic. The environment is the composition.[32]

Kandinsky's statement is inseparable from the fact that the plastic arts since Monet have set a dizzying pace in the creation of new environments. At first limited to radical shifts within the context of the "painting" or the "sculpture," their activities soon spilled out into "assembled" environments, often creating the need for entirely new evaluative criteria. The task of a modern aesthetic is to achieve discursive continuity with such constructs. Just as single "things" gave way to "environments," so too, the single arts of painting and sculpture have become antique, giving way first to hybridizations with other aesthetic forms and now to new aesthetic creations, *sui generis,* often with no recognizable tie to what was only recently known as art. What is most needed, therefore, is a philosophical outlook which does not ask dead questions, that is, questions which focus simply on content. Whether we say with Kandinsky "the environment is the composition" or with McLuhan "the medium is the message," the problem is clear from the philosophical side—the need for a doctrine of relational activity phrased in aesthetic metaphors.

At this juncture William James again offers a point of departure. James has an original approach to relations: they are rooted in a psychology of experience. His view of self-consciousness is characterized by process and function rather than by entity and faculty. And finally, his anthropology, which is Promethean in outlook, is fully aware of chance, novelty, and the centrality of human creativity. Rather than a structured aesthetic theory, it is his life [33] and his philosophical approach to the problem of inquiry which gives us the basis for a modern aesthetic. Using the assumptions of James, let us make an effort to consider the problems of modern art in a way which shows philosophical concern but maintains fidelity to the quality of modern experience.

III. A RELATIONAL AESTHETIC

"Monumentality is an affair of relativity."

—Hans Hofmann [34]

William James took his stand over against the associationist psychology of the nineteenth century. Although he shared the empirical temper of that tradition, he could not accept its view that experience is composed of atomistic elements. The reigning opposition was idealism which, in James's understanding, provided an overarching principle of unity, without any experiential sustenance. Rejecting both views, he countered with his doctrine of radical empiricism.[35] The clearest statement of this position was made by James in the "Preface" to *The Meaning of Truth*, written in 1909.

> Radical empiricism consists first of a postulate, next of a statement of fact, and finally of a generalized conclusion.
>
> The postulate is that the only things that shall be debatable among philosophers shall be things definable in terms drawn from experience. (Things of an unexperienceable nature may exist *ad libitum*, but they form no part of the material for philosophic debate.)
>
> The statement of fact is that the relations between things, conjunctive as well as disjunctive, are just as much matters of direct particular experience, neither more so nor less so, than the things themselves.
>
> The generalized conclusion is that therefore the parts of experience hold together from next to next by relations that are themselves parts of experience. The directly apprehended universe needs, in short, no extraneous trans-empirical connective support, but possesses in its own right a concatenated or continuous structure.[36]

The crucial aspect of this position is unquestionably found in his claim for the "statement of fact." Central to James's radical empiricism, this affirmation has its roots in a phenomenology of the processes of consciousness. He tells us in his essay on "The Stream of Thought" that "If there be such things as feelings at all, *then so surely as relations between objects exist* in rerum natura, *so surely and more surely, do feelings exist to which these relations are known.*"[37] Quite concretely, we should say a "feeling of *and*, a feeling of *if*, a feeling of *but*, and a feeling of *by*, quite as readily as we say a feeling of *blue* or a feeling of *cold.*"[38] And to the extent that we do not, we accept the empiricist prejudice "of supposing that where there is *no* name no entity can exist."[39] In this way, "all dumb or anonymous psychic states have, owing to this error, been coolly suppressed. . . ."[40]

The search for "what" inevitably ends with a "noun" for a

response. The epistemology of common sense seeks names, definitions, and categories. From its critical side, modern art, particularly in its dadaistic overtone, has led an assault on such an approach. In refusing to name its artifacts, or in naming them abstractly, as "# 1," or again, in naming them specifically but with no visual correspondence to the work, this art denies to itself and to the participant any substantive identity. Such a denial does not, however, imply an absence of meaning or of intelligibility. Rather, meaning is located in the ongoing fabric of relations, by which we mean it is found neither in an isolated self nor in an isolated thing but, rather, in the environment constituted by shared participation. Any attempts to extrapolate a fixed meaning for other than functional purposes are denials of this process. James had warned of the dangers involved when connections were thought to be but logical bridges instead of experienced continuities.

> Continuous transition is one sort of a conjunctive relation; and to be a radical empiricist means to hold fast to this conjunctive relation of all others, for this is the strategic point, the position through which, if a hole be made, all the corruptions of dialectics and all the metaphysical fictions pour into our philosophy.[41]

If we wish to understand the meaning of modern art, we have to place ourselves in continuity with the interiorized structuring of each creation. At all costs, we must avoid the temptation to evaluate this art by virtue of criteria derived from a source extrinsic to the qualities of the creative process. Support for such a contention is offered to us in the following text of James: "Knowledge of sensible realities thus comes to life inside the tissue of experience. It is *made;* and made by relations which unroll themselves in time." [42]

In order to sustain this claim, James takes a position which is bold relative to philosophy but obvious from the side of modern painting and sculpture. "Life is in the transitions as much as in the terms connected; often, indeed, it seems to be there more emphatically. . . . These relations of continuous transition experienced are what makes our experiences cognitive. In the simplest and completest cases the experiences are cognitive of one another." [43] The crucial problem, therefore, in the search for the "form" of a modern painting is the inability to relate it to a reality already given.

In the concrete, to seek a morphology of a modern painting, say, of the abstract expressionist school, turns up the following. We do not confront an object but an event;[44] or, in a name used recently for one kind of modern art but more widely applicable, a "happening." The origins of such an event are obscure, unless we accept a psychoanalytic or sociological reductionism. Should we do so, the experiencing of such an event would likewise be conditioned and we would still be faced with the problem of ever varying qualities in such influence.[45] Despite the absence of an inherited identity, we are able to enter into meaningful relationship to modern art. We enjoy, undergo, and are carried along by it. Its form seems to be its process although with no fixed goal. This does not imply looseness of endeavor or of craft. In the paintings of Mark Rothko, for example, one is fascinated by the intense effort to deal with relationship as such, under the specifics of shading, dripping, and ever so subtle internal shifts of color and canvas size. This concern becomes almost obsessive in the work of the late Ad Reinhardt, known as minimal art. The point at issue here is that this galaxy of interiorized relations cannot be rendered meaningful by any appeal to a known object. This does not mean that such paintings are locked up within themselves, but any opening out of their meaning must follow the same nonliteral processes [46] which were central to their creation originally. That the human self can enter into such a process, we shall discuss further on.

Expressions such as "ongoing," "process," "reconstruction," "event," "interaction," so central to a metaphysics of experience, and so often criticized by philosophers as vague, show up again and again in writings by painters and critics.[47] Perhaps the most explicit statement of the position that an ongoing fabric of relations is the source of meaning and intelligibility in a work of modern art was offered by Hans Hofmann. A painter of the first rank, Hofmann was also a teacher and made a serious effort to render in discursive terms his view of modern painting. Holding that a color interval is "analogous to a thought-fragment in the creative process," Hofmann sees such intervals or fragments taking their meaning from their "aesthetic extension," for "any isolated thing can never surpass its own meaning." [48] Actually, he goes beyond James, for according to William Seitz, Hofmann will hold that "the relation between elements, whatever they may be, is always more significant than the elements themselves." [49] Should we not take seriously Hofmann's belief that "relations" rather than isolated "actualities" account for the quality of our response? Seitz clarifies our attitude toward these matters in the following text.

> Traditionally, a painting used to begin as a rough sketch of the main lines or areas of a preconceived image, and this is still often the case; but with Hofmann, painting is from the first stroke a continuing establishment and re-establishment of life relationships. As it progresses, the work moves toward a more perfect integration of all its parts—toward a relational unity.[50]

We need not remain within the rhetoric of painting in order to establish the significance of relations for the modern theme. Perhaps if we were to look at a more aggressive art form, like modern jazz, our meaning would become clearer. Outside of a relational setting, jazz is meaningless, for it proceeds by a series of interwoven tensions. A jazz group is especially revealing, as single members create their music in line with their respective insight but over against other members of the group. We have tension between personal mastery of the instrument and the demand for improvisation; between the developing structure of each contribution and, overall, an open system. The entire performance is carried on with a sense for group responsibility.[51] The viability of these tensions is manifested only as experienced. It cannot be predicted or planned, as there are no formal or abstract correlations. The qualities of a jazz performance cannot be extrapolated and taught as such. The jazz master is one whose distinctive originality enables the fledgling to create in his own vein; thus, each to his own vision but as a shared experience. Such indirect communication is necessary, for we do not have duplication of experiences or the performance of others' versions. Yet, in a jazz group, the participant senses when the group is not sharing the same experience, articulated by each in his own manner. And, in turn, the experiencing public sense when it "comes off." As in the plastic arts, intelligibility is manifest when one is carried along by the possibilities and relations of the medium in question. This is a cardinal instance of Dewey's contention that *"connections* exist in the most immediate non-cognitive experience, and when the experienced situation becomes problematic, the connections are developed into distinctive objects of common sense or of science." [52]

In jazz the experienced situation becomes meaningful because of the technique. More than any other single factor, as for example the instruments used or the melody as point of departure, it is technique which is decisive in bringing about a creative advance. In the plastic arts, correspondingly, every shift in material used creates a new locus of relations, new problems and, lately, entirely new art forms. In his essay on "The Structuralist Activity," Ronald Barthes states: "It is not the nature of the copied object which defines art (though this is a tenacious prejudice in all realism), it is the fact that man adds to it in reconstructing it: technique is the very being of all creation." [53]

At this point, it should be obvious that modern art sustains an important shift in the meaning of person. No mere copier of forms or even a discoverer [54] of forms hidden, man becomes the creator of forms. The rhetoric of the artist and the critic, on this issue, has often been extreme. Apollinaire, for example, in his work on *The Cubist Painters,* traces the existence of the "world" to the creative work of the artist.

It is the social function of great poets and artists to renew continually the appearance nature has for the eyes of men.

Without poets, without artists, men would soon weary of
nature's monotony. The sublime idea men have of the
universe would collapse with dizzying speed. The order
which we find in nature, and which is only an effect of art,
would vanish. Everything would break up in chaos. There
would be no seasons, no civilization, no thought, no
humanity; even life would give way, and the impotent void
would reign everywhere.[55]

In an exchange of views between the critic Herbert Read and
the founder of constructivism, Naum Gabo, a similar position is
taken, although more modestly stated. Gabo puts it this way.

I maintain that knowledge is nothing else but a construction of ours and that what we discover with our knowledge
is not something outside us or a part of a constant and
higher reality, in the absolute sense of the word; but that we
discover exactly that which we put into the place where we
make the discoveries. . . .[56]

In his essay on "Human Art and Inhuman Nature," Read
simply maintains that some modern artists set out "to invent an
entirely new reality." [57] But these contentions, and they are
representative of the many manifesto-declarations of novelty
that abound in modern art, are too pat; they protest too much.
They have meaning in that they clearly delineate the opponent,
a mimetic or spectator view of the world. The problem, however,
is more complex and surely the creative capacity attributed to
the modern artist is more subtle than the replacing of one total
view by another. A "new reality" is only one kind of novelty and
it is rarely achieved. Further, in time, it too shall be replaced
and rendered obsolete. The revolution of modern art is better
found in the attitude it takes to all reality, whether obvious to
common sense, surreal, or invented.[58] What is novel is not
simply new creations, but a way of approaching all art.
The genuine sense of novelty is achieved by virtue of our
focusing on processes rather than on products; and by our

energizing of relationships, both given and created. If we wish, this approach can be applied retrospectively to classical art, for although it may violate the original intention, the implications of such art would then be considerably widened. No doubt this is why so many modern artists claim profoundly personal relationships with individual classical artists, while creating, in their own vein, a radically different style. From the outside, the well-known fact of the influence of classical drawing on abstract expressionism is difficult to absorb and seems to demand a massive reconstruction of the notion of continuity. Yet, in morphological terms, the internal struggles to achieve the dynamics of line are quite continuous. The key is to dwell within and capture the rhythm, the ongoing dialectic. The identity or nonidentity of extrapolated forms is peripheral to real aesthetic insight, and is not necessary for purposes of understanding or comparison. Gardner Murphy describes a wider sense of creative activity that parallels our description of artistic creation.

. . . creative activity is the very nature of the primitive life-process itself. The concept of the open system really means that living things are not only intent on their own growth and development, but that they are directing evolutionary processes in accordance with a dynamic which is organismic, rather than mechanical.[59]

That such an inner dynamic, with its own logic, is characteristic of the processes of experience and amenable to human interaction is a distinctive position of William James. In a series of texts, written at different times, he lays the problem bare.

James, in a morbid state and on the edge of suicide, entered this liberating text in his "Diary": "Life shall [be built in] doing and suffering and creating." [60] The full meaning of his commitment at that point is made clear in his subsequent essay on "The Sentiment of Rationality."

If we survey the field of history and ask what feature all

great periods of revival, of expansion of the human mind, display in common, we shall find, I think, simply this: that each and all of them have said to the human being, "The inmost nature of the reality is congenial to *powers* which you possess." [61]

The confidence in the capacity of man to transform his environment proceeds from James's view that the human self and the flow of experience share the same basic relational patterns. The human self, in James's view, has no inherited identity. Gordon Allport writes of James:

There is, he thinks, no such thing as a substantive self distinguishable from the sum total, or stream, of experiences. Each moment of consciousness, he says, appropriates each previous moment, and the knower is thus somehow embedded in what is known.[62]

The interaction between the human self and the environment is the decisive factor in engendering the experience of identity. The fabric of man's life is a relational schema; it not only deals with the exigencies for human identity but, within conditioned structure, yields the imaginative construction of the meaning of the world. In his *Principles,* James had held to the natively formulating character of conscious activity. The selective work of the mind follows interest, practical or aesthetic.[63]

Out of what is in itself an undistinguishable, swarming *continuum* devoid of distinction or emphasis, our senses make for us by attending to this motion, and ignoring that, a world full of contrasts, of sharp accents, of abrupt changes, of picturesque light and shade.[64]

By the time of *Pragmatism,* published in 1907, James sees the activity of man as even more aggressively constructive.

In our cognitive as well as in our active life, we are

creative. We add, both to the subject and to the predicate part of reality. The world stands really malleable, waiting to receive its final touches at our hand. Like the kingdom of heaven, it suffers violence willingly. Man engenders truth upon it.[65]

As with the modern artist, James's world does not give itself to any conceptually extrapolated or finalized version. "Whatever separateness is actually experienced is not overcome, it stays and counts as separateness to the end." [66] The world cannot be had whole, from any single perspective. Indeed, two minds cannot know one thing, except by a pragmatic verification of a shared experience.[67] Unity is a process achieved only *durcheinander* and not *all einheit*. He rails against the "block universe," holding rather to a "multiverse," unfinished, tychastic, and shot through with novelty.[68] In the search for meaning in a processive world, James gives to man the decisive role; man is the creator of forms.

Notwithstanding all these positions of James and the strength of their supporting texts, rendered almost stereotypical by the commentaries on his thought, we should focus on another perspective too often overlooked. First, we should not forget the full text, cited above (n. 61) of James's remark in "The Sentiment of Rationality." While it is true that he emphasizes the "powers which you possess," he describes man's relationship to his environment as one of "congeniality" and not one of dominance. Further, he stresses the presence of the "inmost nature of the reality," to which such "congeniality" is directed. It can be said that James did not stress adequately his insight into the relational fabric of the affairs of nature, concentrating, rather, on the "energies of men" and the fluid quality of the human self. Yet he was aware of such dynamics and came to hold that only by acknowledging this texture in the activities of nature as experienced can we do justice to the creative thrust of human activity. Rather than the oversimplified emphasis on novelty, as proceeding wholly from the self (a caricature of the modern artist), James presents a taut relationship between a constructing and manipulating consciousness, and the activity of a continually related flow of experience.

A second balancing factor in James's view was found in our earlier discussion, when we indicated James's contention that "life is in the transitions." A text in *Pragmatism* spells out this belief and gives meaning to his affirmation of that "inmost nature of the reality" which challenges the creative activity of man. "Our experience meanwhile is all shot through with regularities. One bit of it can warn us to get ready for another bit, can 'intend' or be 'significant' of that remoter object." [69] Relative to man's needs, including his desire to enhance, experience is malleable. But it is no dummy, for "Experience itself, taken at large, can grow by its edges. That one moment of it proliferates into the next by transitions which, whether conjunctive or disjunctive, continue the experiential tissue, can not, I contend, be denied." [70]

Man, therefore, is called upon to create meaning, to engender truth. This activity places man at the center of the flow of experience. The modern artist has shown that the resources of human imagination are virtually limitless and that man has only begun to articulate the possible dimensions of the human self. Nevertheless, we must maintain that it is a "world" which we wish to create. We seek more than a dazzling array of self-preening evocations of the human psyche. Relations must be forged between the processes of the human self and the affairs of our living space, our topography, our cities, and our artifacts. Modern art, in the last decade, has become aware of this need and, as we shall attempt to indicate, has begun to offer a viable aesthetic for contemporary man. So that modern art on behalf of modern man, in carrying on this endeavor, may avoid the temptation to become overly impressed with the novelty of the effort, at the expense of the task, let us close this section with a stern and incisive warning by William James.

Woe to him whose beliefs play fast and loose with the order which realities follow in his experience; they will lead him nowhere or else make false connexions. [71]

IV. EXPERIENCE OF THE ORDINARY
AS AESTHETIC

Works of art are . . . celebrations, recognized as such, of the
things of ordinary experience.

—John Dewey [72]

The philosophy of radical empiricism, with which John
Dewey [73] was fundamentally in accord, is thematically rearticu-
lated in his *Art as Experience.* Published in 1934, the book was a
development of Dewey's remarks as the first William James
Lecturer at Harvard University. Dewey's range of concerns and
the incisiveness of his judgments make this one of his outstanding contributions and deserving of ever more analysis.[74] Quite
aside from these significant general considerations, recent artistic events press us to evaluate the book, especially the first
three chapters, from a perspective quite unknown to Dewey. In
a word, his sections on the "live creature," "ethereal things,"
and "having an experience" are profound philosophical delineations of the art of the last decade. Dewey's views provide a point
of departure for a contemporary aesthetic, rooted in the very
fabric of the human condition and capable of transforming our
cultural attitudes. Taking James's sense for relations and his
processive anthropology, Dewey deals with the interaction of
man with his environment. He goes beyond James, by virtue of
his insight into the sociological dimension of all inquiry, his ever
present sensitivity to the struggle for values and his acute
awareness of man's effort and need to control his social
environment. It is not excessive to say that Dewey has initiated
an inquiry into experiences of which the contemporary art of the
ordinary, collage, assemblage, found-objects, mixed media,
environmental sculptures, ready-mades, junk art, pop art, kinetic art, and happenings are intensifications and symboliza-
tions. His view of the aesthetic situation as a phenomenology of
the live creature, rhythmically tied to his environment, was
anticipatory of today's artistic structurings of such interactions.

And, in line with the contention of the present essay, Dewey's book offers sustenance for our belief in the viability of the American philosophy of experience, for purposes of enlightened analysis of the contemporary cultural situation.

At the very outset of his book, Dewey tells us that our "task" is to "restore continuity between the refined and intensified forms of experience that are works of art and everyday events, doings and sufferings that are universally recognized to constitute experience." [75] Given the full implication of Dewey's subsequent analysis, the term "restore" is to be read as "build," that is, to achieve relational continuity between the intrinsic rhythms of the human self as a live creature and the attempts to structure enhanced versions of his environment. Two obstacles prevent successful rendering of this continuity. First, our approach to art has been dominated by theoretical statements of its meaning and, more serious, has failed to maintain the relationship between aesthetic refinement and experiential bedding from which such art proceeds.

> *Theories* which isolate art and its appreciation by placing them in a realm of their own, disconnected from other modes of experiencing, are not inherent in the subject-matter but arise because of specifiable extraneous conditions. [This approach] deeply affects the practice of living, driving away esthetic perceptions that are necessary ingredients of happiness, or reducing them to the level of compensating transient pleasurable excitations. [76]

Aesthetic enhancements are too often things apart, and when sought out, are approached for reasons extraneous to the very mode of experiencing which generated them in the first place. The second obstacle then becomes clear, for having systematically separated aesthetic delight from reflective awareness, we become correspondingly anaesthetized to the aesthetic qualities inherent in the live creature. The establishing of continuities between the life of the person and artistic creation cannot take place by the acknowledgment of this art as "great," but only by the intensification and qualitative reconstruction of patterns of feeling already deeply felt.

Theory can start with and from acknowledged works of art only when the esthetic is already compartmentalized, or only when works of art are set in a niche apart instead of being celebrations, recognized as such, of the things of ordinary experience. Even a crude experience, if authentically an experience, is more fit to give a clue to the intrinsic nature of esthetic experience than is an object already set apart from any other mode of experience.[77]

Dewey then devotes an entire chapter to an examination of the rhythms of ordinary experience. He speaks of the "humdrum," "slackness," "dissipation," and "rigidity" as factors in preventing the integration of personal anticipations [78] and affections with the larger patterns of the human situation.[79] In this aesthetic ecology, Dewey stresses the need to be continuous with animal life and to have one's senses on the *qui vive*.[80] All should be turned to living tissue; suffering and celebration become related aspects of maturation. "The live creature adopts its past; it can make friends with even its stupidities, using them as warnings that increase present wariness." [81] He repeats, in a number of different ways, the significance of having sensitivity to relations. Order is a becoming, a transactional relationship between "doing" and "undergoing." Consistent with our viewpoint on modern art, Dewey insists that "order is not imposed from without but is made out of the relations of harmonious interactions that energies bear to one another." [82] Said another way, form in modern art is the theme of continuity which wends its way through the creation of the work of art, acting not as a constant element but as a living function, holding in tension that narrow otherness of vision and technique. Entering into this process, the live creature must do more than witness. "For to perceive, a beholder must *create* his own experience." [83] And, finally, the person must create the continuities between the rhythm of his own life lived and the experienced participation with those refinements and enhancements present in the world of art.

The recent explosion of that art generally referred to as "art of the ordinary" is created out of the very texture of the continuities sought by Dewey. It takes seriously his claim that "art is thus prefigured in the very processes of living." [84] As early as the Futurist Manifesto of 1912, Boccioni tells us that we can use "furry spherical forms for hair, semicircles of glass for a vase, wire and screen for an atmospheric plane" and in our artistic work overall, we can incorporate "glass, wood, cardboard, iron, cement, horsehair, leather, cloth, mirrors, electric light, and so on." [85]

Taking assemblage as a cardinal instance of art of the ordinary,[86] we isolate two attitudes, each of which have importance for a contemporary aesthetic. First, any material, found or constructed, can be aesthetically meaningful. What is most important, and here the plastic arts have broken far more ground than other art forms, is the willingness to abandon a hierarchy of material, of composition, and to deny the delineation of acceptable aesthetic forms. The most dramatic instance of this is to be found in the "Watts Towers" of Simon Rodia.[87] Built singlehandedly and under construction for thirty-two years, Rodia abandoned the "Towers" as forever unfinished. They are found in his yard, hard by a railroad siding, in the now well-known depressed area of Watts, Los Angeles. Soaring some one hundred feet high, they are built of steel webbing, concrete, broken dishes, cups, 7up bottles, tiles, and scrap of every kind. Enclosed by a high wall, they are multicolored and shaped as rising spirals or simulations of crowns and grottoes. Crossing and recrossing the lines of sculpture, architecture, and industrial design, they threaten always to be sentimental or grotesque. But they are not. As assemblage, they press upon us a renewed experience of the regenerative powers of the human hands,[88] and bring to the surface how deeply affectionate we are toward our entire setting and all that touches us as human. It would be good to admit to this natively aesthetic quality in our ordinary experience.

A second attitude emerging from the art of the ordinary is the narrowing of the gap between nostalgia and immediacy. Following the criteria of Marshall McLuhan, we render environments aesthetic when they are no longer experienced. Thus, romantic poetry is written in the machine age.[89] Our age is one in which the gap between differently experienced environments has shrunk almost to an imperceptible level. The metaphor of our times is "instantaneity"; the transistor replaces the wire. One experience is "had" differently, at different times and for different purposes. Aspects of our present environment have many aesthetic qualities, heretofore unacknowledged. If we widen the scope of the meaning of aesthetic quality, immediate experience yields new riches. Junk art, found objects and ready-mades, all aspects of our immediate experience, are offered to us for purposes of aesthetic participation. Lawrence Alloway draws the following implications from these activities.

> Junk culture is city art. Its source is obsolescence, the throw away material of cities, as it collects in drawers, cupboards, attics, dustbins, gutters, waste lots and city dumps. Objects have a history: first they are brand new goods; then they are possessions accessible to few, subjected often to intimate and repeated use; then as waste they are scarred by use but available again. . . . Assemblages of such material come at the spectator as bits of life, bits of environment. The urban environment is present then, as the source of objects, whether transfigured or left alone.[90]

This art tends to draw us in from the side of creation rather than observation. The artist, himself, makes of us a more intimate aspect of his art. "By actively participating in the aesthetic transaction the spectator becomes himself a part of the artist's total material." [91] Correspondingly, the extraordinary range of what is offered as aesthetic and the variant number of ways in which this can take place encourages all of us to render aesthetically our immediate environment. Collage alone has revolutionized the experience of art for young children. Liberated from dealing with formal design perspective and encouraged to utilize all materials, especially those at hand, the child can now forge experienced continuity between what he feels deeply and what he creates as artifact. The end of the Euclidean values of proportion, symmetry, and total accountability has opened the way for each of us to work at a new kind of structuring; one that is continuous with our experience rather than irrelevant to it or even a violation of our actual sensibilities.

The decisive insight of contemporary art is that it does not claim hold of an eccentric, albeit exciting, aspect of human life but, rather, creates out of a sense of the most properly human dimensions. Its credo is, in effect, that to be human is to humanize. The art process is the human process brought to a specific angle of vision, with a claim about man's activity which throws light on the entire range of human affairs. We stand then with Dewey who, in a paraphase of Keats, held that the truly ethereal things are made by man.[92]

V. A PSYCHEDELIC/CYBERNETIC AESTHETIC

We have stressed the lag between philosophical articulation and the activities of the contemporary art scene. Even if we were able to generate some energy devoted to closing this gap, we may still find ourselves badly dated. For as we write, two movements of great vitality appear upon the cultural scene. Each has an unusual potentiality for reworking the human situation: the effort to expand human awareness psychedelically [93] and the attempt to extend the human perimeter by means of electronic technology. Both of these revolutions are continuous with the concerns stated above and both share, with modern art, the critique of man's confinement within the geometric or linear view of human experience. Positively these efforts are directed to the massive and crucial problem of how to structure affectivity in a technological society.

The relationship of personal life to the need and experience of community is characterized in our time by a major tension. On the one hand, the scope of our experience has been broadened in a shattering way. Paradoxically this has also increased the intensity of our experiences. "As electrically contracted, the globe is no more than a village. Electric speed in bringing all social and political functions together in a sudden implosion has heightened human awareness of responsibility to an intense degree." [94] Politics enjoins astral physics. We domesticate the heavens and cut distances in a savage onslaught on the limitations of time and space. From another side and at the same time we have an equally profound effort to probe the inner man, from both a behavioral and speculative point of view. Perhaps we can say that the poles of contemporary experience are nothing less than the astral and the nuclear.[95]

For some, in order to develop a sense of community in our present environment, it is necessary to shift the focus of concern from the biological and even the sociological to the activities of cybernetic technology, as a resource for metaphors used to articulate the human endeavor. In a quite different direction, we find those thinkers who hold that we should reconstitute human experience and thereby human feelings and language by virtue of psychedelic activity. Both of these commitments, whether to have us "tuned in" or "turned on," stress total involvement. Institutions such as the school, the church, and our political bureaucracy have shown themselves largely bankrupt in providing nutrition for the human person. Sensibility, affectivity, and a relevant liturgy of celebration are hard to come by. Still we must admit that the psychedelically inspired "trip out" has major difficulties, since the landscape for such a trip often (though not always) remains painfully introverted. The total resource for the lived experience becomes heightened but correspondingly narrowed. The psychedelic community has exclusivity at its core. On the other hand, the revolution in electronic technology extends the hegemony of man and even, some contend, renders our planet but a probe. Yet, here too, we face divisiveness. Few of us can participate directly in planetary experience and many of us find ourselves hopelessly cut off from a world so distant from common experience, from the use of our hands, and even from the use of our machines.

Modern art has moved steadily in the direction of liberating the human person to enjoy his immediate experience. As Martin Buber says, "all is hallowed" and the ordinary sings a distinctive song of its own. Is the psychedelic-cybernetic revolution continuous with this attitude or is it to be another catastrophic break in our experience? Perhaps we are once again faced with the paradoxical situation wherein the dazzling quality of our insights moves us forward at one level only, but generates a feeling of anomie and loneliness for the larger community. The question confronting us can be asked in simple terms. Given the increased extension of man and his growing hegemony over nature, can he achieve a response, in concert, equal to those startling intensifications of personal experience brought on by psychedelics? In a cybernetic technology can we achieve affectivity and personal sensibility, in all aspects of the human situation on a communitywide basis? If philosophy has a contribution to make, it could urge that the last half of this century would do well to view the economic and political questions as, at bottom, aesthetic.

NOTES

1. William James, *Psychology—Briefer Course* (New York: Henry Holt and Co., 1892), p. 165.
2. Although we use the term "modern art" as a functional canopy for all of the major art activities of our century, in this essay the plastic arts are mainly in focus. The references to contemporary art stand for recent events in the modern art tradition.
3. "Inquiry" as used throughout this discussion refers to man's transactional quest. He is informed by the world at every turn, literally through his skin and in his dreams, as well as by virtue of more conventional means. Man also informs the world; again literally by creating the contexts in which his awareness takes place. Rooted in Kant, this tension between man getting and begetting the world is of irreducible importance in modern art.

4. Ronald Barthes, "The Structuralist Activity," *Partisan Review* (Winter 1967), p. 84.
5. Has any major cultural prognostication turned out to be so wide of the mark as the judgment of Ortega y Gasset on the viability of the new art? Cf. *The Dehumanization of Art* (Garden City: Doubleday Anchor Books, 1956), p. 5: "Modern art, on the other hand, will always have the masses against it. It is essentially unpopular; moreover, it is antipopular."
6. Gillo Dorfles, "The Man-Made Object," *The Man-Made Object,* ed. Gyorgy Kepes (New York: George Braziller, 1966), p. 2.
7. The driftwood sculpture of Louise Nevelson is a notable contemporary effort to create "environments" or, better, "worlds," out of apparently relationless materials. In an interview in the *New York Times,* April 28, 1967, she said: "I am asking for an environment to suit me. Look darling, there is no world. We objectify the world in form. That is the world." The combine-paintings of Robert Rauschenberg and the mixed media of Edward Kienholz are other imaginative examples of the limitless array of new human constructs.
8. Marshall McLuhan, *Understanding Media—The Extensions of Man* (New York: McGraw-Hill Book Company, 1964), pp. 7-21. The same point is made from the side of a theory of criticism as found in Barthes, *op. cit.,* pp. 82-88.
9. An interesting comment on the machine, that is, a typewriter, as a shift in poetic media is found in an analysis of the poetry of Charles Olson by M. L. Rosenthal, *The New Poets* (New York: Oxford University Press, 1967), p. 146.
10. There are exceptions to this charge, although rarely found within the context of philosophy itself. One effort to construct a modern aesthetic is reaching its zenith with the publication of the first volume in Susanne Langer's *Mind: An Essay on Human Feeling* (Baltimore: Johns Hopkins Press, 1967).
11. An outstanding example of this problem is found in the six-

volume study edited by Gyorgy Kepes under the general title of *Vision and Value* (New York: George Braziller, 1965-66). With multicontributors to each volume ranging over the cultural and aesthetic problems which challenge us, philosophical perspective can be garnered only indirectly. The issues in question, however, have philosophical significance at almost every turn.

12. Cf. Allen S. Weller, "Art: U.S.A.: Now," *Art: U.S.A.: Now,* ed. Lee Nordness (New York: Viking Press, 1962), pp. 249-252, for a commentary on the increased importance of the reflective statement by the contemporary artist.

13. Herbert Read, "Realism and Abstraction in Modern Art," *The Philosophy of Modern Art* (New York: Meridian Books, 1957), p. 99. Cf. also Herbert Read, "The Limitations of a Scientific Philosophy," *The Forms of Things Unknown* (New York: Meridian Books, 1963), pp. 15-32.

14. Cf. Dore Ashton, "From Achilles' Shield to Junk," in Kepes, *The Man-Made Object*, p. 194. In speaking of the dadaists, she comments that "when they incorporated shreds of daily life in their work they did so with a dual and often equivocal purpose—both to deride and explore."

15. Thomas B. Hess, *Willem de Kooning* (New York: George Braziller, 1959), pp. 15-16.

16. For a significant comparison, cf. "Innovation in Science," *Scientific American,* vol. 199, no. 3 (September 1958), *passim.*

17. An illustration of our meaning of "field" is found in the analysis of "field composition" by Charles Olson in his essay on "Projective Verse," *The New American Poetry, 1945-1960,* ed. Donald M. Allen (New York: Grove Press, 1960), pp. 386-397.

18. An important but separate endeavor would take on the interrelated origins of the artistic event. Sociological, historical, and psychoanalytical matrices of interpretation, no one of them wholly reductionistic, are themselves irreducible conditioners of the aesthetic quality in each of our experiences. For a preliminary statement, cf. Arnold Hauser, *The*

Philosophy of Art History (New York: Alfred A. Knopf, 1958), pp. 21-116.

19. Hess, op. cit., p. 15.

20. Herbert Read, "The Modern Epoch in Art," The Philosophy of Modern Art, p. 29.

21. William James, "Notebook," cited in Ralph Barton Perry, The Thought and Character of William James, vol. 2 (Boston: Little, Brown and Co., 1935), p. 700.

22. Perry, op. cit., vol. I, pp. 108-109.

23. Jacques Barzun, "William James and the Clue to Art," The Energies of Art (New York: Harper & Row, 1956), p. 325.

24. William James, "The Stream of Thought," The Writings of William James—A Comprehensive Edition, ed. with an Introduction and Annotated Bibliography by John J. McDermott (New York: Random House, 1967), p. 45. Referred to hereafter as Writings.

25. James, Psychology—Briefer Course, p. 165.

26. William James, "A World of Pure Experience," Writings, p. 207. Cf. also "Pragmatism and Common Sense," Writings, p. 442: "Everything that happens to us brings its own duration and extension, and both are vaguely surrounded by a marginal 'more' that runs into the duration and extension of the next thing that comes."

27. Only by an acknowledgment of man's dwelling on the fringe can we understand the risk-oriented, strenuous ethic of James as well as his much maligned doctrine of "the will to believe."

28. William C. Seitz, Claude Monet—Seasons and Moments (New York: The Museum of Modern Art, 1960), p. 24.

29. William James, "The Stream of Thought," Writings, p. 46.

30. Wassily Kandinsky, "Reminiscences" (1913), in Robert L. Herbert, Modern Artists on Art (Englewood Cliffs: Prentice-Hall, 1964), p. 26.

31. We draw here from the tradition of American social psychology, especially the work of Charles Horton Cooley, George Herbert Mead, and Gardner Murphy. See, e.g., Murphy, "The Human Natures of the Future," Human

Potentialities (New York: Basic Books, 1958), pp. 302-329.

32. Robert Goldwater and Marco Treves, eds., *Artists on Art* (New York: Pantheon Books, 1947), p. 451. Cf. also, Weller, *op. cit.,* p. 12: "In a sense, the physical facts of nature become less and less important to us in themselves; we have gone beyond a stage in which recognition and identification of material forms is of primary significance. It is the tension between forms, the effects of movements on shapes and qualities, the active spaces which surround solid masses, which seem to be the most tangible things with which many artists need to work. There are of course striking parallels to the social and economic situation of our times. The great problems of our period are not material ones; they are problems of basic relationships."

33. The contemporaneity of James's questions and attitudes becomes obvious to the reader of the biography by Gay Wilson Allen, *William James* (New York: Viking Press, 1967).

34. Cited in William Seitz, *Hans Hofmann* (New York: The Museum of Modern Art, 1963), p. 50.

35. The historical and philosophical factors in the development of James's radical empiricism are extensively presented by Perry, *The Thought and Character of William James,* vol. II, *passim.* The relevant texts are found in *Writings,* especially pp. 134-317.

36. James, *Writings,* p. 314. This mature view is consistent with James's essay of 1884, "On Some Omissions of Introspective Psychology" *(Mind,* 9, pp. 1-26), which became the basis for his chapter in the *Principles of Psychology* entitled "The Stream of Thought." Further, this position maintains the fundamental viewpoint of "The Function of Cognition" *(Writings,* pp. 136-152), written in 1885, and rephrased throughout James's writings, particularly in the group of essays published in 1904 and 1905 under the generic theme of radical empiricism. Of significance for our subsequent remarks in Section IV, these essays of James play a decisive

role in the maturation of John Dewey's metaphysics. Cf. John Dewey, "Experience, Knowledge and Value—A Rejoinder," *The Philosophy of John Dewey,* ed. Paul Arthur Schilpp (New York: Tudor Publishing Co., 1951), p. 533, n. 16: "Long ago I learned from William James that there are immediate experiences of the connections linguistically expressed by conjunctions and prepositions. My doctrinal position is but a generalization of what is involved in this fact."

37. James, "The Stream of Thought," *Writings,* p. 38.

38. *Ibid.*

39. *Ibid.*

40. *Ibid.*

41. James, "A World of Pure Experience," *Writings,* p. 198.

42. *Ibid.,* p. 201.

43. *Ibid.,* pp. 212-213. Cf. John Dewey, "The Experimental Theory of Knowledge," *The Influence of Darwin on Philosophy* (New York: Henry Holt and Co., 1910), p. 90: "An experience is a knowledge, if in its quale there is an experienced distinction and connection of two elements of the following sort: *one means or intends the presence of the other in the same fashion in which itself is already present, while the other is that which, while not present in the same fashion, must become so present if the meaning or intention of its companion or yoke-fellow is to be fulfilled through the operation it sets up.*" A later statement on relational continuities, notably in the realm of aesthetics, is found in Christopher Alexander, "From a Set of Forces to a Form," in Kepes, *The Man-Made Object,* pp. 96-107.

44. Cf. Daniel Abramson, in Nordness, *Art: U.S.A.: Now,* p. 134. "De Kooning's painting is never a situation but rather, an entire event."

45. The problem of reductionism in aesthetic interpretation deserves far more analysis than it has received. For strong statements, cf. Norman Brown, "Art and Neurosis," *Life Against Death* (New York: Random House, 1959), pp. 55-

67; Erich Neumann, *Art and the Creative Unconscious* (New York: Harper & Row, 1966); and Arnold Hauser, *op. cit.,* pp. 43-116.

46. Cf. Robert Goldwater, *Primitivism in Modern Art,* rev. ed. (New York: Vintage Books, 1967), p. 98. Without objects, we have "implications far beyond the canvas itself." He cites a remark of Georges Duthuit that "the painter remains in intimate contact not alone with a motif, but also with the infinite nebulousness. . . ." Goldwater then states that "Emotionally as well as in its formal structure, the picture becomes a symbol whose very generality increases its possible meaning." We can crystallize this in Jamesian terms by holding that the lines of meaning stretch out beyond the finished work and are picked up by any number of responses, be they primitive rejoinders to sheer color and shape, aesthetic in the formal sense, or historical and sociological evaluations. Each work of art has a future as well as a past, in that it extends and proliferates its connections out beyond the field in which it was brought to fruition.

47. Cf. for example, Herbert, *op. cit.;* Hans Hofmann, *The Search for the Real and Other Essays,* ed. Sara T. Weeks and Bartlett H. Hayes, Jr. (Cambridge: The M.I.T. Press, 1967); and Hans Hofmann, "The Color Problem in Pure Painting—Its Creative Origin," in Frederick Wight, *Hans Hofmann* (Berkeley: University of California Press, 1957).

48. Seitz, *Hans Hofmann,* p. 50.

49. *Ibid.*

50. *Ibid.*

51. Cf. André Hodeir, "On Group Relations," *Toward Jazz* (New York: Grove Press, 1962), pp. 73-93.

52. John Dewey, in Schilpp, *op. cit.,* pp. 532-533.

53. Barthes, *loc. cit.*

54. The reigning confusion involved in our notions of creativity, innovation, and discovery is given incisive analysis from the side of a philosophy of science, by Norwood Russell Hanson, "The Anatomy of Discovery," *Journal of*

Philosophy, vol. 64, no. 11 (June 3, 1967), pp. 321-352. An interdisciplinary approach to discovery and innovation, especially with regard to the problem of form, is found in Lancelot Law Whyte, ed., *Aspects of Form* (Bloomington: Indiana University Press, 1961).

55. Guillaume Apollinaire, *The Cubist Painters* (New York: George Wittenborn, 1962), pp. 14-15.

56. Naum Gabo, cited in Herbert Read, "Realism and Abstraction in Modern Art," *The Philosophy of Modern Art,* p. 97.

57. Herbert Read, "Human Art and Inhuman Nature," *The Philosophy of Modern Art,* p. 76.

58. Cf. André Malraux, cited in *The Modern Tradition,* ed. Richard Ellmann and Charles Feidelson, Jr. (New York: Oxford University Press, 1965), p. 517: "I name that man an artist who *creates* forms, be he an ambassador like Rubens, an image-maker like Gislebert of Autun, an *ignotus* like the Master of Chartres, an illuminator like Limbourg, a king's friend and court official like Velazquez, a *rentier* like Cezanne, a man possessed like Van Gogh or a vagabond like Gauguin; and I call that man an artisan who *reproduces* forms, however great may be the charm or sophistication of his craftsmanship."

59. Gardner Murphy, "The Enigma of Human Nature," *Main Currents* (September 1956), no pagination.

60. James, "Personal Depression and Recovery," *Writings,* p. 8.

61. James, "The Sentiment of Rationality," *Writings,* p. 331.

62. Gordon Allport, *Becoming* (New Haven: Yale University Press, 1955), p. 51.

63. James, "The Stream of Thought," *Writings,* p. 71.

64. *Ibid.,* p. 70. Texts like this abound in the *Principles.* Cf. McDermott, Introduction, *Writings,* pp. xxxi-xxxv. James makes a specific reference to the artistic activity as "notoriously" selective and, therefore, having "superiority over works of nature" *(Writings,* p. 72). Compare these texts to that of the American painter, Robert Motherwell, in William C. Seitz, *The Art of Assemblage* (New York: The Museum of Modern Art, 1961), p. 97: "One cuts and

chooses and shifts and pastes, and sometimes tears off and begins again. In any case, shaping and arranging such a relational structure obliterates the need, and often the awareness of representation. Without reference to likeness, it possesses feeling because all the decisions in regard to it are ultimately made on the grounds of feeling."

65. James, "Pragmatism and Humanism," *Writings,* p. 456. And with Lawrence Durrell, "Does not everything depend on our interpretation of the silence around us?" Cf. *Justine* (New York: Pocket Books, 1961), p. 250.

66. James, "A World of Pure Experience," *Writings,* p. 212.

67. James, "How Two Minds Can Know One Thing," *Writings,* pp. 227-232.

68. Cf. William James, *A Pluralistic Universe* (New York: Longmans, Green and Co., 1909); or *Writings,* pp. 277-304, 482-581.

69. James, "Pragmatism's Conception of Truth," *Writings,* p. 432.

70. James, "A World of Pure Experience," *Writings,* p. 212.

71. James, "Pragmatism's Conception of Truth," *Writings,* p. 432.

72. John Dewey, *Art as Experience* (New York: Capricorn Books, 1958), p. 11.

73. In addition to material in Schilpp, *op. cit.,* a recent statement of Dewey's aesthetics is found in Monroe Beardsley, *Aesthetics—From Classical Greece to the Present* (New York: The Macmillan Co., 1966), pp. 332-342. For a relevant collection of Dewey texts, cf. Richard J. Bernstein, *Experience, Nature and Freedom* (New York: Liberal Arts Press, 1960). Creative reinterpretations of Dewey's thought are found in Robert C. Pollock, "Process and Experience," *John Dewey, His Thought and Influence,* ed. John Blewett (New York: Fordham University Press, 1960), and John Herman Randall, *Nature and Historical Experience* (New York: Columbia University Press, 1958).

74. For the scattered work on Dewey's aesthetics, cf. references in Beardsley, *op. cit.,* pp. 391-392.

75. Dewey, *Art as Experience*, p. 1.
76. *Ibid.*, p. 10.
77. *Ibid.*, p. 11.
78. Speaking of anticipation of what is to come, Dewey gives depth of meaning to James's contention that "life is in the transitions." Cf. *ibid.*, p. 50: "This anticipation is the connecting link between the next doing and its outcome for sense. What is done and what is undergone are thus reciprocally, cumulatively, and continuously instrumental to each other."
79. Dewey, *Art as Experience*, p. 40.
80. *Ibid.*, p. 19.
81. *Ibid.*, p. 18.
82. *Ibid.*, p. 14.
83. *Ibid.*, p. 54.
84. *Ibid.*, p. 24.
85. Seitz, *The Art of Assemblage*, p. 25.
86. We acknowledge the complexity of the contemporary art scene. From the side of the artist, for example, differences between assemblage and pop art are considerable. In addition to Seitz, *The Art of Assemblage*, one can find these distinctions in Lucy R. Lippard *et al.*, *Pop Art* (New York: Frederick A. Praeger, 1966) and Gregory Battcock, *The New Art* (New York: E. P. Dutton, 1966).
87. It is extraordinary and depressing that the pathos of the "Watts Towers," relative to our time, has not, to my knowledge, been discussed. The "Towers" were constructed by Simon Rodia, an Italian immigrant and tilesetter, as a monument to opportunity for the disfranchised. Just recently, they looked down upon a new group of deprived, who at the time were destroying Watts as a monument to the hopelessness of their plight. The setting was the same, but some continuities are not as fruitful as others.
88. Cf. Henri Focillon, "In Praise of Hands," *The Life of Forms in Art* (New York: George Wittenborn, 1948), pp. 65-78.
89. Cf. Marshall McLuhan, "Address at Vision 65," *The American Scholar*, vol. 35 (Spring 1966), pp. 196-205.

90. Seitz, *The Art of Assemblage,* p. 73.
91. Weller, *op. cit.,* p. 462.
92. Cf. Dewey, "The Live Creature and 'Etherial Things,' " *Art as Experience,* pp. 20-34.
93. Cf. R. E. L. Masters and Jean Houston, *The Varieties of Psychedelic Experience* (New York: Holt, Rinehart and Winston, 1966).
94. McLuhan, *Understanding Media,* p. 5.
95. Cf. R. Buckminster Fuller, "Conceptuality of Fundamental Structures," *Structure in Art and Science,* ed. Gyorgy Kepes (New York: George Braziller, 1965), pp. 66-88.

CHAPTER TWO

The Community of Experience

and

Religious Metaphors

Under our eyes a new stoicism is coming to birth from the death of God even as the old arose upon the tomb of the gods; it, too, is a stiffening at the extreme limit of doubt. . . .

This is the dominant spiritual state of a world in which every attempt at explanation having foundered, the scientific after the theological, the impossible is assuming its most uncompromising meaning. . . .

Not only is this world an irrational world, the mystery of which—pregnant as much of promise as of anguish—blurs its outlines: it is, too, a world positively, fully and definitively absurd, alien to reason as to goodness, deaf to every call uttered by man. It is not that it merely returns distressing replies to the questions we ask, but, far worse: it does not reply at all, because it has nothing to say in response.

—Emmanuel Mounier [1]

THE PROBLEM OF BELIEF

In the world described by Emmanuel Mounier, it would seem that we should fall back upon ourselves and look to the future in terms of our own energies. Still, how can human life, collectively understood, sustain such a vision, such a lonely vigilance on behalf of human values, stripped of their guarantee and lighted only by their human quality. I speak not of this person, nor of that person, not of Camus, nor of William James, nor of John Dewey, nor of Hannah Arendt, but rather of those who gather together without such insight and live in and off the "everyday." We cannot, after all, in Buber's phrase, live only with the "spasmodic breakthrough of the glowing deeds of solitary spirits." [2] No, we must enter into a "relational event," a "living center," a community of human beings. And this in turn involves us in a shared belief as directed to the worth of our efforts. No single idea, no single rubric, no single tradition can account for our quest for human unity and a creative relationship with the world. Speaking of such a quest, Erich Fromm tells us that "Man has to answer this question every moment of his life. Not only—or even primarily—with thoughts and words, but by his mode of being and acting." [3] Is this asking too much of man, to confront his situation without recourse to a given and collective source of security? For a complex host of reasons modern thought seems to say that contemporary man has no alternative; that he clings to securities which at best are no longer relevant and which at worst are an impediment to the development of genuine human values. This is not a quixotic or isolated response on the part of contemporary thought, for its roots are many and varied. The world of Kant with man as a Copernican center and religion seen within the limits of reason alone, the insight to self-deception in thinkers as disparate as

Marx, Dostoevsky, and Freud. Process and logical relations replacing substance and a Euclidean logic under the press of Hegel, Bergson, James, and Whitehead. At every turn paradox invades clarity.

Catastrophic events in our history—totalitarian madness and the threat of nuclear obliteration—seem to arise headless and show themselves to us as our own creations before we can evaluate their meaning and control their direction. We no longer have a *deus ex machina.* We are weary of "final solutions" and of total explanations ever to be corrected. Is it any wonder that in our age belief and unbelief join hands in the shadows of doubt and uncertainty. The viewpoint of our time was brilliantly anticipated by an American nineteenth-century writer, unsung, Benjamin P. Blood. In his work, *The Flaw in Supremacy,* Blood writes:

> Reason is but one item in the mystery; and behind the proudest consciousness that ever reigned, reason and wonder blushed face to face. The inevitable stales, while doubt and hope are sisters. Not unfortunately, the universe is wild—game-flavored as a hawk's wing. Nature is a miracle all; the same returns not save to bring the different. The slow round of the engraver's lathe gains but the breadth of a hair, but the difference is distributed back over the whole curve, never an instant true—ever not quite.[4]

Now if we can be pleased that contemporary culture has submitted to critical examination the last remnant of a world not of our making, but yet filled with demands which have kept us from our true problems, we cannot say that the end of outworn certitudes and the liberation of man from historical ideologies, religious or otherwise, are themselves adequate to our situation. For death of God or no, where there is no vision, the people perish. Or should we accept Ernest Becker's description in his *Revolution in Psychiatry,* where he speaks of our age as "The Wistful Age"—"never before had so many seen man's shortcomings so clearly, and been able to do so little about it."[5]

New problems loom large before us. Having overextended our beliefs in the past, dare we believe in the future? Having been seduced over and over again by our own commitments, can we again galvanize our energies to build a truly human order in response to emerging needs rather than as a continuity of some prefabricated view of man's destiny? Stripped of the religious symbolism of the past, can we develop an entirely new sense of affectivity, a new liturgy, a new source and way of celebration? Can we learn how to gather together out of a sense of human solidarity rather than in response to ritualized obligations? And throughout, can we maintain a living reverence for our traditions, religious and otherwise, held both in common and in highly stylized forms as roots of the plural way in which we have grown; or are we condemned to regard as obsolete all that has come before us? Put another way, to begin anew could mean, on the one hand, that we have been re-created by the dramatic bequest of our past in its splendor as well as by the challenge of its stupendous inadequacies. While acknowledging complex roots we would nonetheless be starting afresh. On the other hand, to start anew could mean that we wander aimlessly, cut off from traditional beliefs, wavering as to further commitments and without insight to a viable future. John Taylor, in a recent study of the masks of society, speaks of our situation thus:

> We live afflictedly, we men of the twentieth century, in a rubble of broken faiths. Our buildings we have rebuilt. Our outward desolations we have mended or buried and concealed. We nevertheless leave untouched and unresolved the most profoundly urgent question of our social condition. The question is very simply stated. It is this: What are the conditions essential to the dignity of persons in any form of human community? [6]

These questions and others similar should be the object of our concern and energies. Why then do we insist upon defending and attacking previously held beliefs as to man's situation, when by their very nature, and even at their best, they were limited both in implication and in symbolic formulation by constricted cultures of one form or another? We should remember that, paradoxically, our past beliefs take on genuine contemporaneity when they are seen as pointing to unrealized possibilities in man's understanding of himself rather than as end points already achieved. Apparently believers and unbelievers, rationalists and skeptics, find this circle of knowledge games hard to break.

Perhaps for our purpose here we could see these questions as two: first, the nature of belief in this new setting and, second, the possibility of a renewed belief in human community. Let us utilize the thought of William James as a way into the problem of belief. The persistent inadequacy of the response to James on this matter should be taken as an indication of the general refusal to take seriously the possibility of a new approach to the nature of belief. From the side of the religious tradition he is said to be an agnostic, though the *Will to Believe* was written against a form of agnosticism. From the side of science he was said to be a mystic, although he was an empirical, if not an experimental, psychologist and he was convinced of the clinical as well as the aesthetic dimensions of his findings in the *Varieties of Religious Experience*. From the side of philosophy he was seen as a poet, perhaps because he saw philosophy as the "habit of always seeing an alternative." In effect, he is a liberating thinker in that his analysis of our problem proceeds from the actual situation and not from the ingrained habits of academic disciplines.

Now with James we confront one statement of the tension between certitude and suicide. In a series of hallucinatory experiences, as well as what is described simply as his "personal crises" of 1869-70, James forges a doctrine of "belief in belief" which, he tells us, "to be sure can't be optimistic." Indeed, for James "Life shall [be built in] doing and suffering and creating." [7] Belief becomes an energy rather than a knowledge. The critics of this position say that James does not face squarely the problem of verification. It is said that he hedges and allegedly,

like the wager of Pascal, tries to guarantee safe passage no
matter how the question ultimately turns out. All these criticisms
of James, and they persist into our own day, are based on an old
logic, a tired and unimaginative way of describing man's fate.
James himself, in 1879, in an essay whose title alone teaches us
much, "The Sentiment of Rationality," offers us a clue to the
development of a truly modern doctrine of belief.

If we survey the field of history and ask what feature all
great periods of revival, of expansion of the human mind,
display in common, we shall find, I think, simply this: that
each and all of them have said to the human being, "The
inmost nature of the reality is congenial to *powers* which
you possess." [8]

We stand then in an ongoing environment, saturated with
possibilities for truly human life, which can be realized only by
the "Energies of Men." This is a position of trust, of belief, if
you will, in the meaningful encounter of man with his world. It
is precisely this situation which John Dewey, in his *Common
Faith*, calls religious. He states, "Faith in the continued disclos-
ing of truth through directed co-operative human endeavor is
more religious in quality than is any faith in a completed
revelation." [9] In that man's powers are congenial (not impotent,
not without limit—but congenial) to the thrust of nature, belief
becomes then a way of relocating ourselves with regard to
human needs. Belief does not offer a privileged position,
invoked as a defense against novelty and the cruel implications
of human folly. It is not only that James teaches us to believe in
the future of man but more so that he teaches us to believe in
the present of man, a present teeming with rich leads of all
kinds. Such leads, such implicitness, such seminal meanings, if
you will, do not offer themselves right off—at face value. They
become manifest in terms of man's struggle within his environment and relative to his goals. They do not yield themselves to
an agnostic standpoint or to an arrogant confidence as to how

things really are. Belief, in James's sense, can liberate them. In religious language we refer here to the endowed, to the sacred, better still, to the sacraments, which if properly understood in contemporary terms offer us ways to revitalize our human center, precisely at those happenings which are most decisive for us: our birth, our coming of age, our marriage, our life's work, our death, and on through our life overall. In his *Hasidism* Buber states that "Every thing desires to become a sacrament." [10] We can think of no aspect of our traditions more relevant, with more capacity to enrich our lives. It is then to be lamented that we so often leave these events buried in symbols no longer meaningful or as directed to aspects of our lives no longer operative.

Let us then place belief midway between certitude and nihilism. Let us see it characterized by trust, by affection, by a sense of novelty, and by hope. Those traditions, especially religious, which have told us through the centuries that we know, for sure, the objects of our belief, have violated not only the character of genuine belief but also the mysterious openness of genuine religious experience. It is a deep tragedy that so much of our energy is expended in explicating and even defending caricatures of our once viable traditions. Even ecumenism, from one point of view a rich opening of the spirit, is from another a witness to a long-standing and dreary history in which self-righteous interpretations of what is fundamentally inexplicable have divided us one from the other and cut off all of us from the human quest. In sociological terms, belief must cease its relationship to finality; it must turn to the future rather than to the past.

We should accept here the position of Erich Fromm, who tells us that "reason cannot be effective, unless man has hope and belief." He goes on to state that:

> Goethe was right when he said that the deepest distinction between various historical periods is that between belief and disbelief, and when he added that all epochs in

which belief dominates are brilliant, uplifting, and fruitful, while those in which disbelief dominates vanish because nobody cares to devote himself to the unfruitful.[11]

We should add, however, that events do not come to us by their nature fruitful and unfruitful. This is what James would mean by his statement that "belief helps to create the fact." James deplores those who hang back as though the resolution of man's problem rests in other hands or as though in any significant issue we can be sure of all the elements before coming to a judgment. He comments:

So far as man stands for anything, and is productive or originative at all, his entire vital function may be said to have to deal with maybes. Not a victory is gained, not a deed of faithfulness or courage is done, except upon a maybe; not a service, not a sally of generosity, not a scientific exploration or experiment or textbook, that may not be a mistake. It is only risking our persons from one hour to another that we live at all. And often enough our faith beforehand in an uncertified result *is the only thing that makes the result come true.*[12]

If James and, in this matter, his existentialist successors show us the way to extricate belief from certitude, they do not show us how to believe together. Such a tradition gives to us a rich feeling about personal life and about the qualities of human activity, but in our time we know all too well that such individualized energies are often buried in the complexities which confront us at every turn. Certainly we wish to accept the view that nothing final can be said until the last of us has had our say, but can such a view of a man, of belief, of energy and openness, persist in the larger community, or is it to be restricted to isolated genius, largely ineffectual for the problems which beset us?

In this way we come to the most crucial question in the problem of belief and modern man, namely: Are we able to believe together as a community without suppressing our differences? And can this belief have truly religious significance for us, that is, open us to the endowed and sacred quality of all that is, while yet not offering a hierarchy of meanings fixed or specifically holy things which divide us from our brother? Can we actually celebrate this belief? Celebrate it in the way of historical religion, that is, liturgically, or in the way of contemporary protest movements, with song and ritual born of adversity? Or is it to remain an abstract goal, a containment keeping us from destroying each other but without building new symbols of human solidarity and affection? Thus John Dewey at the conclusion of *Human Nature and Conduct,* by virtue of a behavioral analysis of our situation, can say:

> Within the flickering inconsequential acts of separate selves dwells a sense of the whole which claims and dignifies them. In its presence we put off mortality and live in the universal.
>
> The life of the community in which we live and have our being is the fit symbol of this relationship. The acts in which we express our perception of the ties which bind us to others are its only rites and ceremonies.[13]

COVENANT AND EXPERIMENT

> But because being here amounts to so much, because all this Here and Now, so fleeting, seems to require us and strangely concerns us. Us the most fleeting of all. Just once, everything, and for once. Once and no more. And we, too, once. And never again. But this having been once, though only once, having been once on earth—can it ever be cancelled?
>
> —Rainer Maria Rilke, *Duino Elegies* [14]

In order to come to grips with the processes of communal life, we should perhaps reconsider the notion of a covenant, although now in terms of a modern relationship between belief and liberty. It is not, I would hold, without meaning that the American tradition began with a renewed version of the covenant and in those terms developed a tradition of liberty, a tradition now threatened, significantly, by our inability to arrive at a more extensive covenant with the world community. Nor is it unrelated that the greatest obstacle to a genuine covenant of religious belief has been the inability to confront the question of liberty. We cannot say it too strongly: covenant and liberty are, for us now, and for the future of man, inseparable necessities.

Speaking of the covenants of civilization, John Taylor cites Job 29:14, "I put on justice, and it clothed me." Taylor remarks, "In that simple sentence is the whole burden of the Hebrew's sense of history: in community he is clothed; cut off, he is naked and there is no other nakedness." [15] We must remind ourselves, however, that the community is not given to us as such. It is to be attained. And the process of attaining it is the fabric of our life together. In *Between Man and Man* Buber describes the religious dimensions of community.

> We expect a theophany of which we know nothing but the place, and the place is called community. In the public catacombs of this expectation there is no single God's Word which can be clearly known and advocated, but the words delivered are clarified for us in our human situation of being turned to one another. There is no obedience to the coming one without loyalty to his creature. To have experienced this is our way.[16]

In theological terms, the living virtue, the one we suggest to our children as an option, becomes hope rather than faith.[17] And the experimental attitude takes precedence over the need to sustain and clarify previous commitments. Journey becomes a meaningful activity despite an unclear understanding of our ultimate future. We do not affirm that such an emphasis on process over against a corresponding concern for arrival need be an optimistic one. Gabriel Marcel, for one, sees man on a journey, but it is one in which he must "perpetually remind himself that he is required to cut himself a dangerous path across the unsteady blocks of a universe which has collapsed and seems to be crumbling in every direction." [18] The challenge and terror of the modern situation was perhaps best put by Karl Jaspers. "As compared with man in (previous) eras, man today has been uprooted, having become aware that he exists in what is but a historically determined and changing situation. It is as if the foundations of being had been shattered." [19] Whatever the merits of Jaspers's philosophical assessment of this situation, namely, that it proceeds from a breakup of the identity between thought and being, we can accept his statement that:

we live in a movement, a flux a process, in virtue of which changing knowledge enforces a change in life; and in turn, changing life enforces a change in the consciousness of the knower. This movement, this flux, this process, sweeps us into the whirlpool of unceasing conquest and creation, of loss and gain, in which we painfully circle, subject in the main to the power of the current, but able now and then to exert ourselves within a restricted sphere of influence. For we do not only live in a situation proper to mankind at large, but we experience this situation as it presents itself in specific historical circumstances, issuing out of a previous situation and progressing towards a subsequent one.[20]

Still other thinkers—Dewey, Bergson, Buber, and Whitehead, for example—accept the developmental character of the human situation but are more sanguine about its possibilities. Whether he regrets or not, it would seem that contemporary man, for the most part, accepts the journey as the source of his communal experience, rather than as a goal specifically delineated. Cannot we say that at present we deny the possibility of a viable eschatology? Or at the very least, hold to an eschatology viable only as mediated by the values and hopes of each generation. In such a framework the goal is to be constructed rather than found or awarded.

This attitude gives a decidedly different context to the present effort to formulate questions about man's destiny. For one thing, our religious options are reduced to the bone. We cannot, after all, participate in the affairs of the larger community and still appeal to our variant traditions, which have strands of exclusivity and self-righteousness built into their very fabric. To dilute certitude and affirm the sacred character of temporality, effects a notion of community characterized by concession, compromise, and an opening outwards. In this regard perhaps we should look at the recent notions of containment and coexistence as mediating insights between the traditional effort to maintain a resolute hold on our previous beliefs and the modern approach to belief which holds to the evolution of new possibilities for reconciliation. Thus far such a conciliatory attitude has been generated, for the most part, by fear of repeated and increased catastrophe. Even for such a limited reason the fruit of this approach is beginning to emerge, namely, the healing and teaching quality of time passing. In larger terms, relative to the world community, we can phrase the present dialectic as a tension between suppressed violence (with sporadic and depressing exceptions) and the bold belief in the liberating quality of time, without corresponding guarantees of ultimate resolution.

This tension between certitude and novelty must be viewed as a central religious and philosophical concern in any effort to assess the possibilities for building a truly human community. Contemporary thought on this matter has as its irreducible beginning point the modern critique of certitude. Certainly, the early work of Sartre, standing for philosophical nihilism, is correct in its critique of the overextended religious and intellectual commitments of Western culture. Accepting this critique, is it possible for us to affirm a genuine future for man, without our being liable to "bad faith"? It is obvious that such an effort cannot be Pollyanna in any sense. We must take full cognizance of the complex and interrelated sociopsychological factors involved in human growth, factors too often missed entirely by philosophical and theological evaluations. As our recent experience demonstrates in a telling way, we must pay particular attention to those seeming irrational dimensions of human life, disruptive personally as well as on a colossal scale. Such persistent accompaniments to the human struggle have too often been overlooked by previous versions of man's future.

Perhaps we should put it this way. Can vision and concern as to man's immediate destiny, when trimmed of its pretense and overarching claims beyond the call of experience, liberate sufficient energy and commitment to the human struggle, necessary to the structuring of a noble and creative life? In effect, can we have an evangelical approach without dogmatic assurance? Heretofore it would appear that we have been better able to generate intense concern over those beliefs that are divisive of human solidarity rather than on behalf of those that celebrate the slow maturation of man's search for ways of reconciliation and collective growth. In this way the precipitous claim of a final goal for some single form or gathering of human activity has too often shut out the possibilities of development and novelty not explicitly articulated by that goal. We would offer that this is most often a religious corruption of the anthropological process and has to be radically reworked if we are to face the actual limits which bind us in our historical situation.

If we focus on the development of American culture, we confront important versions of this clash between the sanctity of time and the loyalty to a vision of an ultimate future. As a matter of fact, the religious dimensions to the anthropological question are preeminent and persistent in the whole of American life. Unfortunately, traditional interpretations of American cultural history have accepted a radical separation between our religious origins and the subsequent "secularization" of those beginnings. Given this affection for simply secular history, important later developments, religious in origin but profoundly cultural in implication, as the evangelical awakenings of the eighteenth and nineteenth century, as well as the Social Gospel movement, have been kept to the side of cultural history. Neglected in such a method is the extraordinary continuity between the early religious vision of America and the continued seminal role of this insight in the culture at large. A glance at the way in which the first three generations of American Puritans worked through the conflict between doctrine and experience will prove instructive, for their fundamental problem is still with us.[21] At what point does the doctrinal stand taken violate the actualities in which we find ourselves, so as to prevent further exploration? And granted that doctrine cannot remain perpetually impervious to experience, what becomes a living relationship between these antagonists and how does a tradition maintain continuity in the face of such persistent reworkings?

From one point of view the Puritans went under. In other terms, however, they built themselves into the structure of American life and perhaps, in the long run, into that of world culture. Conceding their style, their metaphors, and their living habits, they bequeathed their vision as to a temporalized covenant and their religious sensibility. The Puritan experience, therefore, is not obsolete but continues to play a role in the growth of human awareness. From the perspective of process this is a creative and fruitful development. From the perspective of orthodoxy this was a calamity. The history of the first century of American puritanism supports the generalization running through this essay, namely, that religious insight must renew itself out of affairs and needs of human living. When it drifts loose from such interaction and perpetuates only its self-sustained version of human life, it is proper that it go under, or at least, along institutional lines, be radically reconstructed. A profound religious insight should be able at that time to bequeath dimensions to the human situation which outlive the demise of its peculiar style. The Puritans had the deepest sense of renewal in Christian history. They combined the Abrahamic sense of man's journey with a salvific vision found in the early church. Rooted in a diaspora, Christian in outlook, and imbued with the spirit of the Hebrew Bible, they faced the problem of humanizing a hostile environment. In view of the utopian and millenarian framework given to thought and activity associated with the New World, the Puritan experience has been often evaluated as the failure of an unrealizable goal.

In an essay written for the *Eranos Yearbook* and recently republished, Mircea Eliade summarizes the recent literature about the eschatological and even apocalyptic dimension to the Puritan colonization.[22] He draws the conclusion that contemporary efforts to understand these origins betray a need to begin *ab initio* and construct anew an eschatological vision. We can agree with Eliade that "The 'novelty' which still fascinates Americans today is a desire with religious underpinnings. In 'novelty,' one hopes for a 're-naissance,' one seeks a new life." [23] But that this new life deals with "the metamorphosis of the American millenarist ideal"—in that we accept "the certainty of the eschatological mission, and especially of attaining once again the perfection of early Christianity and restoring paradise to earth" [24]—is a contention of another kind. Such a position is a reflection of the belief that religious vision is evaluated precisely in proportionate relationship to its ability to take us beyond the confines of our own experience, personal and collective. Thereby, Eliade, as so many other commentators, fails to see the religious quality of the pragmatic reconstruction offered to meet the press of actual events.[25] To find an awareness of these historical events and a delineation of the religious response to them, we must look to the sociologists and cultural historians. They in turn, however, are often insensitive to the religious quality of such a transformation.[26] Both approaches are limited by a highly defined understanding of what constitutes religious experience. This understanding will have to be broadened considerably by contemporary thought if we are to explore and encourage the novel qualities necessary to a living and extensive religious experience in our time.

Now if we take a closer look at the Puritan experience, we find that those who view it as primarily a failure to realize an eschatological ideal are wide of the mark. More to the point, was the effort of the Puritans to institutionalize the covenant consistent with the political and social exigencies of their time and place? The history of Calvinist doctrine in the hands of the American Puritans is a revealing instance of the transmutation of theological assertions for purposes of grounding a more

extensive society while there is still commitment to the fundamental Christian concern for redemption. Perry Miller, in his
essay on "The Marrow of Puritan Divinity," has shown how the
American Puritans systematically reworked the notion of a
covenant.[27] Centering it in human activity, they reformulated
the tension between a covenant of grace and that of works in a
way which has provided much of our subsequent attitude to
polity and community. The Puritan denial of a Church,
understood as separate from the way in which men are
communally gathered together, has been, we believe, immensely
fruitful for American society. And since that time American life
has been most nobly renewed under evangelical emphasis when
the body politic, as such, is regarded as the locus of our most
important undertakings.[28]

   The last such effort to use religious language directed toward
communal renewal was that of the Social Gospel movement at
the turn of the century.[29] Although this attempt was concerned
in an incisive way with a temporal doctrine of the kingdom, its
use of scriptural language and an inability to break decisively
with theological problems contributed to its undoing. The
succeeding effort at social amelioration, led by Dewey, stripped
itself of such language and attempted to create an entirely new
discourse about values and conflicts in the community. With
regard to concern and sensitivity, Dewey can be read as fully
continuous with the Puritan evangelical tradition. Despite his
most profound efforts, however, he could not deal adequately
with the religious quality of even his own version of the human
situation. Subsequent utilization of Dewey's approach was
simply crude in any assessment of the religious question. When
in our time we have need for a political awakening, fully
consonant with pragmatic valuation as articulated by Dewey, we
should strive to render our activities celebratory. The difficulty
confronting us is that both traditional political and religious
institutions are no longer an adequate let alone rich resource for
a celebratory language. A morphology of ameliorative social
movements in America shows that they begin with a jeremiad,
then a diagnosis and finally an effort at collective consciousness-

raising. The key factor in this process is the development of a new language, one that not only reflects criticism of the past but also opens us out to new possibilities, as witness the recent formulations of black American consciousness and woman's consciousness.

We, in the middle of the twentieth century, have witnessed the emergence of world culture. America can no longer strut before the world as one above many. Much of our previous rhetoric, political and religious, is outworn and sterile, when it is not offensive. The task seems clear: we must develop a new celebratory language, rooted in contemporary American experience, pluralistic in style and able to resonate creatively throughout the fabric of world culture.

NOTES

1. Emmanuel Mounier, *The Spoil of the Violent* (New York: Cross Currents, 1961), pp. 9-10.
2. Martin Buber, *I and Thou,* 2d ed. (New York: Charles Scribner's Sons, 1958), p. 54.
3. Erich Fromm, *Beyond the Chains of Illusion* (New York: Pocket Books, Inc., 1963), p. 189.
4. Cited in William James, *The Will to Believe and Other Essays* (New York: Longmans, Green and Co., 1896), pp. viii-ix.
5. Ernest Becker, *The Revolution in Psychiatry* (New York: The Free Press, 1964), p. 200. This study has considerable importance for the last section of this paper, as it advocates in psychiatric terms a new approach to human behavior based on the work of James, Dewey, and G. H. Mead.
6. John F. A. Taylor, *The Masks of Society—An Inquiry Into the Covenants of Civilization* (New York: Appleton-Century-Crofts, 1966), p. viii.
7. Henry James, ed., *The Letters of William James,* vol. I (Boston: The Atlantic Monthly Press, 1920), p. 148.
8. William James, "The Sentiment of Rationality," *op. cit.,* p. 86.

9. John Dewey, *A Common Faith* (New Haven: Yale University Press, 1934) 1955), p. 26.

10. Cited in Jacob Trapp, ed., *Martin Buber—To Hallow This Life* (New York: Harper and Brothers, 1958), p. 157. A full discussion of this problem is found in Martin Buber, "Symbolic and Sacramental Existence," *The Origin and Meaning of Hasidism* (New York: Horizon Press, 1960), pp. 151-181.

11. Fromm, *op. cit.*, p. 195.

12. James, "Is Life Worth Living?" *op. cit.*, p. 59.

13. John Dewey, *Human Nature and Conduct* (New York: The Modern Library, 1930), pp. 331-332. It is of note that Dewey's rhetoric on religion in this volume, so long an object of scorn by those of religious convictions, is now commonplace in the writings of religiously oriented contemporary criticism (see *ibid.*, pp. 330-331).

14. Rainer Maria Rilke, "Ninth Elegy," *Duino Elegies* (New York: W.W. Norton and Co., 1939), p. 73.

15. Taylor, *op. cit.*, p. 23.

16. Martin Buber, "Dialogue," in *Between Man and Man* (London: Routledge and Kegan Paul, 1947), p. 7.

17. See for example Max Born, "What Is Left to Hope For?" *Cross Currents*, vol. 16, 3 (Summer 1966), 257-264.

18. Gabriel Marcel, "Value and Immortality," *Homo Viator* (Chicago: Henry Regnery Co., 1951), p. 153.

19. Karl Jaspers, *Man in the Modern Age* (New York: Anchor Books, 1957), p. 2.

20. Jaspers, *op. cit.*, p. 3.

21. The American Puritan approach to the conflict between doctrine and experience is treated by Perry Miller, *Errand into the Wilderness* (Cambridge: Harvard University Press, 1956). In American history the most egregious instance of our maintaining doctrine in the face of countervailing experience was our sustenance of the war in Vietnam.

22. The essay by Eliade, "Paradis et Utopie: Geographie Mythique et Eschatologique," in *Vom Sinn der Utopie*, *Eranos Yearbook, 1963*, now appears translated in Frank E.

Manuel, ed., *Utopias and Utopian Thought* (Boston: Beacon Press, 1966), pp. 260-280.

23. Eliade, *art. cit.,* p. 268.
24. *Ibid.,* p. 269.
25. Cf. Eugene Fontinell, *Toward A Reconstruction of Religion* (New York: Doubleday and Co., 1970).
26. For a sharp critique of the type of cultural history which is innocent of the qualities peculiar to religious conviction see Alan Simpson, *Puritanism in Old and New England* (Chicago: Phoenix Books, 1955).
27. Miller, *Errand,* pp. 48-98.
28. We do not minimize that with the advent of modern nationalism such affection for the body politic can cross the line to a vicious and collective *hubris.* At this point the covenant, religiously understood, becomes a corrective. This problem requires detailed treatment, but it does not change our discussion, for the modern church has proven inadequate in both directions.
29. See for example Charles Hopkins, *The Rise of the Social Gospel in America, 1865-1915* (New Haven: Yale University Press, 1940), and Robert T. Handy, ed., *The Social Gospel in America, 1870-1920* (New York: Oxford University Press, 1966).

CHAPTER THREE

Deprivation and Celebration: Suggestions for an Aesthetic Ecology

This isolated line and the isolated fish alike are living beings with forces peculiar to them, though latent. . . . But the voice of these latent forces is faint and limited. It is the environment of the line and the fish that brings about a miracle: the latent forces awaken, the expression becomes radiant, the impression profound. Instead of a low voice, one hears a choir. The latent forces have become dynamic. The environment is the composition.

—Wassily Kandinsky [1]

I

Perhaps we may be allowed to sound an introductory positive note as accompaniment to the extensive turbulence which characterizes contemporary American culture. At this time we are witnessing an extraordinary intensification of the experience of self-consciousness along with a parallel growth in our sensitivity to environmental problems. Dissatisfaction in our culture proceeds not only from the traditional critique of inadequate surroundings but also from the escalating awareness of the complex needs of the human person. Contemporary man suffers more, or at least complains more, in part because he has come to believe and feel that his needs are infinitely more complex. While such a development has obvious political and social roots, the thrust of this presentation will be to show that in large measure the revolution in our time is aesthetic—that is, a revolution in feeling. And we contend that one of the meanings of contemporary art is the light it casts on this transformation of human needs and possibilities.

The all too characteristic attempt to deal with this revolution by a mere shift in the external functions of our institutions is now proving to be abortive. In his book *Symbolism*, Whitehead spells out the implications of an insensitive approach to institutional transformation.

It is the first step in sociological wisdom, to recognize that the major advances in civilization are processes which all but wreck the societies in which they occur: —like unto an arrow in the hand of a child. The art of free society consists first in the maintenance of the symbolic code; and secondly in fearlessness of revision, to secure that the code serves those purposes which satisfy an enlightened reason. Those societies which cannot combine reverence to their symbols with freedom of revision, must ultimately decay either from anarchy, or from the slow atrophy of a life stifled by useless shadows.[2]

Whereas Whitehead refers to the "symbolic code," we speak here of man's "affectivity." The important question confronting proponents of social change has to do with how men actually feel about their situation. Efforts to ameliorate the human condition must be sensitized in a very specific way as to what those persons in question "care for"—in a word, that toward which they are affectionate. The failure to achieve this sensitivity looms large as a factor in generating the savage contemporary critique of the "do-gooder," the "liberal," and the establishment-sponsored programs for social welfare. Too often our programs attempt to help people become what we *assume* they should become. Too often we impose our own social style on others, even in some instances our own social trap. We claim that such programs are liberating although we rarely have any understanding of the strength of the variant life-styles with which we tamper.[3]

We look back, for example, on the recent efforts at urban renewal. The diagnosis seemed obvious: a ramshackle environment complete with all the attendant physical and social evils. The solution seemed equally obvious: destruction of the environment and either relocation to a new context or a subsequent return to the rebuilt neighborhood. Now, quite aside from the fact that the hard-core poor were rarely provided opportunity to return, another, more subtle problem existed. For even when the original occupants were returned to public housing, they seemed not to take care of these new dwellings. The first reason offered was typically insensitive: "What can you expect of such people? They are incorrigible." A later reason was more humane but nonetheless paternalistic and wide of the mark: "Such people have had no experience in caring for a new environment. They have to be taught."

It is only in our time and only when we listen to the people involved, in their own language, that we come close to understanding this problem. A neighborhood, a block, a tenement is not simply an external setting. Rather it is a complex field of relationships that form an ecological network, the strength of which is often beneath the surface. The human organism struggles for salvation, no matter how impoverished his context. He does this by building himself into his environment by means of establishing confidence in a number of relational ties. They may involve "landmarks"—a candy store, a playground, a house of worship, a merchant tradition, or perhaps vicarious participation in the passing scene. Such relations become internalized, that is, taken for granted. Their full power, their function as lifelines become manifest only when they are uprooted. The problem thus becomes obvious. With the cutting of these inexplicit yet deeply felt ties, people become estranged, and while thrashing about in search of a recognizable hold, they tend to reject a new and comparatively alien environment.[4] It is imperative, therefore, that our diagnosis of social ills include a recognition of the positive factors at work in the situation under evaluation. The more serious our affliction, the deeper the affection we have for those aspects of it which are humanizing. Little if any growth is achieved if by our social changes we truncate these relations, especially in view of the failure of contemporary pedagogy to develop in many of our people the ability to make new ones from scratch.

John Dewey has told us that "order is not imposed from without but is made out of the relations of harmonious interactions that energies bear to one another."[5] Why, then, do we fail to recognize that personal growth does not usually proceed from an imposition of values, however noble in intent, but must rather be continuous with the experienced situation in which a person finds himself? Such growth, particularly when found in the midst of social and economic impoverishment, often does not appear to be impressive when judged by standards external to the undergoing of the experience, as, for example, long-standing sociological sanctions primarily related to the problems and aspirations of another time. Many of us still assume that the mere shift from one environment to another is equivalent to a personal breakthrough, as though mobility guaranteed depth of participation. In fact, the external character of the environment is not a necessary guarantee of the quality of involvement. The personal growth of which we speak, no matter what the setting, signalizes an integration of the needs and possibilities of the person, taken, in Dewey's phrase, as a "live creature." That an environment should generate and sustain such a development in the person is obvious. That it should not systematically prevent such growth is equally obvious. Where we seem to be in the dark is in the evaluation of specific environments. We seem quite incapable of recognizing and sustaining the redeeming factors in what has come to be known as a deprived environment, just as we ignore the lethal factors in those considered to be more acceptable. A contrast of the worlds of Henry Roth and James Agee with those of John Updike and John Cheever gives aesthetic intensity to the long-standing questions about the relationship of affluence and personal growth. One of the reasons for failure to recognize and strengthen the humanizing dimensions of impoverished environments is that, on methodological if not psychological grounds, contemporary efforts to engender social change often fall victim to a colossal instance of "vicious intellectualism," as phrased by William James. "The treating of a name as excluding from the fact named what the name's definition fails positively to include, is what I call vicious intellectualism." [6]

James warns us that the consistent use of certain "names" is not a necessary indication that the experiences so named have maintained an equal consistency in meaning and import. Names of large and complex experiences such as "city," "poverty," and "black" have developed an illegitimate clarity over the years. Upon deeper analysis, particularly when sustained by the articulation of persons actually involved, we find that many of our assumptions are seriously out of touch with the nature of the situation as experienced. It is instructive in this regard to acknowledge the new use of the term "visibility" when applied to "black people" and the "poor," for it refers to the upending of the mass stereotypes which have resulted from structuring our definitions in such a way as to preclude new data. Assessing the "failures" of black Americans in the context of immigrant success and the attribution of the circularity of hard-core poverty to lack of initiative are glaring instances of such stereotypes. In each case, when challenged, these assumptions have been shown to misdirect our attention and keep us from confronting even the most obvious causal factors in these massive social problems.

More subtle dimensions of our lives—the nature of the learning process, for example—have shown themselves to be surprisingly opaque when analyzed by traditional concepts. Many of our people are profoundly alert to their situation and are responsive in an original and creative way to their environment, yet judged by most of the criteria we have enshrined, they would be found bereft of insight. Again, it is instructive to remember that the previous extensive revolution in our educational system also involved a break with a massive stereotype— namely, the contention that interest and social relevance were inversely related to the importance of what was to be learned. Symbolized by the new psychology of William James and the pedagogy of John Dewey, the breakthrough in educational practice at the turn of the century involved a radical relocating of the question. The experience of the child as a child rather than as a small adult became the focal point, and from this proceeded extensive changes in what we call the aesthetic setting: the design of the classroom, its furniture, and the overall provision for continuity between the school as environment and the needs and interests of the child. Unfortunately the results of this breakthrough have themselves now become stereotypical and often function to prevent articulation of the considerably new needs and style of more recent generations. As then, a new aesthetic setting for inquiry is necessary. The phrase "Tell it like it is" has roots not only in the anguish of the black revolution and in the hippie critique of the middle class but also in a more generalized attack on the bifurcation between our experience directly expressed in aesthetic terms and statements about experience. These latter statements are accused of becoming a world unto themselves, complete with seductive metaphorical changes intended to indicate contact with reality.

In this last regard, our capacity for self-deception seems unlimited. Too often we credit ourselves with an awareness of others' experience simply on the basis of a mere shift in our language. We domesticate or legitimize the most radical protest by borrowing its phrasing and thereby claim institutional awareness and accommodation. On a more profound and integral level, however, such language as "black argot" or "poverty speak" is rooted in a very different version of the world and cannot be absorbed. As a way of preventing such a shallow response, the disfranchised have taken to expressing themselves in obviously aesthetic terms, peculiar to their own sense of experience. Gatherings of the poor, blacks, and now students tell a remarkably similar story in pointing to this gap between radically different styles of articulation. The present revolution, therefore, addresses itself not so much to the values in question, on which there is considerable agreement, but rather to our way of interacting or, in Dewey's phrase, to our way of "having an experience." What is being sought, then, can be phrased as a new cultural pedagogy in which the "affective" dimension moves from the periphery to the center, as a resource for evaluating the quality of our environment. I offer here that contemporary art, taken in the broad sense, is incisive about this need and yields significant philosophical and methodological approaches, which would prove liberating if we were to adopt them in our attempt to bring about basic institutional changes. Further, again on methodological grounds, it would be salutary if our efforts to bring about social change were influenced as much by the arts as by developments in the natural and social sciences. Let us now attempt to offer some sustenance for these contentions.

II

The fundamental question has to do with our basic understanding of human activity. Although seldom put so crudely, the fact is that a common attitude is reflected in the statement that man is a thing among things, manipulable from the outside. Other images are only slightly below the surface, holding that man is a box, a container, a chessman externally moved upon a world board with a finite number of places to occupy. Perhaps we should call this a euclidean geometric anthropology, in which man "fits in" and the angles "prove out" in the end. For those of us who credit a life of reflection, for the supposed avoidance of this attitude, we are now warned by the fact that the very institutions created to sustain such insight have recently been among those accused of gross personal manipulation.

Now, if there is any generalization we can make about contemporary art, it has to do precisely with this approach to human activity. To bathe ourselves in the variant art styles of our time is to come away with the conviction that man is an energizer and a maker of worlds,[7] rather than a derivation from worlds already made. In an effort to stress the novel aspects of creative experience, contemporary art has introduced the performing of "happenings." While it has to be admitted that, despite the claims of increased flexibility, such "happenings" are stylized and even planned, the full implication, however, of such a direction is that man himself is a "happening" and that at any given time, he can "aesthetize" his living. Coupled with recent experiments in the theater, we find here a concretization, from the side of art, of Dewey's insight into the rhythm and activity of the "live creature." Dewey even anticipated the contemporary artistic commitment to immediacy and its denial of the tendency to store up for another generation,[8] He tells us that "the time of consummation is also one of beginning anew. Any attempt to perpetuate beyond its term the enjoyment attending the time of fulfillment and harmony constitutes *withdrawal from the world.*"[9] Out of a different context, Robert Jay Lifton describes this development in the assessment of human activity, as the creation of "a new kind of man—a 'protean man.'" He continues:

As my stress is upon change and flux, I shall not speak much of "character" and "personality," both of which suggest fixity and permanence. Erikson's concept of identity has been, among other things, an effort to get away from this principle of fixity; and I have been using the term self-process to convey still more specifically the idea of flow. For it is quite possible that even the image of personal identity, in so far as it suggests inner stability and sameness, is derived from a vision of a traditional culture in which man's relationships to his institutions and symbols are still relatively intact—which is hardly the case today. If we understand the self to be the person's symbol of his organism, then self-process refers to the continuous psychic recreation of that symbol.[10]

Lifton's understanding of the self as the "person's symbol of his organism," contrary to the use of the term "self-identity," enables us to avoid blocking off the necessary awareness of the novel qualities in our experiencing. Rather than taking the creative artistic process as a departure from life ordinarily lived, we should see it as an articulation of possibilities inherent in the flow of each person's experience. In this vein, with contemporary art as the focus, we gain access to a new set of metaphors, considerably more viable in any consideration of human activity.

Contemporary art presents us with an open system. Order is maintained, but at the service of novelty. The future is anticipated not as a codification of our intention, rather as a harbinger of surprise. Indeed, intention itself emerges with clarity only when we are far into the creative process, and is often retrospectively reconstructed when our work takes a surprising turn. More specifically, the work of contemporary art is largely themed by a tension between the pressure for improvisation and the need to maintain some structural continuity, at least to the satisfaction of the artist. So demanding is the burden of improvisation that the beginning artist of our time often feels compelled to start from scratch and create an entirely new environment. Thus we have a dizzying array of new approaches in which the artist, by his work, not only avoids even the broadest imitation but, in deeply personal terms, challenges the assumptions about the nature of art prior to his contribution. Consequently, what is striking about this art is the variety of technique and, above all, the materials used, for both are decisive factors in the creating of a new environment. Also it is rare that works by different artists now reveal enough in common for us to utilize the comparative method to evaluate them. Generic terms like "pop art," "combine paintings," "mixed media," and "assemblage" are merely catch-holders and lack clear criteria of distinction and evaluation. We come closer to the quality of this art if, upon confrontation, we do our best to participate in the artist's "managing process," with an eye to our own experience. Contemporary art does not tend to create objects of honor. Rather, it honors the act of creating, and it celebrates the personal as an aesthetic dimension. In some instances of electronic sculpture, the observer becomes a direct participant, a co-creator, as his body scent or sounds are taken as factors in the activity of the sculpture. The contemporary artist, at his best, is pressing us to aesthetically reconstruct our own environments rather than to have us participate vicariously in idealized versions of a world distant from our own experience. We should pay heed here to John Dewey, who wrote that works of art are "celebrations, recognized as such, of the things of ordinary experience. Even a crude experience, if authentically an experience, is more fit to give a clue to the intrinsic nature of esthetic experience than is an object already set apart from any other mode of experience." [11]

The element which binds Dewey's metaphysics to the contemporary "art of the ordinary" is to be found in the dimension of affection. It is necessary to have a genuine care for common experience, if celebration is to take place. By virtue of an emphasis on improvisation, the affirmation of the potential majesty of the ordinary, and the denial of rationalistic criteria for aesthetic evaluation, contemporary art has shown itself to be of relevance for certain attempts to revitalize personal life now under the press of vast institutional bureaucracies. If we truly seek a new cultural pedagogy, the task before us is to bring about a decisive movement from the pervasive experience of deprivation to one of celebration. If we think in terms of human ecology, such a shift would involve two major approaches. First, we hold that the nature and worth of our interactions, biological and sociological, should not be evaluated apart from their "affective" quality, as self-consciously experienced and articulated by the participants. Second, we should rejuvenate the aesthetic dimension of common experience inclusive of the technological, both industrial and electronic.[12] Both of these approaches cannot be limited to personal belief, as a sort of therapy, but the community has to indicate some sanction for these attitudes by building them into our institutions, the school for example. With the generalized attitudes of contemporary art as a backdrop, let us open the question of an aesthetic ecology.

III

The basic difficulties in an aesthetic ecology emerge when we move from rural to urban experience. It has not been enough noticed that such a development really means a change from nature as the resource to artifact as the resource, for the purpose of building a personal environment. There is a profound and unsettling paradox at work in American culture which has given rise to considerable difficulty in our attempt to face the now dominant urban experience. In an almost mythic sense, we are tied to the land, although in increasing numbers our experience of it is either vicarious or in an artifactual context, as in a park. Yet we have failed to mythologize the urban environment so as to provide experiences necessary to human growth—namely, among others, nesting, creative participation in daily ritual, and celebration of odds and ends—recognized to be worthy by the larger community.[13]

We have, perhaps, taken too much for granted in man's adaptation to an urban context. What is involved in the urban child being a "sitter on curbs" rather than a "swinger of birches"? Does "concrete" blunt affection? Can man truly achieve a sense of continuity with his setting when he works through technological intermediaries? The fact that modern man dwells in the city does not of itself indicate that he is affective toward it. Some say that we have repressed our sense of space and our enjoyment of a more organic setting. In this view, we merely tolerate the urban setting as necessary to other goals. I suggest that the increasing acceptance of such a view spells disaster for city life. While it is unquestionable that certain offensive characteristics of urban experience, such as congestion, air pollution, and social afflictions, have to be drastically reduced, a corresponding positive task also awaits response. We have failed to articulate, for purposes of common experience, the aesthetic quality of a technological environment. Our nostalgia for the things of nature, however repressed, has kept us from the marvels of sound, design, texture, and light which constitute modern urban life.[14] I do not believe that the aesthetic dimension of the city is to be found primarily in its museums or resources for the performing arts. Indeed, a too heavy dependence on such institutions has perhaps warped our sense of the aesthetic and caused us to think of much of our surroundings as paltry and trivial, and, worse, to treat them in that vein.

For Dewey, the basic problem was "that of recovering the continuity of aesthetic experience with normal processes of living." [15] To anaesthetize these processes is to set the stage for deprivation, which not only results from the absence of conditions necessary to basic human life but proceeds as well from an inability to draw nourishment from a person's immediate situation. Whatever the paucity of our environment, if we enter into it as an active, engaging self, making relationships and building a personal style, this will constitute some growth. In this way, our basic attitude would be characterized by a reaching, a cresting—that is, by being open to new possibilities. Deprivation is the loss of this ability and can be found even in environmental settings rich in detail. Now, one of the causes of this situation is that too many of our experiences are proscribed, so that our responses are external and perfunctory. This is particularly true of the myriad of artifacts which we encounter in our everyday experience, many of them fascinating in vernacular design but unsanctioned by traditional artistic judgment. In still other instances a cultural hierarchy of values is at work, ascribing the worth of situations apart from the person's potential relationship to them. Paraphrasing John Cage, we hear the "names" of sounds and see the "names" of things, often ranked in importance by an objective order and rarely touched by us in a personal way.[16]

We might strike a parallel here by a reference to the development of modern art since impressionism.[17] Speaking in broad terms, modern art has attempted to upend the fixed character of aesthetic values and of late has contended that any material and any technique, given a relational context, can bring forth a work of art. This sense of the new, of beginning again in personal terms, is given statement by Thomas Hess, writing on the painter Willem de Kooning: "The crisis of modern art presupposes that each shape, even a plain oval, be re-invented— or, rather, given an autochthonous existence in paint. Nothing could be accepted or received on faith as a welcomed heritage." [18] Perhaps the most revealing style of this concern of modern art is found in that of assemblage, which has considerable symbolic meaning for our discussion of ecology. Assemblage is historically rooted in futurism, with its concern for a "completely renovated sensitiveness," [19] and in dada, which, in the words of Tristan Tzara, held that art would be created by "materials noble or looked down upon, verbal clichés or clichés of old magazines, bromides, publicity slogans, refuse, etc.—these incongruous elements are transformed into an unexpected, homogeneous cohesion as soon as they take place in a newly created ensemble." [20] In assemblage the context is the source of meaning. The materials shed their prior meanings and regather along different, even drastically different, lines of intelligibility. Nothing belongs anywhere until it is present. And with every new entry to the assemblage, all the other entries are reconstructed in their meanings. One of the intriguing factors here is that the masters of assemblage are very young children, for they are the least dominated by definitions of materials and, in the pejorative sense, by "proper" space, color, and texture relationships.

Now, if we phrase the other side of our parallel, the attempt to forge a viable aesthetic ecology involves us in issues very similar to those found in the development of modern art. Celebration cannot take place if it is a response to experiences whose worth and meaning are predetermined by criteria alien to our own experience—to our having and undergoing. Deprivation cannot be ameliorated if we assign worth to activities as proportionate to their place in a hierarchy of values, independent of our experiencing and unreconstructed by our participation. Learning is not going to be a rich experience if it is tied solely to the economic ladder or if competition becomes its dominant theme. We are not going to have affection for our environments if their worth is determined by a comparison with a fixed and largely unobtainable standard.

Assemblage has much to teach us here. Out of bits and pieces, some old, some new, some thrown away, some kept out of nostalgia, we assemble a new environment and return life and meaning to these fragments. As an application of this approach, we can look at the city as a great pyramid with clear delineation as to top and bottom. Depending on our personal position in this arrangement, experience is exhilarating, trying, or simply oppressive. At its best, however, the city yields to another vantage point, as a masterpiece of assemblage. In this instance the technological has aesthetic quality, and the unity achieved is not hierarchical but is rather built up out of a coalescence of relational wholes, each giving to its participants a sense of control, of management, of enjoyment, and, above all, continuity with their most immediate needs. The question is not how far we go but how rich is the journey. At the conclusion of *Human Nature and Conduct,* John Dewey says it better.

Within the flickering inconsequential acts of separate selves dwells a sense of the whole which claims and dignifies them. In its presence we put off mortality and live in the universal. The life of the community in which we live and have our being is the fit symbol of this relationship. The acts in which we express our perception of the ties which bind us to others are its only rites and ceremonies.[21]

NOTES

1. Cited in Robert Goldwater and Marco Treves, eds., *Artists on Art* (New York: Pantheon, 1947), p. 451. Cf. also Lee Nordness, ed., *Art U.S.A. Now* (New York: Viking Press, 1962), p. 12, for a statement by Allen S. Weller: "In a sense, the physical facts of nature become less and less important to us in themselves; we have gone beyond a stage in which recognition and identification of material forms is of primary significance. It is the tension between forms, the effects of movements on shapes and qualities, the active spaces which surround solid masses, which seem to be the most tangible things with which many artists need to work. There are of course striking parallels to the social and economic situation of our times. The great problems of our period are not material ones; they are problems of basic relationships."

2. Alfred North Whitehead, *Symbolism* (New York: Capricorn Books, 1959) (1927), p. 88.

3. Contemporary social science and literature abound in material on the complexity of cultural styles. Cf., e.g., the work of Oscar Lewis, especially *La Vida: A Puerto Rican Family in the Culture of Poverty—San Juan and New York* (New York: Random House, 1966).

4. Cf. Theo Crosby, *Architecture: City Sense* (New York: Van Nostrand, 1965), pp. 76-83. For the importance of local landmarks, cf. Kevin Lynch, *The Image of the City* (Cambridge, Mass.: M.I.T. Press, 1960), p. 48.

5. John Dewey, *Art as Experience* (New York: Capricorn Books, 1958), p. 14.

6. William James, *A Pluralistic Universe* (New York: Longmans, Green, and Co., 1909), p. 60.

7. The work of Edward Kienholz and Louise Nevelson is especially pertinent in this context. Cf. also Allan Kaprow, *Assemblage, Environments, and Happenings* (New York: Abrams, 1965).

8. The most perceptive comment on the sense of immediacy which characterizes recent art is to be found in an essay by Leo Steinberg. After reading Exodus 16, he comments: "When I had read this much, I stopped and thought how like contemporary art this manna was; not only in that it was a God-send, or in that it was a desert food, or in that no one could quite understand it—for 'they wist not what it was.' Nor even because some of it was immediately put in a museum—'to be kept for your generations'; nor yet because the taste of it has remained a mystery, since the phrase here translated as 'wafers made with honey' is in fact a blind guess; the Hebrew word is one that occurs nowhere else in ancient literature, and no one knows what it really means. Whence the legend that manna tasted to every man as he wished; though it came from without, its taste in the mouth was his own making.

"But what struck me most as an analogy was this Command—that you were to gather of it every day, according to your eating, and not to lay it up as insurance or investment for the future, making each day's gathering an act of faith." "Contemporary Art and the Plight of Its Public," in *The New Art*, Gregory Battcock, ed. (New York: E.P. Dutton & Co., 1966), pp. 46-47.

9. Dewey, *op. cit.*, p. 17. Italics added.

10. Robert Jay Lifton, "Protean Man," in *Partisan Review*, vol. 35, no. 1 (Winter, 1968), 13.

11. Dewey, *op. cit.*, p. 11.

12. The electronic analysis of organismic experience is given some structural treatment in Lucien Gérardin, *Bionics* (New York: McGraw-Hill, 1968).

13. Cf. John Kouwenhoven, "To Make All Things New," in *The Arts in Modern American Civilization* (New York: The Norton Library, 1967), pp. 103-136.

14. Cf. the *Vision and Value Series*, ed. Gyorgy Kepes, particularly the volumes entitled *Education of Vision, The Man-Made Object*, and *Sign, Image and Symbol* (New York: George Braziller, 1965, 1966, 1966). Cf. also

Kouwenhoven, *op. cit., passim,* and David Pye, *The Nature of Design* (New York: Reinhold Publishing Corp., 1964).

15. Dewey, *op. cit.,* p. 10.
16. Cf. John Cage, *Silence* (Cambridge, Mass.: M.I.T. Press, 1966).
17. For a discussion of this development from the side of a metaphysics of relation, cf. John J. McDermott, "To Be Human Is to Humanize: A Radically Empirical Aesthetic," in Michael Novak, ed., *American Philosophy and the Future* (New York: Charles Scribner's Sons, 1968), pp. 21-59.
18. Thomas Hess, *Willem de Kooning* (New York: George Braziller, 1959), pp. 15-16.
19. Cited in William C. Seitz, *The Art of Assemblage* (New York: The Museum of Modern Art, 1961), p. 30.
20. Seitz, *op. cit.,* p. 39.
21. John Dewey, *Human Nature and Conduct* (New York: The Modern Library, 1930), pp. 331-332.

CHAPTER FOUR

Life Is in the Transitions:
Radical Empiricism
and Contemporary Concerns

You see also that it stands or falls with the notion I
have taken such pains to defend, of the through—and—
through union of adjacent minima of experience, of
the confluence of every passing moment of concretely
felt experience with its immediately next neighbors.
—William James [1]

I

The decided increase in publications, both editions and
commentaries, have pointed to a definite renascence of interest
in American classical philosophy as represented by Peirce,
James, Royce, Dewey, Santayana, and Mead. Two major tasks

await such a revival of interest: first, to present and clarify the textual tradition; second, to utilize the insights of that tradition in an effort to confront the significant problems of our time. In this essay, we focus on the second task, relating James's radical empirical empiricism to some of our more recent problems, in the hope that a different formulation may assist remediation. Although basically a late-nineteenth-century thinker, James's thought is highly relevant to contemporary culture; indeed, we can say that the philosophy of William James acts as a vestibule to much of twentieth-century life.

Before proceeding to the substance of these issues, two methodological concerns are in order. First, care must be exercised that in formulating relationships between contemporary concerns and the thought of William James, we do not wrench his language and ideas out of their setting so as to create anachronistic and misleading patterns of influence. It cannot be contended, for example, that James anticipated the specifics of new developments in depth psychology, theories of interpersonal relations or proxemics, the new subtleties of cultural anthropology, and the vast import of developments in transportation and electronic media. James was a man of the industrial revolution, of steamships, the telegraph, and the train. His experienced sense of time, while "speeded up," was fundamentally antique, that is, measurable by the traversing of space.

Despite these cautions, James's thought nonetheless functions in an extraordinarily anticipatory way. For one thing, if not the first, James was the most outspoken proponent of a distinctively contemporary view of cosmology, unabashedly post-Copernican and highly sensitized to the role of novelty and the constitutive role of human life. He was also committed to an overthrow of the centuries-old "substance"-oriented description of reality, attempting to replace it with a relational and process-oriented metaphysics, far more flexible and in keeping with the subsequent developments in the disciplines of our own time. James's critique of previous positions paved the way for a more free-wheeling approach to the problems of inquiry and description, and while not worked out in detail, his own theories and approaches, however inadvertently, foreshadowed major shifts in priorities and concerns in psychology, the arts, and even social psychology.

The significance of James's thought for social psychology leads to the second methodological question. How, it may be asked, can such significance be ascribed to a thinker so notoriously concerned with the individual and so singularly free of apparent insight to matters social or to the sociological context for inquiry, later explicated so brilliantly by John Dewey? A first response to this question has to do with James's language. Granted that he does not invoke a sociological vocabulary, he nonetheless assumes a fundamental social matrix in his epistemology, for the pragmatic method has to do with consequences, testing, and experimentation as subject to verifying in a world of experience other than one we simply think about. Put another way, James was adamantly opposed to evaluating ideas relative only to other ideas, professing that ideas carry their weight as applied to actual situations, many of them inevitably social.

Second, unless a sociology is explicitly reductionistic, it must honor some assumptions about the nature of human activity from a philosophical and psychological perspective. James's thought on human behavior, while nurtured on his abiding sensibility to individual experience, is yet characterized by perceptions significantly germane to social psychology. And as both G. H. Mead and John Dewey have attested, their own developments in social theory would be inconceivable without James's breakthroughs in psychology and his metaphysics of relations.

With these methodological cautions behind us, let us set up the approach to our present considerations. After a brief reminding exposition of James's doctrine of relations, we shall examine in some detail two contemporary problems in what is hopefully the Jamesian manner. An attempt will be made to recast the diagnosis of our present situation, characterized as it is by the language of alienation and anomie, in the direction of less emphasis on the quest for human certitude and more emphasis on affectivity and the texture of our actual experiences. For James, after all, "experience itself, taken at large, can grow by its edges." [2] The manifestations of living occur in time, with both events and meanings internal to that process, never yielding to a transcendent point of view.[3]

II

As is well known, James stated the basic contentions of his philosophy, that is, radical empiricism, on a number of occasions. Despite some surface ambiguity, a careful reading of James will show it to be clear, both textually and thematically, that for him pragmatism is a methodological application of his radical empiricism. In that sense, to call James simply a pragmatist is misleading and, indeed, without radical empiricism as a metaphysical base, pragmatism is subject to the savage philosophical critique it has received.

In 1897, as part of the Preface to *The Will to Believe,* James wrote:

> Were I obliged to give a short name to the attitude in question, I should call it that of *radical empiricism.* . . . I say "empiricism" because it is contented to regard its most assured conclusions concerning matters of fact as hypotheses liable to modification in the course of future experience; and I say "radical," because it treats the doctrine of monism itself as an hypothesis. . . .
>
> He who takes for his hypothesis the notion that it [pluralism] is the permanent form of the world is what I call a radical empiricist. For him the crudity of experience remains an eternal element thereof. There is no possible point of view from which the world can appear an absolutely single fact.[4]

In 1904, James wrote to François Pillon that "my philosophy is what I call a radical empiricism, a pluralism, a 'tychism,' which represents order as being gradually won and always in the making." [5] And finally in 1909, James offered his clearest version of radical empiricism when he wrote a Preface to *The Meaning of Truth,* significantly, a book intended to answer the critics of his *Pragmatism:*

> Radical empiricism consists first of a postulate, next of a statement of fact, and finally of a generalized conclusion.
>
> The postulate is that the only things that shall be debatable among philosophers shall be things definable in terms drawn from experience. [Things of an unexperience-able nature may exist *ad libitum,* but they form no part of the material for philosophic debate.]
>
> The statement of fact is that the relations between things, conjunctive as well as disjunctive, are just as much matters of direct particular experience, neither more so nor less so, than the things themselves.
>
> The generalized conclusion is that therefore the parts of experience hold together from next to next by relations that are themselves parts of experience. The directly ap-prehended universe needs, in short, no extraneous trans-empirical connective support, but possesses in its own right a concatenated or continuous structure.[6]

Now for our present purpose, two major themes emerge; first, the contention that in our experience at large we are given continuity but not Unity; and second, this continuity is due to our affective or feeling grasp of the relationships which set up all of our activities, conceptual as well as perceptual. This second claim is what James calls a "statement of fact" and what Arthur Bentley [7] calls the "Jamesian datum," capable of experimental verification. If it is not so that relations are equally and affectively experienced as are the poles of the relationship then James's thought is but a string of brilliant asides, declining considerably in positive and philosophical merit. Further, given that his negative statement about no possibility of seeing the world whole or as a single fact is seemingly true, as twentieth-century thought attests over and over, his doctrine of relations provides the only meaningful source of intelligibility. The accuracy of James's "statement of fact" is, therefore, no idle matter, for with the rejection of an overarching, transcendent principle of explanation, man is forced back into an unreflective "taking things as they come" or the intellectual encapsulations of a solipsism. Accepting James's radical empiricism and consistent with its claims, let us sketch an approach to the discussion of two contemporary concerns, alienation and repression.

III

One of the cardinal concerns of our century has been the increased presence of the experience of alienation. The language of articulation for this situation has been either Marxist, following the renewed awareness of the *Economic and Philosophic Manuscripts* (1844), or existentialist, following the writings of Camus, Sartre, Marcel, Jaspers, and Heidegger. In both Marxist and existential traditions, however profound their differences, there exists the common theme of deep distrust of the classical European institutions—the church, class structure, and philosophy, especially the claims fostered by centuries of confidence in the ultimate intelligibility of nature as open to reason. The collapse of these claims in a series of intellectual revolutions, from Copernicanism, through Luther, Hume, Kant, the romantic poets, Marx, and Nietzsche, abetted by the irrational terrors of the holocaust have generated a rootlessness and despair in much of Western contemporary thought. The writings of Cioran and Ellul are a witness to the loss of hope, and the vigorous interest in Eastern thought as well as the writings of Joyce and N. O. Brown yield a return to the doctrine of the cycle and the rejection of historical novelty.

By contrast, an analysis of alienation from the perspective of James's experience and thought will prove illuminating. Although James [8] has said that a man is not educated unless he has "dallied" with suicide, as he did, and although most interpreters focus on James's multiple neuroses, such as his psychosomatic neurasthenia, insomnia, and transcontinental restlessness, leading Gay Wilson Allen [9] to imply that James was on the edge of a nervous breakdown all his life, nonetheless his philosophy was not characterized by alienation. The reasons for this are extremely instructive, not only relative to an interpretation of James's life, but as a harbinger of a creative response to our own problems. Taking fundamental issue with the interpretation of James as a neurotic and insecure person, we offer that the key to his philosophy can be phrased as first, his rejection of a derivative ethics and of a derivative sense of self, and second, his affirmation of local intelligibility as present in the experience-continua of human activity. This rejection and affirmation feed off each other. James is willing to chance the dangers of radical novelty even in the deepest recesses of personal life precisely because he believes that all of our experiences are affectively related and carry with them distinctive meanings. Paradoxically, James holds that the real threat to human life is security, for it prematurely blocks us from sources of intelligibility which often yield themselves only on behalf of personal risk.

For James, alienation is the inability to make relations. To accept a derivative ethics or an a priori meaning of the self, as in the classical doctrine of the soul, is to abort the making of relations. On the other hand, to be without such an inheritance is not to be cut completely adrift, for while "my belief, to be sure, *can't* be optimistic . . . I will posit life (the real, the good) in the self-governing *resistance* of the ego to the world. Life shall [be built in] doing and suffering and creating." [10] In effect, James sees the human task as constituting meaning, not *ab ovo* from the power of the mind as in philosophical idealism, but in selective and rejective response to the press of events upon us.

Alienation can be described as the experience of disconnections in those areas of life in which we are vulnerable. No event, situation, or circumstance is by nature alienating. Human beings have withstood, nay flourished under the most objectively dehumanizing and terrifying of experiences. Just as the "liver" is the relational manifold of our bodies so too do we have a psychological relational manifold, which has as its task to anticipate needs, set balances, and warn us against misleading directions. James writes in the *Pragmatism:* "Woe to him whose beliefs play fast and loose with the order which realities follow in his experience; they will lead him nowhere or else make false connexions." [11] He is not pointing to ultimate alienation, that is, the inability to make sense of the world, for that is a result of an illegitimate expectation in the first place. Rather, he is pointing to the instances of alienation which occur when we do not guard against the twin dangers of prometheanism and the laissez-faire acceptance of the world as conceived by others. When James states that "the inmost nature of the reality is congenial to powers which you possess," [12] he affirms a metaphysical possibility but he offers no guarantee. Although James is fond of talking about powers, energies, and leads, he also assumes a highly developed sense of self-awareness and self-protection. After all, the abandonment of an inherited self, while liberating, is nonetheless challenging and even dangerous. If the world is not given as meaningful and the self is but our capacity to be meaningfully present, then the making of relations becomes equivalent to who we are.

There are a number of ways in which we are alienated, that is, prevented from making relations. The traditional meaning of alienation, to be "cut off," we describe as relation-starvation, and given James's understanding of human activity, it is but one source of alienation. Other sources can be described as relation-saturation and relation-seduction. Before detailing these terms, a brief statement of James's fundamental world view will be helpful. Reality is a network of concatenatedly related objects or things, rendered as such by human conceptual decision, in keeping with the possibilities and limitations structured by nature on its terms and historically rendered by previous human activity. Human experience is an aware flow within the activities of reality at large, which in turn is also in process, unfinished, and broken into by novelties relative to the patterns already set up. For the most part we live our lives focally, that is, within a familiar range of experiences rendered clear to us by our conceptual systems or simply accepted by habituation. Ideally this focus opens outward, reaching toward a fringe of experiences, often vague and inarticulate but subtly continuous and profoundly meaningful. Religious experience, unusual psychic experiences, aesthetic experiences, drug experiences, psychophysical breakthroughs as in Yoga, and the range of allegedly neurotic and psychotic experiences are potentially rich possibilities at the fringe.

Speaking diagnostically, then, about human well-being, James's philosophy offers the following cautions and suggestions. First, if our focus is concave, we tend to duplicate our experiences or at a minimum, no matter their actual differences, they are slotted in an already articulated and accepted conceptual scheme. James refers to this as "vicious intellectualism," which is "the treating of a name as excluding from the fact named what the name's definition fails to include...." [13] This attitude becomes increasingly defensive, even shrill in overestimating the importance and reach of our focus and in time develops a hostility to experiences not already included within our range. In effect, we tend to identify and evaluate experiences only in terms already familiar to us and sanctioned by us.

Self-encapsulating, this approach results in relation-starvation and in an increasing narrowness of person. What is to be lamented is not the decrease in the quantity of relations formulated, although that is often, if not necessarily, a factor, but in the absence of novelty, differentia, and, in short, the developing in ability to be open to experience. In this pillbox mentality, novelty is ever a threat so we burn out the relational ground around us. Little comes to our consciousness which is not duplicative or replicative. It is as if we lived our lives in imitation of the way we were taught to diagram sentences as children. We were told to focus on Subject (noun/pronoun), Verb (active/passive), and Object (direct/indirect). Yet most of the action is found in our use of gerunds, participles, adjectival clauses, prepositional phrases, to say nothing of expletives, argot, and grunts. In a word, relation-starvation is cancerous. More specifically, it is a cancer of the psychological "liver," for not only does it represent the stark absence of most novelty, but more seriously, it generates an increasing incapacity to make anything of the little novelty which does break through. To live within an increasingly concave focus is to give the impression of security and confidence. Yet, this masks a deep experience of alienation, for with a decrease in the capacity to make relations, the experiences we have already undergone become threadbare and lifeless.

By contrast, if our focus is convex, we have the advantage of reaching out and thereby reconstituting our frame of reference, flooding us with enormous possibilities, for, as James tells us, anything that makes a difference anywhere, makes a difference elsewhere.[14] These differences may be slight or they may be dramatic, thus forcing us to reconstitute the importance of experiences undergone long ago. James contends that every experience we have is fringed with relational possibilities. To live in the world is to be in the presence of inference. James's view of the fringe is not that of a world separate or totally unknown. It resides within the possibilities of the perceptual field, linked by relationships open to human awareness, even if not to clear and defined statement. We make our way to and throughout the fringe hand over hand as it were, with all senses on the *qui vive*, alert to pitfalls and dead ends, ever within hailing distance of our point of origin. Just as we have no inherited self, so too do we not have a permanent foothold. We do, however, "selve" ourselves in the vast, teeming flow of experience and in so doing, we constitute a foothold, ever changing but ever present.

We caution here that the liberating possibilities which emerge in opening ourselves to new experiences and to the novel relational implications of heretofore ordinary experiences are not brought off without attendant dangers. We name the first of these dangers relation-saturation. For many of us, the obviousness of our daily lives heightens the temptation of sheer novelty, such that a change of interpersonal relations, scene, or life-style often carries with it the promise of an enriched life. Yet, the piling up of novelties does not guarantee a significant breakthrough in the quality of our experiencing. The crucial task is always the same; whatever our experiences, we must be able to break them open so that we savor their fullest implications, relative to our needs and hopes. It is essential that we proceed from extensive self-diagnosis, enabling us to make decisions on the kind of novelty which is genuinely nutritious for us. Some of us need multiple novelty of a linear kind, stretched out through changes of place, thing, and person. Others find novelty in the ramifications of the same event, worked through in deeper and deeper patterns of articulation. We are reminded here of the long aesthetic journey of the two "Pablos," Casals and Picasso. The first, Casals, built into his cello, explodes it from inside so that the same piece, the same note is never quite the same. He creates multiple relations out of an intense and creative version of the same locus. The second, Picasso, picks up scraps, pieces, textures, and themes from the world at large and assembles them to make new worlds. Just as the world speaks to itself, as salamanders to mud, so Picasso has everything speak to everything else, in an endless variety of ways. Quantity, then, is not the key to the experience of novelty. Relation-saturation occurs when we move through our lives touching while un-touched. We become voyeurs rather than participants, piling up a string of "experiences" in name only, hash marks vicariously undergone and fundamentally unrelated. In time, we lose the capacity to make relations and undergo a subtle form of alienation. Seemingly "with it," we are carried from novelty to novelty, more like flotsam than of our own doing.

One futher danger lurks behind our quest for novelty, that of relation-seduction. We agree with James that the extreme fringe of our conscious life is revelatory of possibilities otherwise hidden from view. In pursuing these possibilities we must be careful not to "space" our relations too far apart. Extreme discontinuities in the kind of experiences we have can cause us to be "spaced out" beyond the fundamental patterns of famil-iarity necessary to self-sustenance. To !eap over the working relationships in our experiencing is to be seduced by the promise of radical novelty, often to the extent of blocking a return to the necessities of ordinary experience. Extreme hallucinogenic expe-

riences or the mind bathing of religious cults are instances in
point, for despite their acknowledged intensity and possible
illumination, they often sever us from the remaining range of
our life-enhancing relationships. Despite the promise of liberation, many of these highly novel experiences are a trap. Unless
we come to them overland, anticipated relation by relation, their
very intensity can sear off our past, rendering us "strung-out."
We should seek to experience a wide fabric of relations rather
than a single event, which renders the rest of our lives trivial and
tawdry. Concretely, relation-seduction is most explicitly present
in that event which presents to us, either the most profound
liberation or the most singular alienation, namely, our suicide.
Our experience of suicide must be continuous with the needs,
patterns, and anticipations of our life; otherwise it is the
supreme insulating cut, the ultimate discontinuity, marked by
the presence of no return.

Given the philosophical approach of William James, alienation is not an ultimate term, proceeding from the language of
being and nonbeing, of meaning and nihilism. Rather James's
language is one which calls for nutrition and warns of starvation,
points to liberation and warns of entrapment, that is, the
language of affairs and processes rather than that of traditional
metaphysics. And despite his strident emphasis on individuality,
James's approach is more relevant to Marx's analysis of social
alienation than to the social philosophy of the British empiricists
or of the utilitarians. James is a philosopher of descriptions and
diagnoses, who offers us a "phenomenology" of the *Lebenswelt*.
And, in the long run, the import of James's philosophy is that an
analysis of human activity turns out to be an "ultimate"
metaphysics, for there is no reality to be discussed apart from
our participation and formulation. In *The Varieties of Religious
Experience*, he writes, "so long as we deal with the cosmic and
the general, we deal only with the symbols of reality, but *as soon
as we deal with private and personal phenomena as such, we deal
with realities in the completest sense of the term.*" [15]

IV

Turning now to a second contemporary concern, the problem of repression, we again find James's thought to be helpful. The term "repression" can bring to mind a variety of definitions and analyses. It is commonplace to associate repression with the activities of human sexuality as interpreted by Freud. In the area of pedagogy, both Maria Montessori and John Dewey have elucidated the repressive implications of traditional educational institutions and practices. And from Rousseau through Marx to more recent critics such as Sartre, Marcuse, and N. O. Brown, the repressive penalties of political institutions are well detailed. The analysis and comparison of these and other versions of the meaning of repression is a major undertaking all its own. We have in mind here something more modest, namely, a demythologization of the term "repression," such that it could have some positive connotations. Using James's functional approach to our conscious life, the term repression takes on a very different meaning. This is not to say that other interpretations of repression as damaging to personal life are misguided, only that they are too exclusive.

It is to be noted that James, despite his affection for the mysteries of the fringe of consciousness, did not hold to the presence of a secret self, whether it be traceable to the classical claim of a "soul" or to the Freudian claim of an unconscious. James would regard the layers of consciousness—*id, ego,* and *superego*—as abstractions, devoid of subtlety. So too would he regard as reductionistic the flock of post-Freudian nostrums, each of them giving a different single principle of accountability. Perhaps we can say that for James, there is no ultimate explanation of either our personal or historical situation. What we do have is a series of grapplings, context by context, more or less resolving, more or less enriching.

In the stream of consciousness, clarity is attained by negation, that is, by cutting off the myriad of relations that proceed from any given experience and by suturing these cuts so that one can name the remainder. Such clarity is often necessary to prevent us from being overwhelmed by the implicitness and inferentiality of our experiences. What we call knowledge is a pragmatically inspired compromise to enable us to hold our own somewhere between our need for identity and our need to grow, that is, to be open to leads and ramifications. *In the Jamesian context, repression means the shelving of an event such that it is temporarily banished from the realm of its own implications.* Such an approach need not be dangerous to the person, for within the functional exigencies of human activity some leads should not be followed, dependent upon the overall assessment of the weakness and capacity of the person involved.

It has to be granted that Freud's contention that repression leads to a festering and sublimated articulation, often violent, has considerable empirical support. A major reason for this situation, however, is that within the fabric of Western culture, human beings are burdened by the pressure to come clean, to have our experiences hang together in a causal and rational sequence. Psychoanalysis and its more recent offshoots, such as encounter groups, transactional analysis, and varieties of psycho-drama, have as their predecessor the resolute possibilities of the long-standing tradition of Christian confession. Despite the claim of an aggressive unconscious at work in human life, ironically, contemporary therapy from Freud forward is addressed to a rational resolution of these hidden difficulties. James would reject both ends of this description. He uses terms such as fringe and subliminal to accentuate the reaches of conscious life, holding that we have access to all aspects of our experience while at the same time denying that we can account for any experience undergone in any final or complete sense. A radical empiricist holds that experiences "speak" to one another and their relations are as much a part of our experience as the poles of the relationship.

> Life is in the transitions as much as in the terms connected; often, indeed, it seems to be there more emphatically, as if our spurts and sallies forward were the real firing-line of the

battle, were like the thin line of flame advancing across the dry autumnal field which the farmer proceeds to burn. In this line we live prospectively as well as retrospectively. It is "of" the past, inasmuch as it comes expressly as the past's continuation; it is "of" the future in so far as the future, when it comes, will have continued *it*.[16]

If every experience has to be undergone such that we are affectively aware of its relations, fore and aft, then it might well be necessary under certain circumstances to mute the implications until a more propitious time. We cannot deny having had a specific experience, but we may be able to hold off the relational bathing that every experience brings. Granted that the strategy of functional repression is always a distinctively personal decision, we can, nevertheless, point to some generalized situations in which such a strategy is feasible. First, we point to those experiences to which we look forward with intensive anticipation, yet prove to be abortive. We have in mind here not only the classic rites of passage, such as our first party, first sexual contact, and first public performance but also a host of subsequent events in which our imaginative projection of realization turns out, in fact, to be sullied. Unless we are very mature, we run the risk in such situations of tying failure to intensity of effort, an extremely crippling relationship. Better, then, that we should shelve or "repress" our failure until we can set up subsequent patterns of realization following upon intention and anticipation. In that way, human life comes very much to resemble our use of a "junk drawer," into which we put our memorabilia, rarely to be taken out and then only when the pain has lessened or ceased.

A second occasion of functional repression has to do with those positive experiences whose implications are so extensive that a vast rearranging of our priorities and sensibilities would be required if we were to absorb them into our immediate frame of reference. Not every good is good for us. Love generates loyalty, and loyalty generates exclusivity. Time spent is time taken from somewhere, someone else. Everything we experience extracts a price and often we must say no if we are to say yes, although both responses are to potentially enriching occasions. In time some of these conflicts are resolvable, whereas our third example of functional repression holds out no such hope. We refer to those experiences which now stand outside the possibilities of remediation or resolution because of the passing of time, as for example, guilt attendant upon the death of others or frustration due to forever missed opportunities. For these events, there is no healing, only a lifelong process of slowly ameliorative absorption into a wider range of understanding. On such events, James is quite clear, seeing them rooted in the actuality of our experience, while interpretively, they float loose, unrealizable, warnings to the fact that "whatever separateness is actually experienced is not overcome, it stays and counts as separateness to the end." [17]

As with our earlier discussion of alienation, so too with a consideration of repression, it is necessary to realize the importance of James's functional approach and his steadfast suspicion about apodictic judgments. No experience is unrelated as undergone, for at the minimum the "haver" of the experience proceeds from a perceptual point of view and thereby constitutes a context for and to some extent the quality of the experience. How the experience is had is inseparable from our knowledge of the experience. In his essay on "The Thing and Its Relations," James writes:

In a concatenated world a partial conflux often is experienced. Our concepts and our sensations are confluent; successive states of the same ego, and feelings of the same body are confluent. Where the experience is not of conflux, it may be of conterminousness (things with but one thing between); or of contiguousness (nothing between); or of likeness; or of nearness; or of simultaneousness; or of inness; or of on-ness; or of forness; or of simple with-ness; or even of mere and-ness; which last relation would make of however disjointed a world otherwise, at any rate for that occasion a universe "of discourse." [18]

The upshot of this is that for James, repression need not have its point of origin in an unintelligible motivation or irrational source. Similar to all of our experiences, repression occupies a role in the sliding stream of events, which for reasons of deep personal self-awareness functions on behalf of quiescence, hiddenness, and a time-biding until the organism can relate the repressed event to a more ongoing, obvious dimension in the flow of our experience. Furthermore, in a world riven with tychastic events, experiences rendered out of sorts, repressed, or held at arm's length can be recovered and rejuvenated due to favorable and surprising interventions in our lives. In James's philosophy, no experience can be spoken for once and for all. Opposing the absolutistic arrogance found in the conceptual systems of the philosophers, James writes in a "Notebook" in 1903 that:

> All neat schematisms with permanent and absolute distinc-
> tions, classifications with absolute pretensions, systems with
> pigeon-holes, etc., have this character. All "classic," clean,
> cut and dried, "noble," fixed, "eternal," *Weltsanschauu-
> ungen* seem to me to violate the character with which life
> concretely comes and the expression which it bears of be-
> ing, or at least of involving a muddle and a struggle, with an
> "ever not quite" to all our formulas, and novelty and
> possibility forever leaking in.[19]

V

The fundamental contribution of William James to any morphological analyses of the human condition is that he thickens the discussion. Radical empiricism involves an accep-tance of a far wider range of continuous and experienced relationships than that usually associated with the normal confines of the human self. It gives to novelty and chance a much greater role in our understanding of the fabric of the world. The philosophy of James calls for a never-ending series of descriptions and diagnoses, each from a specific vantage point but no one of them burdened with having to account for everything. For James, the world is much like "the pattern of our daily experience," [20] loosely connected, processive, and pluralistic. The crucial factor in our understanding of the world in which we live is the affective experiencing of relations. So multiply involved are we that the attainment of deep insight to our "inner life" leads us to participate in no less than the very rhythm of the world at large. If we live at the edge, what we most find in this rhythm are surprises, relational novelty everywhere. Nothing is clear until the last of us has our say and the last relation is hooked. Rare among philosophers, William James believed this.

> In principle, then, as I said, intellectualism's edge is broken; it can only approximate to reality, and its logic is inapplicable to our inner life, which spurns its vetoes and mocks at its impossibilities. Every bit of us at every moment is part and parcel of a wider self, it quivers along various radii like the wind-rose on a compass, and the actual in it is continuously one with possibles not yet in our present sight.[21]

NOTES

Unless otherwise cited, references to William James will be to John J. McDermott, ed., *The Writings of William James—A Comprehensive Edition* (New York: Random House, 1967; The Modern Library, 1968), hereafter cited as *Writings*. For a more detailed statement of the meaning of radical empiricism, cf. John J. McDermott, Introduction to William James, "Essays in Radical Empiricism," *The Works of William James*, ed. Frederick Burkhardt (Cambridge: Harvard University Press, 1976), pp. xi-xlviii.

1. "A Pluralistic Universe," *Writings*, p. 808.
2. "A World of Pure Experience," *Writings*, p. 212.
3. Cf. James, *Ibid.*, p. 201. "Knowledge of sensible realities

thus comes to life inside the tissue of experience. It is *made;* and made by relations that unroll themselves in time."

4. *Writings,* pp. 134-135.

5. "The Letters of William James," *Writings,* pp. xxxvi-xxxvii.

6. *Writings,* p. 136.

7. Cf. Arthur Bentley, "The Jamesian Datum," *Inquiry into Inquiries,* ed. Sidney Ratner (Boston: The Beacon Press, 1954), pp. 230-267.

8. "The Letters of William James," *Writings,* p. xiv.

9. Cf. Gay Wilson Allen, *William James—A Biography* (New York: The Viking Press, 1967), pp. vii, xii.

10. "Diary," *Writings,* p. 8.

11. "Pragmatism," *Writings,* p. 432.

12. "The Sentiment of Rationality," *Writings,* p. 331. This is also the sentiment of Walt Whitman. "The press of my foot to the earth springs a hundred affections. They scorn the best I can do to relate them." *Leaves of Grass,* no. 14.

13. "A Pluralistic Universe," *Writings,* p. 503. In his chapter on "The Stream of Thought," James holds that we tend to believe "where there is *no* name no entity can exist." *Writings,* p. 38. To the extent that this is true, we obviate most of the subtleties in our experiencing.

14. Cf. "Pragmatism," *Writings,* p. 379.

15. "Varieties of Religious Experience," *Writings,* p. 768.

16. "A World of Pure Experience," *Writings,* pp. 212-213.

17. *Ibid.,* p. 212.

18. "The Thing and Its Relations," *Writings,* p. 221.

19. Cited in Ralph Barton Perry, *The Thought and Character of William James,* Vol. II (Boston: Little, Brown and Co., 1935), p. 700.

20. "A Pluralistic Universe," *Writings,* p. 509.

21. *Ibid.,* pp. 296-297.

CHAPTER FIVE

From Cynicism to Amelioration: Strategies for a Cultural Pedagogy

Cultural Pedagogy: The Common Source of Our Personal Expectations, Sensibilities, and Evaluations

I

Time moves fast in America. We are a people for whom event and obsolescence are almost simultaneous. The intense and sometimes shrill critique of our institutions which rent the air of the last decade has now retreated to an eerie whisper, with only nostalgia on which to feed. We live in a culture that is suffering severe withdrawal symptoms, a culture which no longer has confidence either in its achievements or in the efficacy of its complaints. We ask, were those criticisms and protests of the last decade so far off the mark that they quickly became irrelevant, or did they cut so deep that they inflicted a near-fatal wound? And again, was our earlier cynicism about institutional reform

118

so telling that its outcome was inevitably a response of boredom to our world, to others, and even to ourselves?

In our judgment the critiques issued in the previous decade cut deep, but they need not be fatal, at least not if we face them squarely. Undoubtedly, the aesthetic and political countercultures of the last decade still have much to teach us about our present situation and, above all, about directions for our future. As with most radical movements in American history, their demise does not obviate their significance or the subtle spreading of their bequest. We offer that in at least three major areas of American cultural sensibility, we have undergone a subtle but important shift in our experience and in our expectation. Specifically, we point to our attitude toward scientific progress, our experience of time, and our confidence about institutional transformation. To avoid coming to grips with these concerns is to render naive any subsequent commentary on a new cultural pedagogy. We regard the recent counterculture movements as an exacerbated symptom, an early warning system, pointing to the need for us to reconsider long assumed styles and priorities. And if it can be said that we have experienced a heightened sensitivity to the presence of an underlying disorientation in our culture, it cannot be said that we have been able thus far to articulate adequately the cause and nature of this disorientation. Our failure to recast the nature of our expectations and our modes of inquiry, relative to the kinds of experiences we have been having, has led to deepening frustration and an erosion of energy.

Our first consideration has to do with science. We have come to distrust science as a guarantor of salvation and with the advent of this distrust, have become decidedly skeptical of the inevitability of progress. The theme of progress to which we as Americans have paid aggressive allegiance in the past once convinced us, however indirectly, that the future was to be an improvement.[1] In colloquial terms, an American was convinced that tomorrow would be better than today and if we paid dues, things would work out. The price to be paid for such improvement was rarely stated and, if known at all, was discovered only in retrospect. In the past, the assessment of our immediate situation, especially in its negative import, was diluted by the confidence we had in a healing and fruitful future.

The promise of science as the harbinger of guaranteed progress induced in us a cultural myopia, whereby we lost sight of the many implications of such progress, and in certain instances we even lost sight of the steep and perhaps catastrophic prices to be paid for such advances. The contemporary energy and ecological crises are salient examples of such myopia. Revealing, too, is the offensive gap between the achievements of American experimental medicine and the inept character of our national health-care delivery system. Yet, those who attempted to resist the lure of dramatic progress as found in the linear breakthroughs of scientific research, often applied indiscriminately, were castigated by the use of the simplistic but psychologically devastating charge of anti-intellectualism. This charge was made despite the fact that a truly intellectual position should be skeptical of any breakthrough, no matter how dramatic, when it cannot account for the relational setting from which it proceeds and for the range of effects which it is sure to have.

At this point in our history, it seems that we have become considerably apprised of the gravity of unreflective progress. Discovery does not thrill us as it once did but rather evokes in us a wariness, for we know too well that breakthroughs in one area all too often carry with them ghastly by-products, some of them timed to erupt generations hence, as witness the aberrant use of the drug thalidomide. And we are no longer necessarily impressed by the ostentatious conquest of the frontiers of knowledge if those conquests generate, sustain, condone, or are even indifferent to patterns of dehumanization elsewhere. This legitimate skepticism about the excessive claims and authority of science soon degenerated, however, into generalized attacks on intellectual research and reflective inquiry overall. At the height of the counterculture movements this attitude was reduced to the banal confrontation between relevance and irrelevance, the definitions of which remained elusive and self-serving. In some quarters the diagnosis cut deeper, amounting to nothing less than a "bleak cynicism" in response to the institutional forms of contemporary society.[2]

II

Now, from one point of view, the emergence of a widespread cynicism should not come as a complete surprise. As our century moves into its last quarter, the long-standing confidence in eschatological redemption is at its lowest ebb. The theological promises of Christianity and the more recent sociological promises of Marxism are now more utilized as contributors to a liberated present than they are trusted to deliver a paradisiacal future. Even more modest formulations of a political and social future, such as the varieties of democracy, have shown themselves capable of massive self-deception. Searing events of recent historical memory such as the holocaust, totalitarian labor camps, Hiroshima, Biafra, and Vietnam seem to lend an imprimatur to the assumption that the historical significance of life is folly and that progress is illusory. Certainly, if the meaning of progress is wedded to an assured future, then we are doomed to disappointment, traceable not only to the catastrophic events which pockmark our century but as well to that inevitable death which closes out every human life. From the point of view of a cultural pedagogy, that is, institutional efforts to enhance personal life, what troubles us here is not the necessary acknowledgment of the irreducible character of these historical facts but the reemergence of an appeal to an ancient resolution, the doctrine of the cycle. Now used as something of a speculative *deus ex machina,* the emphasis on patterns of cultural return and repetition is held to account for the meaning of human life in a way that is virtually independent of the development of our social, political, and institutional history. Many contemporary social and religious movements in America are characterized by this deemphasis on local intelligibility and by a withdrawal from the exigencies of social and political change. Introverted in style and concern, these movements are less counterculture than they are indifferent to the larger social webbing in which they reside. Whether they be orthodox in presentation as the Hare Krishna or more pluralistic as in the countless versions of Zen, Yoga regimen, Tai Chi, or Meditation, they have selectively appropriated the language and themes of ancient traditions and congealed into an ahistorical response to contemporary life.

Actually a more accurate view of the doctrine of the cycle will show that its contemporary adherents are advocating a simplistic and misleading version of what in fact is a host of complex interpretations of the fabric of reality. Surely the ancient traditions of Buddhism and Hinduism cannot be described in the simple terms of a commitment to historical repetition. For example, despite his entitling of a major work *The Human Cycle,* the important twentieth-century Indian thinker Sri Aurobindo has a deep sense of political evolution.[3] So too was there also a deep awareness of change and growth in the fundamental notion of Greek thought, the *apeiron,* which yields the being and becoming of all reality. Likewise can it be said of those modern Western European thinkers who focus on the theme of recurrence, such as Vico, Nietzsche, and James Joyce, that they are superbly attuned to the nuances and messagings of their respective cultures.

Nonetheless, it can be attributed to such generalized approaches to the human saga, that they harbor a deep skepticism about the efficacy of building the future day by day and reveal also an aggressive distrust of the claims of novelty, so important to the practitioners of linear history. Even James Joyce, who, in all of literature, has given us perhaps the most exquisite and evocative description of our immediate experiences, repeatedly stresses the recurrence and internalization of our conscious life. The wisdom and imagination so characteristic of these cyclical versions of human life should not cloak from view that they lead to an erosion of political energy. Indeed, in reference to the more contemporary, counterculture use of these traditions, a polemic would contend that a return to the doctrine of the cycle as a principle of explanation is a rationalization on behalf of the refusal to confront the ultimate inexplicability of historical processes. In turn, this rationalization breeds a consequent justification of an abandonment of personal responsibility for the quality of our collective social and political life.

Lest the reader be unconvinced of the straight line between cyclic consciousness and severe dubiety about social and political ameliorative efforts, we cite the work of Norman O. Brown. Not to be relegated to the status of a counterculture guru, Brown offers us a biting and perceptive critique of the social and psychological assumptions of contemporary society, only to prophesy its healing by an appeal to the cycle. Beginning with *Life Against Death*,[4] Brown assaults linear history as the source of our deepest troubles. He cites with favor Stephen's comment in Joyce's *Ulysses* that "history is a nightmare from which I am trying to awake." [5] For Brown, "psychoanalysis can provide a theory of 'progress,' but only by viewing history as a neurosis." [6] The building of a civilization is the supreme act of self-deception, trapping us in a series of bad-faith flights from death. Subsequently, in an impassioned Phi Beta Kappa address in 1961, Brown points to the "way out." Reminiscent of the prophetic utterances of Emerson's address more than a century ago, but with a vastly different message, Brown elicits the source of our liberation.

> And so there comes a time—I believe we are in such a time—when civilization has to be renewed by the discovery of new mysteries, by the undemocratic but sovereign power of the imagination, by the undemocratic power which makes poets the unacknowledged legislators of mankind, the power which makes all things new.
>
> The power which makes all things new is magic. What our time needs is mystery: what our time needs is magic. Who would not say that only a miracle can save us.[7]

This text is no isolated or transient remark of Brown, for he repeats most of it in his most recent book, appropriately entitled *Closing Time*.[8] In an admittedly brilliant commentary on Vico and Joyce, Brown's theme in *Closing Time* is stated as:

> First the age of the gods, then the age of heroes, then the age of men. The origin is sacred; the decline is secularization, process is profanation.[9]

In effect, Brown holds that to build a civilization is to mislead and to be misled. He contends that the deepest realization of aesthetic sensibility requires that we "drop out" from the affairs and burdens of linear time. In *Life Against Death*, he writes that a "city is itself, like money, crystallized guilt." [10] In a later essay, "From Politics to Metapolitics," Brown holds that:

> Technological rationality can be put to sleep so that something else can awaken in the human mind, something like the God Dionysus, something which cannot be programmed.[11]

What, then, is this "miracle" which will save us? Brown answers: nothing less than a return to our origins, to "primitive simplicity," where we await and greet the "return of the Gods." [12] And what should we do in the meantime but witness the "return of barbarism," which signals the second, or third, or fourth coming. Perhaps Brown has a remark of Emerson in mind, "when half-gods go, the gods arrive." [13] Yet, should we not ask whether, upon arrival shall the gods stay, and more importantly, whether there are gods at all? Surely these are open questions, and they press us to ask still another. What of us now, that is, in fundamental human terms, what do we do while waiting? At a minimum, in the interim, we should remind ourselves that the doctrine of the cycle is not the only bequest of antiquity relative to the meaning of history and time.

At this point in contemporary culture, we should renew awareness of an alternative approach to the meaning of history, namely, that nurtured by the Hebrew Bible and which succeeding generations of Jewish life have brought to world consciousness. No longer exclusively Jewish, and in some recent traditions, dramatically secularized, this ancient vision stresses historical lineage, prophecy with political responsibility, accrued wisdom and salvation in time upon the earth. For this tradition, the lesson of time has been that the focus should not concentrate so much on the goal as on the journey, which in turn, carries its own worth. The future stretches before us, unguaranteed, its quality for better or worse in our own hands. Chary of mysticism, secrets, false gods, cycles, and ever wary of broken promises, this vision of historical destiny made its way into the modern world. One of its most seminal reformulations occurs in the emergence of seventeenth-century Puritanism, notably, the founders of America. Ostensibly Christians, the Puritans were more so children of the Hebrew Bible, committed once again to the journey, to salvation on the land, and to the entwining of the political and religious covenant. In no way pollyanna, the Puritan attempt to found Zion in the wilderness was deeply sensitized to the travails of time, yet refused to accept a *deus ex machina*, whether of ideological or eschatological origin. The history of the Puritan ethos in America is a complex one, and we do not deny that its "orthodox" followers of the nineteenth century are shallow and legalistic. Unfortunately, it was a function of such subsequent emptiness that much of American thought generated a doctrine of progress minus a deep sense of tragedy. The original Puritan sensibility, however, transformed in name and language, emerged anew in the American philosophers Emerson, James, Royce, and especially Dewey. For them, as for the Puritans and the Jewish tradition, nostrum-mongerers were to be denied their seductions. Taking up against false gods, false promises, and the illusions of ultimate salvation, they did not look for a "way out" of history. To the contrary, they attempted to understand, enhance, and ameliorate the human journey, which inexorably takes place as history. When developing a cultural pedagogy, we should pay heed to the classical

American philosophers who help us to avoid cynicism while simultaneously cautioning us against the seductions of ideology and final solutions.[14]

III

Prior to turning to the qualities of a cultural pedagogy as rooted in the thought of John Dewey, we should bring to the fore the main lines of another recent critique of contemporary society, that of Herbert Marcuse. Diagnostically similar to the critique of Norman O. Brown, Marcuse's book, *Eros and Civilization,* also provides an imaginative reading of Freud's *Civilization and Its Discontents.*[15] The disagreements between Brown and Marcuse are not to be found in their critique of society, past and present, but rather with regard to the possibilities for the future. In a text that seemingly could have been written by both of them, Marcuse holds that:

> . . . progress itself according to its explicit concept, is laden with disturbing activity, transcendence for its own sake, unhappiness, and negativity. It becomes an unavoidable question whether the negativity inherent in the principle of progress is perhaps the motive force of progress, the force that makes it possible. Or, to formulate it in another way that establishes the link to Freud: Is progress necessarily based on unhappiness and must it necessarily remain connected to unhappiness and the lack of gratification? [16]

Brown, of course, believes that progress is necessarily based on unhappiness (read repression) and that it will remain so, for that is precisely what is meant by human history as neurosis. Marcuse, more deeply committed to Marx than is Brown,[17] contends otherwise and points to the need for "revolution in the capitalist world." [18] For Brown, the way out of the cave is to move from the politics of sublimation to symbolism, that is, to the realization that our chains are "magical." They will fall from us as we come to liberated self-consciousness, a liberation effected by the confrontation with our own inevitable death and the rejection of all sublimated posturings of immortality. In his ingeniously rich "book," *Love's Body*,[19] Brown invokes selective literary instances from our cultural past on behalf of his fundamental message. "From literalism to symbolism; the lesson of my life. The next generation needs to be told that the real fight is not the political fight, but to put an end to politics. From politics to metapolitics. From politics to poetry." [20]

On this matter, Marcuse was quite clear. The cave is a battleground, and the chains are real. Coming to liberated consciousness does not of itself guarantee the way out.

> Waking up from sleep, finding the way out of the cave is work within the cave; slow, painful work with and *against* the prisoners in the cave.... There are those who do this work, who risk their lives for it—they fight the real fight, the political fight.[21]

In a subsequent attack on the apolitical wing of the counter-culture, Marcuse writes what has to be a parody of Brown's position or, at least, of the position of those who claim to be influenced by him. Marcuse stresses the need for individual liberation, which in turn is an overcoming of the bourgeois individual. "But the bourgeois individual is not overcome by simply refusing social performance by dropping out and living one's own style of life. To be sure, no revolution without individual liberation, but also no individual liberation without the liberation of society." [22] Granted, for Marcuse is right in his insistence on a "dialectic of liberation," in which the individual is conjoined with the processes of radical social change. Marcuse is not innocent of the fact that such simultaneous "liberations" have not been characteristic of previous revolutionary consciousness, to say nothing of previous revolutions. For Marcuse, the history of mankind has been a "history of domination and servitude." [23] In Marcuse's statement of the causes of this repressive history, he assumes a theme common to both Marx and Freud. However different in style or intent, they both tell us that in the most profound recesses of our consciousness we are self-deceived, and despite social appearances to the contrary, we live secondhand lives.[24] It is this interpretive context that enables Marcuse to write:

> These causes are economic-political, but since they have shaped the very instincts and needs of men, no economic and political changes will bring this historical continuum to a stop unless they are carried through by men who are physiologically and psychologically able to experience things, and each other, outside the context of violence and exploitation.[25]

This is a remarkable text, for it makes clear that nothing less than a revolution in the experience of our bodies is necessary if a genuine social and political revolution is to take place. Marcuse had written earlier that "cultural needs" can "sink down" into our instinctual life and thereby sustain, if not develop, patterns of aggression and guilt, which he takes as requisites for the maintenance of contemporary society.[26] In effect, despite his persistent calling for a "revolution in the capitalist world," Marcuse sees that such a revolution has as its linch-pin the emergence of a "new sensibility," which "expresses the ascent of the life instincts over aggressiveness and guilt." [27] Perhaps we can say that at this point Marcuse brings the wisdom of Freud to bear on the pages of Marx's "Economic and Philosophical Manuscripts of 1844." [28] To Marx's brilliant analysis of alienation, Marcuse carries the message of eros; "aesthetic needs have their own social content." [29] Marcuse is aware that revolutionary consciousness is vacant and counterproductive if it does not proceed from a genuine revolution in personal "sensibility," which, in turn, protects us from those new forms of "social immortality" so omnipresent as the backfill of classical revolutions.

The new sensibility has become, by this very token, *praxis:* it emerges in the struggle against violence and exploitation where this struggle is waged for essentially new ways and forms of life: negation of the entire Establishment, its morality, culture; affirmation of the right to build a society in which the abolition of poverty and toil terminates in a universe where the sensuous, the playful, the calm, and the beautiful become forms of existence and thereby the *Form* of the society itself.[30]

Certainly this is a highly desirable state of affairs, which Marcuse details for our future. And we applaud Marcuse's insistence on the central importance of the new sensibility in any social and political revolution. On a closer look, however, certain difficulties do emerge from Marcuse's version of our situation. The first has to do with the distinction made by Marcuse between rebellion and revolution. In the *Essay on Liberation,* despite his praising much of the aesthetic style of the counterculture, one still had the nagging feeling that his praise was programmatic rather than genuinely enthusiastic. For Marcuse, the significance of modern art, black American music, and new forms of literature and poetry seemed to proceed more from their antiestablishment animus than from their distinctive aesthetic quality. They are to be regarded as rebellious but not as revolutionary. Put stridently, the last pages of Marcuse's chapter on "The New Sensibility" gave the impression that after the revolution, we would all listen to Beethoven. That such a judgment is not excessive finds its support in a line from Marcuse's later work, *Counterrevolution and Revolt:* "Co-option threatens the cultural revolution: ecology, rock, ultramodern art are the most conspicuous examples." [31] Revolutionary consciousness turns out to be "fussy" consciousness, whereby much of the aesthetic sensibility developed in recent decades is to be regarded as merely a step on behalf of the "revolution." In the midst of Marcuse's revolutionary rhetoric, high culture rears its head and the result is condescension. Surely we can agree with Marcuse that "the most extreme political content does not repel traditional forms." [32] Such an acceptance does not mean, however, that we are limited to traditional forms, much less saddled with them. No revolutionary design is necessary to justify the aesthetic significance of the music of Charlie Parker or the painting of Jackson Pollock.

A second difficulty in Marcuse's position is that operatively it seems to contain a vicious cycle. If we accept Marcuse's judgment that the history of civilization has been repressive and has reworked even our instinctual life so as to sustain patterns of aggression and guilt, then who is to effect the revolution? As Marx before him, Marcuse contends that thus far we have not experienced genuine revolution but only rebellion. The historical result has been to replace one political facade, one bureaucratic apparatus, with another, changing rhetoric and intent without effecting genuine liberation.[33] Even given the possibility, which by Marcuse's own strictures seems unlikely, that some of a future generation would come to a liberated consciousness, conjoining sensibility, rationality, and revolutionary commitment, the following problem emerges. How could those in question sustain that consciousness through the travails of a violent revolution and the attendant decisions which arise inevitably in the reconstituting of the economic, social, and political fabric of human life? "Apparatchik" are not born, they are made by the urgency and complexity of such decisions. Is it a parody or a lamentable truth when it is said that after the revolution names change but things are the same?

By way of escaping this circle, Marcuse rests on a veiled restatement of the older Marxist eschatology,[34] that history is on our side. He opens his chapter on "The New Sensibility" by admitting that his theoretical projection would seem "to be fatally premature—were it not for the fact that the awareness of the transcendent possibilities of freedom must become a driving power in the consciousness and the imagination which prepare the soil for this revolution." [35] Marcuse's notion of transcendence is decidedly secular in that it does not reflect a world outside of time. Nonetheless, it is a force which ostensibly will take us to a new "historical stage" [36] and, as a revolution, will be "essentially different." [37] Despite its secularity, this transcendence is more an item of faith than it is of knowledge and, as a social strategy, scarcely more convincing than the invisible hand of the eighteenth-century liberals. Indeed, with regard to the transcendent possibilities spoken of by Marcuse, or for that matter, transcendence of any other stripe, why has it been so hidden, so stingy, so banal? Or perhaps we have looked in the wrong direction, for if the twentieth century is an index, transcendence reveals that we have been in the hands of a *mal genie.* As the Manicheans long ago taught us, the claim of one kind of transcendence invokes the other.

In his response to Marcuse's critique of *Love's Body,* Norman O. Brown had written, "My friend Marcuse and I: Romulus and Remus quarreling; which of them is the *real* 'revolutionary?' " [38] To the extent that either of them wishes to be so called, they are both revolutionary in their critique of existing society. They are very traditional, however, when one considers their confidence in a liberated and unified future.[39] This is a confidence which we regard as dangerously illusory, for it generates judgments about the quality of our present experiences on behalf of a future which has not yet, and may not ever, come to pass. This is not to gainsay that Brown and Marcuse are tellingly perceptive when they argue that any fundamental transformation of human society will trace to a heightening and enhancing of personal aesthetic sensibility. We caution, however, that neither the dialectic of history as bequeathed by Marx nor the chthonic energies released by Dionysus are guaranteed to save us or to protect us from the irreducible problematic of the human situation, our personal and inevitable death. Freud had referred to death as the "immortal adversary" [40] of Eros. At the close of *Life Against Death,* Brown asks if "perhaps" our children can see in that "old adversary, a friend." [41] Perhaps. More likely, our children will see themselves in the same paradoxical situation as our own: called to ameliorate our condition by striving for saving experiences in a world apparently devoid of salvation.

Contrary to much of the commentary on American optimism and historical innocence, this stark version of our situation is a more accurate index of our reflective tradition [42] and is found as a major strand in our philosophical and literary history. The experience and articulation of alienation is a persistent theme of American poets, just as the garrulousness of our political style hides an abiding, irreducible awareness of human finitude and of the novel styles, generation by generation, of human folly and self-deception. An important question emerges here. What are the qualities of a cultural pedagogy if amelioration rather than salvation is the touchstone for evaluation and decision?

IV

Now in an issue as important as the development of a cultural pedagogy, it will not do to state simply that one should cut between the interpretations of Brown and Marcuse, between the doctrine of the cycle and that of revolutionary consciousness. It is true that a staple of traditional American thought has been the avoidance of extremes, but we must also face the fact that in contemporary America, advocates of a centrist position are most often bereft of imagination and have displayed little moral or political courage. And we admit that it would be atavistic to reinvoke the thought of an earlier philosopher, John Dewey, as a solvent for present ills. Despite the incredible range of Dewey's thought, written over a seventy-year span, from the time of Darwin to that of the Korean War,[43] it is important to realize that his philosophy was not wrought out of the two catastrophic events of the mid-twentieth century, the holocaust and the "bomb." Furthermore, Dewey's philosophy takes inadequate cognizance of our now deep awareness of personal and collective self-deception, rendered in political terms as co-optation.[44]

Nonetheless, American culture does harbor a philosophical tradition which can respond to contemporary needs if given sufficient recasting. Granted the dating of exemplification and of some formulations, John Dewey is still the most eloquent and incisive spokesman for a distinctively American cultural pedagogy. We focus here on Dewey's notion of aesthetic experience and its pedagogical significance for our efforts to ameliorate human institutions. We assume as an historical context for this discussion a generalized statement of the notion of experience characteristic of American culture and a radically empirical doctrine of relations, both themes treated in earlier essays in this volume.[45]

At the beginning of his philosophical career, Dewey was an Hegelian. Primarily due to the influence of William James's *Principles of Psychology,* published in 1890, Dewey began to develop his own philosophy of experience. Whether the concern was psychological, epistemological, or educational, the theme of experience became increasingly central, as witness, selectively, "The Reflex Arc Concept in Psychology" (1896), "The Postulate of Immediate Empiricism" (1905), and *Democracy and Education* (1916).[46] In 1917, Dewey wrote an essay on "The Need for a Recovery of Philosophy," which contrasted the orthodox description of experience with what he held to be more "congenial to present conditions." In that contrast, Dewey's version of experience stressed its experimental character, connection with a future, inferentiality, and affectivity. For Dewey, experience is "an affair of the intercourse of a living being with its physical and social environment." Further, "an experience that is an undergoing of an environment and a striving for its control in new directions is pregnant with connections." [47] The physicality, if not sexuality, of Dewey's language should not be overlooked in the present discussion. Lacking the flamboyance of both Brown and Marcuse, Dewey nonetheless is setting the stage for a philosophy of culture in which the activity of the body is the prime analogate for evaluations of social and political life.

In 1925, Dewey published *Experience and Nature,*[48] which gives to his notion of experience its major formulation. Cast as a metaphysics, the book is also a philosophy of culture, as Dewey himself acknowledged in subsequent reflection. While preparing a new, and never to appear, edition of *Experience and Nature* in 1951, Dewey decided to change the title to "Nature and Culture." At that time he wrote: "I was dumb not to have seen the need for such a shift when the old text was written. I was still hopeful that the [philosophic] word 'experience' would be redeemed by [being] returned to its idiomatic usages—which was a piece of historic folly, the hope, I mean. . . ." [49] In his first chapter, "Experience and Philosophic Method," Dewey sets out his fundamental position that "experience is *of* as well as *in* nature." [50] He details this judgment in the following way:

> It is not experience which is experienced, but nature—stones, plants, animals, diseases, health, temperature, electricity, and so on. Things interacting in certain ways *are* experience; they are what is experienced. Linked in certain other ways with another natural object—the human organism—they are *how* things are experienced as well. Experience thus reaches down into nature; it has depth. It also has breadth and to an indefinitely elastic extent. It stretches. That stretch constitutes inference. [51]

Although telescoped in style, this text indicates Dewey's understanding of our fundamental situation, and it provides the basis for his integration of the multiple reflective approaches which constitute a philosophy of culture. The setting is the transaction [52] of the human organism with nature or with the environment. Nature has a life of its own, undergoing its own relatings, which in turn become what we experience. Our own transaction with the affairs of nature cuts across the givenness of nature and our ways of relating. This is *how* we experience *what* we experience. Dewey was a realist in the sense that the world exists independent of our thought of it, but the meaning *of* the world is inseparable from our *meaning* the world. Experience, therefore, is not headless, for it teems with relational leads, inferences, implications, comparisons, retrospections, directions, warnings, and so on. The rhythm of *how* we experience is an aesthetic, having as its major characteristic the relationship between anticipation and consummation, yet having other perturbations, as mishap, loss, boredom, and listlessness. Pedagogy becomes, then, the twin effort to integrate the directions of experience with the total needs of the person and to cultivate the ability of an individual to generate new potentialities in his experiencing and to make new relationships so as to foster patterns of growth. And politics is the struggle to construct an optimum environment for the realizing and sanctioning of the aesthetic processes of living. Finally, the entire human endeavor should be an effort to apply the method of creative intelligence in order to achieve optimum possibilities in the never-ending moral struggle to harmonize the means-end relationship [53] for the purpose of enhancing human life and achieving growth. Dewey sees this effort as central to a philosophy of culture. In a chapter significantly entitled "The Construction of Good," he describes our "deepest problem."

> The problem of restoring integration and cooperation between man's beliefs about the world in which he lives and his beliefs about the values and purposes that should direct his conduct is the deepest problem of modern life. It is the problem of any philosophy that is not isolated from that life.[54]

The beliefs of which Dewey speaks are not foreordained, only to be uncovered by sagacious announcement. They emerge from the struggles of the human organism in its attempt to understand and ameliorate its condition by virtue of *experimental* inquiry. Some might say that Dewey's description of our "deepest problem" is prosaic, for terms such as "integration," "cooperation," "values," and "purposes" are hardly the stuff of highly charged social and political movements. Precisely, for Dewey is describing our "ordinary" experience, which he considers to be a far more accurate description of actual situation than those tantalizing but misleading rhetorical formulations of variant salvation myths. For Dewey, the world is intelligible, although not ultimately so, and thereby his fundamental attitude is neither pessimistic nor optimistic. In the tradition of Emerson, Lester Frank Ward, and William James, Dewey is a meliorist. In contrast to assorted prophets and more strident claimants of social and political vision, Dewey promises little and delivers much. And finally, long before recent counterculture movements Dewey was aware that a heightening of aesthetic experience was of essential importance to *any* form of liberation.

We must admit, however, that Dewey is rarely read this way. To some extent, he is to blame for generating misunderstandings of his position.[55] It is especially unfortunate that he did not integrate sufficiently his aesthetics with his political writings. This gap was exacerbated in his social and political writings of the 1930s, in which he utilized the language of social planning as his way of responding to the competing Marxist and laissez-faire formulations of that time. It is instructive that this period is also represented by his publication of his profound work in aesthetics, *Art as Experience,* in 1934. This work comes at a midpoint between his major writings in social and political philosophy: *The Public and Its Problems* (1927), *Individualism Old and New* (1930), *Liberalism and Social Action* (1935), and *Freedom and Culture* (1939). For our purposes, it will be best to concentrate on the last chapter of *Liberalism and Social Action,* which Dewey titles "Renascent Liberalism" and which is the clearest statement of his politics. We can then bring to bear upon that discussion some of his views about the importance of aesthetic experience.

In his chapter on "Renascent Liberalism," Dewey takes a position which is clearly counter to that held by Brown or by Marcuse, and actually, if it were not anachronistic, we could say that he had them in mind. The chapter begins with Dewey sorting out three obvious interpretive approaches to social and political change. The first is that change does not or should not take place. If it does take place, it is due to a preordained plan, or at a minimum, such change is of no affair of ours, tracing to forces operative elsewhere. This is a veiled reference to laissez-faire liberalism or to its later version in social Darwinism. Dewey regards this position as naive, reflecting as it does that "men's minds are still pathetically held in the clutch of old habits and haunted by old memories." [56] Lamentably, he does not focus on the fact that this position is most often taken by those who have most to benefit by the absence of radical change, especially that brought about by revolutionary intervention.

The second position is that significant change can take place only by means of violence. Dewey traces this propensity for radical solution to deep insecurity based on a long-standing human experience of scarcity. Then, in a text worthy of Marx, Dewey points to the presence of a dramatic difference in an industrial culture.

The conditions that generate insecurity for the many no longer spring from nature. They are found in institutions and arrangements that are within deliberate human control. Surely this change marks one of the greatest revolutions that has taken place in all human history. Because of it, insecurity is not now the motive to work and sacrifice but to despair.[57]

Finally, Dewey offers his own version, which is to acknowledge the inexorability of change, while setting our task as one of directing it by the utilization of social intelligence. The backdrop to this position was written earlier by Dewey in *The Public and Its Problems.* "The creation of a *tabula rasa* in order to permit the creation of a new order is so impossible as to set at naught both the hope of buoyant revolutionaries and the timidity of scared conservatives." [58] Dewey contends that education holds the key to liberation, especially if it develops programs of action for fundamental institutional reform. He is skeptical of the significance of sheerly personal patterns of liberation if they do not coalesce to effect substantial changes in our social and political beliefs, for "the educational task cannot be accomplished merely by working on men's minds, without action that effects actual change in institutions." [59]

Lest the reader think that Dewey was innocent of the obstacles to such institutional change, we cite his statement of 1928.

The notion that men are equally free to act irrespective of differences in education, in command of capital, and the control of the social environment which is furnished by the institution of property—is a pure absurdity, as facts have demonstrated.[60]

And he returns to this theme in "Renascent Liberalism," where he again points to the coercive power flowing from the ownership of property. "It is foolish to regard the political state as the only agency now endowed with coercive power. Its exercise of this power is pale in contrast with that exercised by concentrated and organized property interests." [61] Despite his admission of the coercive power arrayed against the possibilities of liberation, Dewey warns that to accept the inevitability of our present situation is to allow for violence as the only means of effective change. Further, the "reign of the inevitable" prevents the use of intelligence, which in Dewey's judgment should be experimental, innovative, and constructive. We do not stand outside of our institutions as hapless observers, nor are we trapped in an historical past which rigidly programs our present. Each historical context demands its own evaluation and its own strategies for effective transformation. "The radical who insists that the future method of change must be like that of the past has much in common with the hide-bound reactionary who holds to the past as an ultimate fact. Both overlook the *fact that history in being a process of change generates change not only in details but also in the method of directing social change.*" [62]

Dewey then indicates here and in other of his political writings that the decisively new factor in the twentieth century is the availability of an experimental method of intelligence, reflective of the cooperative approach found in the natural sciences. He does not relate this method explicitly at this point to his understanding of the method of experience as found in his pedagogy, nor to his notion of aesthetic experience, although in "Renascent Liberalism" he writes of the need for an "embodiment of intelligence" if we are to "know where to turn for the means of directing further change." [63] Given the events of the last two decades, it would be fair to question Dewey's confidence in science as the exemplary method for the development of social intelligence. On the other hand, he was prescient in his emphasis on aesthetic sensibility as central to a liberated human life. Indeed, Dewey's understanding of experience as aesthetic may turn out to be more politically significant than his explicitly political writings.

Throughout the essays in this volume, we have attempted to show the relevance of Dewey's aesthetics to concrete social and cultural issues. We do not repeat that here, choosing rather in the context of our discussion of Brown and Marcuse, to sketch Dewey's assessment of the kind of sensibility most fruitful for human life. He stands with Emerson, for whom "every ingenious and aspiring soul leaves the doctrine behind him in his own experience. . . ." [64] And with James, for whom "experience, as we know, has ways of *boiling over*, and making us correct our present formulas." [65] In Dewey's philosophy experience is undergone in the transaction of the human organism with nature, a transaction which is clearly an "embodiment." The human existential situation yields generic traits, and for Dewey, the most fundamental are the "stable" and the "precarious." These traits do not divide the world, nor are entities or situations simply one or the other. They are not divisions between self and world, between you and me, between yesterday and today, this and that. Rather, the precarious and the stable live as irreducible entwinings in every event. In Buberian terms, their relationship constitutes our melancholy fate. Make no mistake, ameliorative politics notwithstanding, Dewey's description of our world is not always cheering.

A feature of existence which is emphasized by cultural phenomena is the precarious and the perilous. . . . Time is brief, and this statement must stand instead of the discourse which the subject deserves. Man finds himself living in an aleatory world; his existence involves, to put it baldly, a gamble. The world is a scene of risk; it is uncertain, unstable, uncannily unstable. Its dangers are irregular, inconstant, not to be counted upon as to their times and seasons. Although persistent, they are sporadic, episodic. It is darkest just before dawn; pride goes before a fall; the

moment of greatest prosperity is the moment most charged
with ill-omen, most opportune for the evil eye. Plague,
famine, failure of crops, disease, death, defeat in battle, are
always just around the corner, and so are abundance,
strength, victory, festival and song. Luck is proverbially
both good and bad in its distributions. The sacred and the
accursed are potentialities of the same situation; and there
is no category of things which has not embodied the sacred
and accursed: persons, words, places, times, directions in
space, stones, winds, animals, stars.[66]

The alternating rhythm of the precarious and the stable is also
the alternating rhythm of our "embodiment" in nature, yielding
the penalties and possibilities of temporality. Each of us has our
own rhythm, our own needs. Our experiences move from the
inchoate to the consummatory, a journey striated with blocked
expectations, surprises, bypasses, and periodic realizations.
Dewey urges us to live our lives on the *qui vive,* always alert to
our surroundings as if with animal sensibility. The most perilous
threat to human life is secondhandedness, living out the bequest
of our parents, siblings, relatives, teachers, and other dispensers
of already programmed possibilities. We should be wary of the
inherited, however noble its intention, for it is the quality of our
own experience which is decisive. Failure, deeply undergone,
often enriches, whereas success achieved mechanically through
the paths set out by others often blunts sensibility. We are not
dropped into the world as a thing among things. We are live
creatures who eat experience.

No creature lives merely under its skin; its subcutaneous
organs are means of connection with what lies beyond its
bodily frame, and to which, in order to live, it must adjust
itself, by accommodation and defense but also by conquest.
At every moment, the living creature is exposed to dangers
from its surroundings, and at every moment, it must draw
upon something in its surroundings to satisfy its needs. The
career and destiny of a living being are bound up with its

interchanges with its environment, not externally but in the most intimate way.[67]

The signal achievement of Dewey's approach is that he has shifted the source of evaluation for human life from "what" to "how." Stated otherwise, Dewey is not sanguine about any final resolution to the human condition, especially if it is presented in the form of an all-solving panacea, be it religious or political. He does, however, believe that the human condition, despite its insoluble and perilous character, can be tremendously enhanced if we can learn to assess, celebrate, and sanction the ways in which we undergo our ordinary experience. "How" we experience becomes more of an index to the quality of our life than "what" we experience. Has Brown or Marcuse written anything quite so revolutionary as that? Despite their radical stance on behalf of personal liberation, would they subscribe to either of the following texts from Dewey?

a) An experience, a very humble experience, is capable of generating and carrying any amount of theory (or intellectual content), but a theory apart from an experience cannot be definitely grasped even as a theory.[68]

b) Even a crude experience, if authentically an experience is more fit to give a clue to the intrinsic nature of esthetic experience than is an object already set apart from any other mode of experience.[69]

I think not. Yet Dewey anticipates Brown and Marcuse in sensing that our real enemies are those who destroy aesthetic sensibility, whether they proceed from excessive authority, condescension, or indifference. In a jeremiad stylistically worthy of Cotton Mather, Dewey warns us against the humdrum, slackness, submission to convention, tightness, rigid abstinence, coerced submission, dissipation, incoherence, and aimless indulgence.[70] A genuinely liberated social and political environment is one which encourages the individual, who is, after all, not ready-made,[71] to experience the world in all of its potential intensity. Such a situation does not protect us from the aforementioned generic trait of the precarious from which Dewey believes there to be no final escape. In certain situations the precarious is the source of our terror, whereas in other situations it is the source of our growth. To build a world is to turn the precarious to our advantage, knowing all the while that in some form it shall be with us to the end. Although our endless struggle with the precarious may be an index to an imperfect world, it is also the occasion of our distinctively human celebrations. In Dewey's language, to undergo the experience of the world as precarious is to suffer. It is arrogant to state that suffering is a necessary ingredient for a life of celebration. Yet, who among us has lived a profound, creative, and aesthetically rich life, knowing only the stable? In Dewey's judgment, the basis of a cultural pedagogy is not to be found in a transcendent force, nor in the abandonment of our historical burdens. It is to be found close-up, in the message of our bodies.

> Life itself consists of phases in which the organism falls out of step with the march of surrounding things and then recovers unison with it—either through effort or by some happy chance. And, in a growing life, the recovery is never mere return to a prior state, for it is enriched by the state of disparity and resistance through which it has successfully passed. If the gap between organism and environment is too wide, the creature dies. If its activity is not enhanced by the temporary alienation, it merely subsists. Life grows when a temporary falling out is a transition to a more extensive balance of the energies of the organism with those of the conditions under which it lives.[72]

At first glance this text may appear gentle and comforting. A closer look, however, reveals that alienation and death present themselves in the course of events, and the line between the *temporary* alienation necessary to the enhancement of life and the gap of *permanent* alienation which spells death, physical or spiritual, is a thin one. The blame for crossing it is placed not on nature, nor on civilization, nor on a *deus ex machina,* but on ourselves. In John Dewey's philosophy, the task of overcoming personal and social alienation and reconstituting the processes of living within the flow of time is one which is laced with chance, happy and otherwise, but the responsibility is ours and ours alone.

NOTES

1. From the vast literature about the notion of progress in American thought, we suggest David W. Marcell, *Progress and Pragmatism, James, Dewey, Beard and the American Idea of Progress* (Westport: Greenwood Press, 1974).

2. Theodore Roszak, *Where the Wasteland Ends* (New York: Anchor Books, 1973), *passim.*

3. Cf. Eugene Fontinell, "A Pragmatic Approach to the Human Cycle," *Six Pillars,* ed. Robert A. McDermott (Chambersburg: Wilson Books, 1974), pp. 129–159.

4. Norman O. Brown, *Life Against Death* (Middletown: Wesleyan University Press, 1959).

5. James Joyce, *Ulysses* (New York: Vintage Books, 1961), p. 34 (1934 edition, p. 35).

6. Brown, *op. cit.,* p. 18.

7. Norman O. Brown, "Apocalypse: The Place of Mystery in the Life of the Mind," *Harper's Magazine,* vol. 222 (May 1961), p. 48.

8. Norman O. Brown, *Closing Time* (New York: Random House, 1973), p. 30.

9. *Ibid.,* p. 30.

10. *Ibid.,* p. 283.

11. Norman O. Brown, "From Politics to Metapolitics," *Caterpillar,* vol. 1 (October 1967), p. 80.

12. Brown, *Closing Time,* pp. 24, 25, 41, 63.

13. Ralph Waldo Emerson, "Give All to Love," *Works,* Vol. IX (Boston: Houghton, Mifflin and Co., 1904), p. 92.

14. Ernest Becker is one of the few thinkers steeped in Brown

and other psychoanalytically oriented critics of contemporary society who brings to bear the American temper in his analysis. Cf. especially his posthumous book *Escape from Evil* (New York: The Free Press, 1975).

15. Cf. Herbert Marcuse, *Eros and Civilization* (Boston: The Beacon Press, 1955), and Sigmund Freud, *Civilization and Its Discontents* (London: The Hogarth Press, 1930).

16. Herbert Marcuse, "Progress and Freud's Theory of Instincts," *Five Lectures* (Boston: The Beacon Press, 1970), p. 32.

17. Cf. Norman O. Brown, "A Reply to Herbert Marcuse," in Herbert Marcuse, *Negations* (Boston: Beacon Press, 1968), p. 243. "The idea of progress is in question; the reality of Marx cannot hide the reality of Nietzsche."

18. Herbert Marcuse, *An Essay on Liberation* (Boston: The Beacon Press, 1969), p. 23.

19. Norman O. Brown, *Love's Body* (New York: Random House, 1966).

20. Brown, "Reply," p. 246.

21. Herbert Marcuse, "Love Mystified: A Critique of Norman O. Brown," *Negations,* p. 243.

22. Herbert Marcuse, *Counterrevolution and Revolt* (Boston: The Beacon Press, 1972), p. 48.

23. Marcuse, *Liberation,* p. 25.

24. As a brief textual support of this judgment, we link the following two well-known texts from Marx and Freud.

a) The mode of production of material life conditions the social, political and intellectual life process in general. It is not the consciousness of men that determines their being, but, on the contrary, their social being that determines their consciousness. *(A Contribution to the Critique of Political Economy,* 1859).

b) It is no wonder if, under the pressure of these possibilities of suffering, (from our own body, from

> the outer world, from our relations with other men)
> humanity is wont to reduce its demands for happi-
> ness, just as even the pleasure-principle itself
> changes into the more accommodating reality-
> principle under the influence of external environ-
> ment; if a man thinks himself happy if he has
> merely escaped unhappiness or weathered trouble;
> if in general the task of avoiding pain forces that of
> obtaining pleasure into the background. *(Civiliza-
> tion and Its Discontents,* 1930).

25. Marcuse, *Liberation,* p. 25.
26. *Ibid.,* p. 10n., pp. 10-11.
27. *Ibid.,* p. 23.
28. Cf. T. B. Bottomore, ed., *Karl Marx-Early Writings* (New York: McGraw-Hill Book Co., 1964), pp. 61-219.
29. Marcuse, *Liberation,* p. 27.
30. *Ibid.,* p. 25. Marcuse was not always so optimistic. Cf. *Eros and Civilization,* p. 237: "But even the ultimate advent of freedom cannot redeem those who died in pain. It is the remembrance of them, and the accumulated guilt of mankind against its victims, that darken the prospect of a civilization without repression."
31. Marcuse, *Counterrevolution,* p. 49.
32. *Ibid.,* p. 128. And we support also Marcuse's incisive critique of the anti-intellectualism generated by self-styled "revolutionaries" and vicarious participants in "proletarian ideology" (pp. 126-127).
33. Contemporary China might become an exception to this otherwise accurate judgment.
34. Marcuse, Foreword, *Negations,* p. xix. "It can be seen that precisely the most exaggerated 'eschatological' conceptions of Marxian theory most adequately anticipate social tendencies: for instance, the idea of the abolition of labor, which Marx himself later rejected." This is vintage histor- ical eschatology, for it warns even the prophet against changing his mind.

35. Marcuse, *Liberation,* p. 23.
36. Cf. Herbert Marcuse, *Reason and Revolution* (Boston: The Beacon Press, 1960) (1941), p. 315. "Truth, in short, is not a realm apart from historical reality, nor a region of eternally valid ideas. To be sure, it transcends the given historical reality, but only in so far as it crosses from one historical stage to another."
37. Marcuse, *Liberation,* p. 23.
38. Brown, "Reply," p. 243.
39. Marcuse, *Eros,* p. 236. "The necessity of death does not refute the possibility of final liberation." And Brown closes *Closing Time* with the belief, "here comes everybody" on "the way to the unification of the human race" (p. 109).
40. Freud, *Civilization,* p. 144.
41. Brown, *Life,* p. 322.
42. It is striking that Marcuse, a man of considerable learning in the history of philosophy, literature, and the arts, has never integrated American cultural history into his aggressive and even hostile version of American society. From Marcuse, we have virtually no response to Melville, Whitman, William James, Dewey, Royce, Faulkner, and countless others whose writings reveal both the wisdom and malevolence of America. Certainly Marcuse does not breed confidence in his critique of American society when, in the face of an extensive interpretive literature, he makes slurring remarks about Puritanism as though that term still had only the ambience of sustaining the repression of the body *(Negations,* p. 265; *Liberation,* p. 28). Finally, if self-posturing and self-deception as to the meaning of "doing good" really do constitute the Achilles' heel of America, then nothing Marcuse has written is as incisively critical as Herman Melville's classic, *The Confidence Man.*
43. For a selection of Dewey's writings which show the wide range of his concerns, cf. John J. McDermott, ed., *The Philosophy of John Dewey,* 2 vols. (New York: G. P. Putnam's Sons, 1973).
44. Unfortunately, Dewey responded more to the program-

matic suggestions of the Marxists than to the thought of Marx himself, and, incredibly, he never wrote a serious study of the implications of the thought of Freud.

45. Cf. above, "An American Notion of Experience" and "Life Is in the Transitions."

46. For a critical edition of the writings of Dewey published before 1899, cf. *The Early Works, 1882-1898,* 5 vols. (Carbondale: Southern Illinois University Press, 1969-1972). *The Middle Works, 1899-1924,* are now in the process of being published.

47. John Dewey, "The Need for a Recovery of Philosophy," in McDermott, *The Philosophy of John Dewey,* p. 61.

48. John Dewey, *Experience and Nature* (La Salle: Open Court, 1929) (1925).

49. Sidney Ratner et al., *John Dewey and Arthur F. Bentley, A Philosophical Correspondence—1932-1951* (New Brunswick: Rutgers University Press, 1964), p. 543.

50. Dewey, *Experience and Nature,* 2d ed., p. 4.

51. *Ibid.,* p. 4.

52. Toward the end of his life, Dewey came to prefer "transaction" over "interaction" as his basic mediating term. Cf. S. Ratner, *op. cit.,* pp. 613-614.

53. John Dewey, *Reconstruction in Philosophy* (Boston: Beacon Press, 1948) (1920), p. 73. "When we take means for ends we indeed fall into moral materialism. But when we take ends without regard to means we degenerate into sentimentalism. In the name of the ideal we fall back upon mere luck and chance and magic or exhortation and preaching; or else upon a fanaticism that will force the realization of preconceived ends at any cost."

54. John Dewey, *The Quest for Certainty* (New York: Capricorn Books, 1960) (1929), p. 255.

55. No thinker so chary of ideology has been subjected to such intense and extreme criticism. Dewey has been accused of lowering educational standards, threatening American ideals, having Communist sympathies, and fostering Nazism. The latest critique reports its authors standing on the

Chicago River, "alienated and nauseous," holding Dewey indirectly responsible for the Vietnam War. Historically anachronistic, this essay makes Dewey a scapegoat for much that is wrong in contemporary American society. Cf. Walter Feinberg and Henry Rosemont, Jr., "Training for the Welfare State: The Progressive Education Movement," *Work, Technology and Education* (Urbana: University of Illinois Press, 1975), pp. 60-91.

56. John Dewey, *Liberalism and Social Action* (New York: Capricorn Books, 1963) (1935), p. 59.
57. *Ibid.,* p. 60.
58. John Dewey, *The Public and Its Problems* (New York: Henry Holt and Co., 1927), p. 162.
59. Dewey, *Liberalism,* p. 61.
60. John Dewey, "Philosophies of Freedom," *Philosophy and Civilization* (New York: G. P. Putnam's Sons, 1931), p. 281. Significantly, Dewey sees the classic capitalist ethic as blocking the ameliorative possibilities of science and technology. "The greatest obstacle to that vision is, I repeat, the perpetuation of the older individualism now reduced, as I have said, to the utilization of science and technology for ends of private pecuniary gain. I sometimes wonder if those who are conscious of present ills but who direct their blows of criticism at everything except this obstacle are not stirred by motives which they unconsciously prefer to keep below consciousness." *Individualism—Old and New* (New York: G. P. Putnam's Sons, 1930), pp. 99-100.
61. Dewey, *Liberalism,* p. 64. For a recent political analysis "in the tradition of John Dewey," cf. Peter T. Manicas, *The Death of the State* (New York: G. P. Putnam's Sons, 1974).
62. Dewey, *Liberalism,* p. 83.
63. *Ibid.,* p. 74.
64. Emerson, "Compensation," *Works,* II, 95.
65. William James, *Pragmatism* (New York: Longman's Green and Co., 1907), p. 222.
66. Dewey, *Experience and Nature,* p. 38.
67. John Dewey, *Art as Experience* (New York: Capricorn

Books, 1958) (1934), p. 13. There is historical sensibility here as well, for on page 18 Dewey writes that "the live creature adopts its past; it can make friends with even its stupidities, using them as warnings that increase present wariness."

68. John Dewey, *Democracy and Education* (New York: The Macmillan Company, 1961) (1916), p. 144.

69. Dewey, *Art as Experience*, p. 11.

70. Cf. *ibid.*, p. 40.

71. John Dewey, "Time and Individuality," *Time and Its Mysteries*, ed., Harlow Shapley (New York: Collier Books, 1962) (1940), p. 158.

72. Dewey, *Art as Experience*, p. 14.

CHAPTER SIX

Feeling as Insight: The Affective Dimension in Social Diagnosis

MEDICINE AND PHILOSOPHY

The popular mind is deep, and means a thousand times more than it explicitly knows.[1]

As a teacher and student of philosophy, I welcome the opportunity to participate in a symposium with distinguished medical doctors devoted to rethinking the Hippocratic wisdom of antiquity and searching for new modes of inquiry in the art of healing. The history of philosophy has long been associated with medicine, as the careers of Aristotle and John Locke, among others, attest. Indeed, one of the most creative of nineteenth-century philosophers, William James, had but one earned degree, and that was in medicine. The comparative isolation of medicine as a discipline, particularly from the social sciences, is a phenomenon of our century and has done much to engender the unfortunate mystique which surrounds the practice of medicine and ensuing lack of social consciousness which too often affects public medical policy. And if similar charges can be placed against philosophy and other academic disciplines, the stakes in medical practice are far higher, for what more crucial ingredient of the human condition exists than physical and psychological well-being?

In the move to interdisciplinary studies, now characteristic of university curricula, little is accomplished if the important and powerful professions of law and medicine are left to pursue their professional paths unquestioned and unchallenged. The future of medicine is of secondary concern—it is the future of man and the quality of his environment which are the primary issues.

In this essay, I attempt to present in an interdisciplinary way some parameters relative to the problem of diagnosis as it applies to contemporary American man, especially in his urban setting. I make no claim to special medical knowledge other than the experience of my own body along with the complex and intense interactions of the medical history of my family. The significance of this limited experience is not, however, to be undersold, for it represents the empirical intimacy of everyone's experience with medicine.

Before turning to the problem of diagnosis, and speaking in general terms, the marvel of medicine is to be found in its achievement of an extraordinary correlation between knowledge and implementation. No other discipline has been so effective in obtaining concrete results from speculative and experimental probes. Catastrophic diseases have been wiped out, and we have confidence that those remaining shall be eliminated. In recent years, dazzling reconstructions of essential bodily organs have given an aura of collective genius to medicine, accompanied by the capacity to outstrip human limitations long held to be inviolable. The existence of organ transplants, for example, connotes to the observer a bold transcendence of the boundaries of history and nature. In its intimacy and immediacy, the era of transplants is a more startling breakthrough than that of moonlanding the astronauts. The latter is an extension of man and continuous with nature, but the former is a rebirth, a bypassing of the heretofore inexorable laws of nature, as if man had transcended himself, albeit in single and isolated instances. At a minimum, the horizon of the possible has been immeasurably widened.

For those of us who are not in medicine, there is little question that the creative events of modern medicine are awe inspiring. Many achievements have an exotic ring to them, and they seem to have elicited from even the reflective and informal observer a blank check for medicine to move forward as it wills. A closer look, however, at the activities of contemporary medicine and especially at the role and stance of the physician, yields a more complex evaluation. Without denying the achievement of modern medicine, we might ask the following questions:

Has the extraordinary success in dealing with highly specialized problems been at the expense of healing the entire community? [2] Said differently, has contemporary medicine, as so much of modern science, been guilty of dramatic linear breakthroughs while impervious to the highly negative implications they so often spawn?

Has contemporary medicine defined illness too narrowly, as if the human body has not undergone profound changes traceable not only to a new ecological setting but also to an entirely different social-psychological context?

The foregoing questions focus on human living as actually experienced in affective terms, rather than as speculatively projected. In a word, we are calling for a cultural anthropology in which the affective dimension is at the center of our evaluation of the human condition, rather than peripheral to it. In doing so, relative to medicine, let us examine the diagnostic process, the new understanding of the nature of person, and finally some strands of an environmental aesthetic, significant for an amelioration of that form of pathology described variously as alienation, anomie, or cultural sadness.

PITFALLS OF DIAGNOSIS

Thus, our perceptions of, and our reactions to, other people and what they do or how they feel can be understood better if we consider the functional possibilities, the conditions and effects of their behavior, which are based on representation and openness to the environment.[3]

The euclidean point of view, with its emphasis on the measurable and its abhorrence of loose ends, still has influence. Despite the vast increase in the speculative versions of varieties of the human condition, our methodological approach to understanding others' experiences seems fixed both in point of origin and in the evaluation of implications. Even among those whose responsibility is to grasp the import of another's feelings, the assumptions about the nature of the human self are unrelievedly trite. Although the person who does not acknowledge the staggering change in environment, media, and pace of life in the last fifty years is rare, still more rare is the awareness of the profound transformation this development has worked upon human self-consciousness. The interiorizing, by the human self, of environmental changes has proceeded in an admittedly subtle but nonetheless significant way. It is not too much to say that the delicate fabric of self-consciousness, under the press of modern technology, has been altered in decisive ways, especially with regard to the experience of our bodies.

Despite these developments, social diseases—alienation, anomie, cultural deprivation, stimulant dependencies, and the afflictions of hard-core poverty—are still diagnosed relative to a classical image of human behavior. Erich Lindenmann, a psychiatrist, writes in his foreword to Herbert Gans's book on *The Urban Villagers,* an analysis of the relocation crises of the residents of the "urban-renewed" West End of Boston, that

"The problems of medical care ... and preventive services have been vastly complicated by our ignorance concerning basic attitudes and motivations of various types of people whom we are serving." [4]

If we look at this situation in methodological terms, we find most often that diagnosis proceeds from a fixed point of view, perhaps best resembling a self-fulfilling prophecy. The diagnostician assumes the contours of human behavior as known and deduces from those limits a set of symptom-question relationships, which follow step by lockstep, to one of a number of familiar conclusions.[5] The person diagnosed has a sense of this ritual, and he very much wants to receive a clarifying judgment as to the cause of his discomfort; therefore, he falls into the proscribed pattern. This can be described as an effort to avoid "being different." In analyzing our response to social pressures, Richard Sennett writes that "the enterprise involved is an attempt to build an image or identity that coheres, is unified, and filters out threats in social experience." [6] Sennett then proceeds to describe the burden we are under as we attempt to fit the model of expectancy.

> The jarring elements in one's social life can be purified out as unreal because they don't fit that articulated object, that self-consciously spelled-out set of beliefs, likes and dislikes, and abilities that one takes to be oneself. In this way, the degree to which people feel urged to keep articulating who they are, what they want, and what they feel is almost an index of their fear about their inability of survival in social experience with other men.[7]

In the process of diagnosis, as long as the questions asked are so structured as to elicit traditional responses, the judgments about their meaning are self-sustained. It is not that alternatives are ruled out but rather, not being sought, they never surface. This approach is a cardinal instance of what William James called "vicious intellectualism," [8] wherein we define a situation such that all possibilities not included in the definition are thereby excluded, no matter the shifts in the overall context. From another vantage point, this methodological approach in diagnosis is the opposite of that encouraged by Martin Buber when he tells us that we should experience "from the standpoint of the other." [9] In this regard, focusing simply on the intake interview, we find countless instances of our insensitivity to the plight and standpoint of the "other."

As an evening counselor to an adult college program some years ago, I was struck by the disparity between the reasons for appointments, such as change of schedule and teacher complaints, and the extraordinary range of serious problems unearthed just in casual conversation. Under the guise of academic problems, many persons had a desperate need to discuss deep personal difficulties in their work and family life, and on a number of occasions they introduced into the conversation their recent suicide attempts.[10] The dramatic difference of the experience from the "other side" is caught in this text from Robert Sommer, as he describes reading fifty autobiographies of mental patients.

> I found these books invaluable for understanding the ways in which being hospitalized affected a person's *Weltanschauung.* Christmas and other holidays were times of loneliness and remorse. The admissions routine, which strips a patient of all personal belongings including his wedding ring (to protect his valuables) and his clothing (to send them to the laundry to be marked) and requires him to answer questions asked by people who do not bother to introduce themselves, lies somewhere between the tragic and the grotesque. Almost every case of visual hallucinations in these 50 autobiographies occurred under conditions of reduced visual stimulation, confirming the laboratory studies of sensory deprivation, in which people who are subjected to reduced sensory inputs are unable to focus their thoughts and frequently experience hallucinations.[11]

In assuming that the person or persons under consideration

proceed from the same basic understanding of experience as the one diagnosing, we find ourselves cut off from some of the most important factors in social diagnosis. We may, for example, have profoundly different experiences yet develop the same symptoms, for as David Mechanic comments, "symptomatology and disability are very different aspects of illness and they must be studied independently." [12] As a case in point, a quest for drugs can be generated by an attempt to escape from the pressures of an outwardly successful life as well as from the horrors of a hopeless poverty condition. Surely the spread of heroin use among middle- and upper-class white youth disestablishes our previously held belief that the use of such drugs is a sign of economic and social deprivation. What about our tendency to trace listlessness and an anomic attitude to that classical social affliction, apathy? To the contrary, we now find that such disengagement proceeds frequently from the frustrations attendant upon an inability to convert intense moral concern into concrete forms of public amelioration, or, as we shall consider subsequently, traces to the antiseptic and bland character of much of our physical environment.

OTHER PROBLEMS IN DIAGNOSIS

Turning now to another serious oversight in traditional patterns of diagnosis, we focus on the common assumption that persons with deep afflictions of a personal and social kind have the necessary language to articulate these disturbances. Some years ago, Michael Harrington wrote a book entitled *The Other America*, in which he spoke about the invisibility of the poor, who "are increasingly slipping out of the very experience and consciousness of the nation." [13] One of the reasons for this invisibility is the drastic gap between the conventional understanding of poverty and the actual experiences of the poor. Harrington tried to show that the real malady of hard-core poverty was social-psychological. It was not so much the quantity of their food and clothing but rather the nutritional vacancy of their food, the difficulty in obtaining it, and the unkempt, styleless character of their clothing and furnishings which induced hopelessness and a loss of body tone. In turn, these characteristics generate environmental conditions dangerous to health and erosive of energy and mental stability, illustrating graphically what we now call the vicious circle of poverty. The middle-class remark, "How can they live that way," becomes a telling instance of experiencing others' lives only from the outside.

An anecdote told me by a poverty program caseworker is indicative of how little we know about the needs of others from their point of view. In visiting an abjectly poor community in the Midwest, one literally without even substandard housing or basic sanitation facilities, a social worker asked the people what they wanted most and first. Their answer was startling but revealing: they requested street signs. Upon reflection this event teaches us much, for the people in this community were not only poor in traditional terms—lacking all the fundamentals of living—but they had lost their communal identity as well. Although they may not have articulated it in this way, apparently they felt that street signs would give them a sense of place, a reference point against which they could begin to evaluate their wider needs.[14] It is difficult to judge from the outside what will fulfill the needs of another person's embattled recess of dignity. Years ago, as a young man, I was a volunteer worker at Bellevue Hospital in New York City. My responsibility was to be of service to the patients, all of them indigent, most of them bereft of family and friends, many of them terminal cases. One aged man had lost his arms and legs and did not speak English. Through gestures and halting translation, I learned from him that he would like two cigars of a certain Spanish make. No other type would do. This man, faced with utter experiential deprivation, clung to a qualitative assessment of his world, while asserting an irreducible pride in his taste.

In diagnosing and evaluating social affliction, the tendency is to proceed from a position of "knowing what is best" for those involved and to scoff at the halting and strange complaints that people have. Yet every statement uttered out of the experience of affliction is loaded with inferential meaning. The sensitive diagnostician will not fit these articulations into an a priori context but will strive to unearth their experienced roots so as to better follow the multiple hints and leads which yield genuine insight into the real and felt needs of the person or community.

A still more difficult task for traditional patterns of diagnosis is the ability to penetrate experiences that are difficult to articulate, that is, those experiences we undergo which are vague in delineation or so profoundly different from the expected that we feel awkward in describing them.[15]

Here we can think of the person for whom, by all public accounts, "things are going well," but who nonetheless is restless, on edge, even hostile to his surroundings and his peers. He may suffer from an interiorization of heightened expectations, pressed subtly upon him but not clear to his own consciousness. Under the circumstances, for him to complain seems "foolish" and "thankless," yet he suffers from deep disquiet and irritations, both physical and mental. A pervasive presence of this problem is found in the apparently perverse behavior of those people who are moved from the ugliness of an urban slum to a clean project. In many such situations, these residents proceed to deface their new environment in what seems to be a pathological effort to duplicate the burdens of their original environment. Yet, consider the difficulty; how does a community express its hostility against a "clean" environment in terms that are sanctioned publicly? What is it in their consciousness and their experience which engenders this hostility? [16] No doubt indicative of deep-seated affective and communal needs, this distress defies expression to the larger community,[17] so often characterized by its clear-cut understanding of a hierarchy of social values.

Other experiences that are difficult to articulate abound. In what way, for example, does a person quantitatively rich in friends and family state his deep feeling of loneliness and anonymity? How awkward it has been for young people to justify their disinterest in perpetuating a society allegedly tuned to their every need. Also significant is the expansive role of shame or guilt in the patient's effort to mask his symptoms and throw the diagnostician off the trail, revealing a willingness to continue suffering rather than to admit to a "social" disease or an embarrassing event. How frequent it is that people retreat to a studied anonymity because the complex quality of their experience defies the recognized patterns of expression and explication.

Objective descriptions and evaluations of situations in which other persons find themselves, which fly in the face of the perceptions of those situations by the persons involved, result in a diagnostic charade. While it is true that we can doubt or deny the accuracy of a judgment about factual matters, we cannot deny the accuracy of another's feelings, however self-deceiving the cause. The vital center of diagnosis, then, is the ability to grasp the ongoing activity of the other person so that neither symptoms and complaints, nor their causes, are dealt with apart from the relational process of webbing and rejecting, which is what constitutes how one feels at any given time. It is important to realize that even agreement between the diagnostician and patient on a "cause" of the difficulty should not be interpreted as a clean-cut solution to the problem; people have an endless capacity and need to have answers, even if only to clear their minds. After all, we rarely have a one-to-one relationship between an event and a response. More likely, events bathe our consciousness, churning up patterns of relationship, frequently novel, so that our deepest feelings are framed out of experiences far distant from what appeared to be the causal source. A richer sense of these dimensions should emerge if we sketch some characteristics of a different understanding of the nature of person than that assumed in most diagnoses.

THE PERSON AS RELATIONAL PROCESS

But don't you see that the whole trouble lies here. In words, words. Each one of us has within him a whole world of things, each man of us his own special world. And how can we ever come to an understanding if I put in the words I utter the sense and value of things as I see them; while you

who listen to me must inevitably translate them according
to the conception of things each one of you has within
himself. We think we understand each other, but we never
really do.[18]

Understanding another person is, indeed, difficult to achieve.
Nonetheless, rich insights about the quality and direction of
experiences shared with others is possible in sensitive interpersonal situations. The crucial factor in such a process is to cease
treating the other person as an object; rather, we should make
an effort to reach out beyond those accepted assumptions which
often block us from grasping the distinctive versions of another's
world view. This kind of sensibility has been steadily gaining
ground on both a theoretical and a practical level. Beginning
with William James, Henri Bergson, and the pioneering social
psychology of Charles Horton Cooley and George Herbert
Mead, our century has seen an extraordinary change in our
approach to the nature of the person. More recent efforts in this
direction include the work of Kurt Goldstein, Erik Erikson,
Robert Jay Lifton, Erving Goffman, and the controversial
philosophical psychiatry of Ronald Laing. Further, we have the
imaginative efforts of Edward Hall, Kevin Lynch, and Robert
Sommer, among others, in the comparatively new field of
proxemics or person-space relationships.[19] Of a still more
speculative cast is the work proceeding from existential and
phenomenological sources, such as Jean Paul Sartre, Gabriel
Marcel, and Maurice Merleau-Ponty. Utilizing the concepts of
some of these thinkers, let us sketch some of those qualities in a
person which, if taken seriously, would enable us to perform
more fruitful diagnoses.

JAMES AND BERGSON

The initial breakthrough came in the thought of James and
Bergson as they sought to overcome the traditional penchant for
a dualistic interpretation of the person.[20] In so doing, they
offered a radical reconsideration of the human body. Instead of
claiming that the body is passive and merely receives external

influences which are rendered meaningful by the active work of the mind, James and Bergson developed a position which delineates the body in more aggressive terms. In his book on *Matter and Memory,* Bergson points to the original quality of that image "which is distinct from all the others, in that I do not know it only from without by perceptions, but from within by affections: it is my body." [21] Further, he tells us that "my body, an object destined to move other objects, is then a centre of action; it cannot give birth to a representation." [22] In effect, we lead with our bodies, or better, our bodies are knowers in a primal way. The self, then, is not a privileged redoubt, not an archimedean point within our bodies, but is actually how and when the body acts. In a footnote to his essay on "The Experience of Activity," William James offers us an unusual text on the self as the activity of the body.

> The individualized self, which I believe to be the only thing properly called self, is a part of the content of the world experienced. The world experienced (otherwise called the "field of consciousness") comes at all times with our body as its centre, centre of vision, centre of action, centre of interest. Where the body is is "here"; when the body acts is "now"; what the body touches is "this"; all other things are "there" and "then" and "that." These words of emphasized position imply a systematization of things with reference to a focus of action and interest which lies in the body; and the systematization is now so instinctive (was it ever not so?) that no developed or active experience exists for us at all except in that ordered form. So far as "thoughts" and "feelings" can be active, their activity terminates in the activity of the body, and only through first arousing its activities can they begin to change those of the rest of the world. The body is the storm centre, the origin of co-ordinates, the constant place of stress in all that experience-train. Everything circles round it, and is felt from its point of view. The word "I," then, is primarily a noun of position, just like "this" and "here." Activities attached to "this"

position have prerogative emphasis, and, if activities have feelings, must be felt in a peculiar way. The word "my" designates the kind of emphasis.[23]

Speaking of Bergson, Ian Alexander claims that his "argument will consist in showing how the self inserts into the world and space through the body." [24] And John E. Smith, speaking of James's empiricism, holds it to be a "radically new account of how the self penetrates and is penetrated by the world." [25] It is important to realize that the role of the body, in the swarm of experiences which make up our world, is more than a neutral filter. We "intend" by virtue of our bodily activity. "Intentionality" is not limited to the processes of thinking, but is present in the selective character of our bodily responses. William James, in his *Principles of Psychology,* states that "out of what is in itself an undistinguishable, swarming *continuum,* devoid of distinction or emphasis, our senses make for us, by attending to this motion and ignoring that, a world full of contrasts, of sharp accents, of abrupt changes, of picturesque light and shade." [26]

In a similar vein, Bergson comments that "our representation of matter is the measure of possible action upon bodies: it results from the discarding of what has no interest for our needs, or more generally for our functions." [27] The body, then, becomes a probe, an informing and selecting extension of our very being. We construct the focus of our experience by the activity of our bodies, for "the actuality of our perception thus lies in its *activity.*" [28]

Writing closer to our time, Michael Polanyi, medical doctor and philosopher, comments on the bodily roots of man's thought and creative powers.

Our body is the ultimate instrument of all our external knowledge, whether intellectual or practical. In all our waking moments we are relying on our awareness of contacts of our body with things outside for *attending* to these things. Our own body is the only thing in the world which we normally never experience as an object, but experience always in terms of the world to which we are attending from our body.[29]

The most crucial difference in the post-Jamesian view of the self from that of traditional Western philosophy and psychology is the shift from spectator to constitutor as the delineating mark of self-consciousness. James had written that *"the pursuance of future ends and the choice of means for their attainment are thus the mark and criterion of the presence of mentality* in a phenomenon."[30] The person constitutes a functional point of view and a series of interlocking goals, simultaneously forging relationships in order to sustain this anticipation. Some relationships are ultimately sterile, others obdurate when placed in a wider context. Adjustments and concessions must accompany the efforts of the person to constitute a world frame compatible with needs, interests, and the ever present facticity of the environment. It is, however, the perceiving activity of the person which is dominant, for the ordering of relations is in response to what we bring to the teeming continua of impressions. In effect, we each constitute a world whose perimeters are shared but whose center is distinctly personal and unrepeatable. One recent commentator, Robert Jay Lifton, refers to our time as the creation of "a new kind of man—a protean man."

> For it is quite possible that even the image of personal identity, insofar as it suggests inner stability and sameness, is derived from a vision of a traditional culture in which man's relationships to his institutions and symbols are still relatively intact—which is hardly the case today. If we understand the self to be the person's symbol of his organism, then self-process refers to the continuous psychic recreation of that symbol.[31]

Protean man is an actualizer more than a recognizer, a formulator more than a spectator. Despite the accepted obviousness of the world, man, by virtue of distinctively personal emphasis, structures his own environment, whether by rejection or assimilation, whether by definition or by inference. A line from the lyrics of a contemporary rock group reads, "I see things I wish my eyes could see." [32] The reductionist character of our language often forces us to acknowledge similarities everywhere, thereby denying the novelty which lurks in all of our experiences. It was Sören Kierkegaard who said something to the effect that we live forward but understand backwards, as if upon retrospect the unique character of our experiences is flattened out so that others may understand them without having gone through them. In time this need for clarity becomes suffusive, and we have our present experiences as already sanctioned by the canons of clarity and stripped a priori of their distinctively personal character. In his book on *Becoming*, Gordon Allport offers an ironic comment on this situation.

> Striving, it is apparent, always has a future reference. As a matter of fact, a great many states of mind are adequately described only in terms of their futurity. Along with striving, we may mention interest, tendency, disposition, expectation, planning, problem solving, and intention. While not all future-directedness is phenomenally propriate, it all requires a type of psychology that transcends the prevalent tendency to explain mental states exclusively in terms of past occurrences.
>
> People, it seems, are busy leading their lives into the future, whereas psychology, for the most part, is busy tracing them into the past.[33]

The point at issue is that contemporary man has access to a vast array of experiences and ways of experiencing, many of both becoming available only in the last half-century. He cannot fit into a framework of interpretation which assumes a one-to-one correspondence between the environment, as defined and clarified, and his affective experience of the environment. Recent commentators such as John Cage, Marshall McLuhan, and Edmund Carpenter have made much of the demise of

Gutenberg or literate man, that is, he who experiences serially or linearly, with the major rubric the staccato of print. To this they contrast the emergence of the electronic medium, with its stress on instantaneity and the reemphasizing of the senses, touch, taste, and smell, all of which are explicit body probes. The full ramifications of these judgments are complicated, but despite a flamboyance of style, they seem to characterize the more self-conscious and expressive aspects of our society, particularly the young. The paradox, however, and this is a main thrust of the essay, is that "everyman" seems to be caught between the new experiencing and the contours of our old, desiccated environment. Thus, men learn by means of mass media about the incredible powers of contemporary man—they are placed in touch with global experiences representative of every land and every people. At the same time, especially in the great urban centers, the environment recedes in personal quality, while it takes a shape either hostile to human life or of a scope and function beyond a person's intimate reach. In a word, coupled with the majestic reach of global communication, with its concomitant increase on stress,[34] man's local environment, shrunken in affective dimensions, has become deaesthetized. While not the only factor, this deaesthetization is a major cause of the widespread anomie which affects contemporary man. It is a social disease and works a serious obstacle to the ameliorative goals of a truly social medicine.

DEAESTHETIZATION AS A SOCIAL DISEASE

Life is coexistent and coextensive with the eternal natural environment in which the body is submerged. The body's dependence upon this external environment is absolute—in the fullest sense of the word, *uterine*.[35]

Modern man is well aware of the obvious forms of repression and social affliction. Poverty, prejudice, and violence take their daily toll. We are less aware, however, of more subtle forms of dehumanization, namely, those brought on by the erosion of a genuinely human environment in aesthetic terms. John Dewey once wrote that "no experience of whatever sort is a unity unless it has aesthetic quality." [36] We refer here not to the world of art but to the drama of our doing, undergoing, celebrating, and suffering that comprises the rhythm of everyday ordinary living. Too often this rhythm is submerged in a bland environment, rendering us insensitive to differences, horizons, and crises. In time, we drift through life without variety or intimacy. Dewey writes:

> Things happen, but they are neither definitely included nor decisively excluded; we drift. We yield according to external pressure, or evade and compromise. There are beginnings and cessations, but no genuine initiations and concludings. One thing replaces another, but does not absorb it and carry it on. There is experience, but so slack and discursive that it is not an experience. Needless to say, such experiences are anaesthetic.[37]

How can this be a serious and pressing problem for contemporary man, especially urban man, living as we do in the midst of a technological explosion that has given us marvels of design, communication, and even extraterrestrial experience? We should keep in mind, however, that our analysis is from the perspective of the person rather than from the perspectives of a catalogue of wonders. A closer look at our environment and how we experience it will reveal some severe dislocations.

In the last fifty years we have witnessed a thoroughgoing movement from the affairs of nature to technological artifact as the context of our activity. The shifts from the horse to the automobile and from the stairs to elevator and escalator were aggressive symbols of a new sense of body, wherein we became packaged within a moving environment rather than physically continuous with it. The evolution of the automobile is characterized by an increasing discontinuity of our bodies with that environment, as we became simply steerers of a powerful and largely unintelligible container. The development of a host of appliances and the advent of packaging still further removed us from intimate contact with the fundamental affairs of our daily life. Even our buildings are becoming containers, usually lacking the qualities that relate to the needs of the dwellers, and more often repressing the opportunity for affective participation. James Marston Fitch, Jr., writes:

> To a greater extent than perhaps any other nation, we Americans have become an "indoor" people. A large portion of our lives—working, sleeping, playing—is spent in buildings; buildings over whose design and construction we have little control: buildings whose physical and economic distribution are only remotely conditioned by our needs; buildings whose effects upon our health and happiness is only obscurely understood.[38]

A further source of the present alienation of our bodies from our immediate surroundings is the unfortunate fact that breakthroughs in technology were not accompanied by a rerouting of bodily interests into other areas of experience. I think that it can be said that we witnessed a steady loss in the role of our hands in the penetration and shaping of the world. Small children, as a case in point, are taught the intricacies of set theory and logic and the staggering speculative reach of modern science, but their bodies are still exercised exclusively under the traditional and time-honored ritual of sports and gymnastics. We rarely teach them to sculpt, to mime, or to experience technology tactilely through the spectrum of touch available to them, ranging over the variety of metals and plastics. Nor have we articulated adequately to ourselves a sense of taste and discrimination relative to our technological environment.

Traditionally, nature, which at one time occupied most of our lives, had an obviousness about it. Crops failed; they were not fecund, they had bugs crawling over and through them, or they simply died. Grass became parched, animals diseased, and water stagnant. On the other hand, our praise of nature responded to its colors, lushness, vitality, energy, texture, and its myriad of shapes and sounds, all deep aesthetic qualities. To the contrary, with regard to the world of artifacts, in our daily lives we seem to settle for "new" or "clean" or "convenient" as sufficient evidence of quality. This attitude has generated a sameness as witnessed by domestic housing, especially projects, roads, building facades, shopping centers, motels, and utensils. Consider also the dreariness of the institutional colors found in hospitals, schools, public housing projects, and, above all, prisons.

Our overall pattern seems to be developing subject to an attitude and a policy which we could describe as a systematic attempt to dilute or remove the sensuousness from our daily environment. Our buses and trains become more and more sterile without any visible recognition that they are to be occupied by human bodies. The seats in these vehicles are contoured as though for an indiscriminate lump and the hand straps have disappeared along with other personal amenities. The materials used in these vehicles are brittle or rigid and they neither take color well nor do they press back against our bodies as we touch them.[39] We have apparently lost our sense of tone and shape in the name of an unrelieved triteness, as if our culture were searching for the least common denominator. Mr. Allen Birnbach, a student of mine, is now preparing a photographic montage of New York City subway stations. His work vividly shows that in a systematic fashion we are replacing the extraordinary wall mosaics of those stations with strips of white tile, turning them into replicas of large public bathrooms.

Some may disagree with these judgments by pointing to the presence of exciting exceptions, as exemplified by isolated instances of monumental architecture found in great cities or cultural centers, or on university campuses.[40] It is instructive to realize that such achievements are experienced directly by only a small percentage of our society and serve frequently as a totally unreal horizon from which to evaluate our everyday experience.[41] Thus, Americans seem caught between amazing accomplishments which we admire from afar but do not experience in intimate terms, and an eroding aesthetic vitality in the rest of our environment. When those involved are also poverty-stricken or otherwise socially trapped, this paradox becomes a cruel gap, rendering their environment still more tawdry and uninteresting.

Now what do these concerns have to do with diagnosis and the affairs of medicine? On one level, there is an obviousness to the problem recognized as such by modern medicine; namely, the disproportionate role of mental and psychological stress versus physical activity which characterizes contemporary man. Responses to this problem range from suggestions of periodic vacations to bicycle riding and jogging. While not opposed to these and similar remedies, our version of the problem cuts differently. The problem is not so much that contemporary man has insufficient physical activity, but rather that the environment in which we live is less and less receptive to our bodies and, further, that the nutrition which proceeds from affective stimulation brought on by aesthetic differentiation and rooted in the affective responses of our body has shrunk, especially in proportion to the range of experiences available to our intellect. My contention is that this situation has resulted in many persons experiencing a deep-seated listlessness, and experiential anomie, masked by using a jazzed-up contemporary idiom and the vicarious identification with the worlds portrayed by contemporary film and television, especially sports. This listlessness, not acknowledged as such, gives rise to a series of medical complaints, physical and/or psychological, which defy traditional modes of diagnosis. A pertinent remark on the medical implications of this development is offered by Serge Chermayeff and Christopher Alexander in a comment on the "Pathology of Boredom."

If man is restricted to one extreme, subjected exclusively to the excitement of the large scale, without the contrast of relief of the minuscule, it is easily conceivable that the human organism might atrophy. Human sensibility, which may be seriously blunted by monotonous overstimulation, may also be blunted if it is exercised exclusively in an environment of calculated and automatically controlled physical comfort. Our faculties function best and are best maintained at peak sharpness when effort is required of them. Monotony of any kind—dull or intense—is debilitating. Boredom is a word heard commonly today. It may be that the uniformity of the "air-conditioned nightmare" fatigues both mind and body, that under such conditions the vital side of human life degenerates.

Possibly science will find that this balanced variety is not essential to man's physical well-being, but it seems unlikely. Equilibrium provided in nature for living organisms appears to be a compound of contrasts in a dynamic relationship. The man-made world must provide at least the same.

Today it is prevented from doing so because of two conspicuous invaders. The very instruments that have given man increased dynamic power—total mobility and instantaneous communication—are destroying the equilibrium in the human habitat.[42]

The use of the word "pathology" in the foregoing text is correct, for any situation which cripples or enervates the human organism, however unusual or vague its roots, is a pathological condition. The task of medicine conceived as a social science (which is not exclusive of medicine as a natural science) is to build into its diagnostic procedures a sensitivity to this dimension of contemporary human experience.

As a specific example of this approach consider the problem of drug use among the young and the increasing desire to be on the road, away from the formal structures of classrooms or conventional dress. Often accompanied by a backing away from traditional sanitary habits such as the use of shoes or patterns of hair grooming, the spectrum of these activities, ranging from a studied shabbiness up to the heavy use of hallucinogenic drugs, affirms a heightening of body sensibility. This development can also be read as an assault on the contemporary cosmetic masking of our bodies and an attempt to return to an explicit sense experience of the entire body, especially of a tactile kind.

Unfortunately, the causes of the attitudes among young people are often thought traceable to the classic explanatory scheme involving family conflict or the inherent social rebellion of youth. Environmental structures, however, play an important causal role in the disaffection of a younger generation. Over against the vast increase in mobility and the extraordinary heightening of sensory experiences by virtue of electronic media, contrast the average school building as an environment for adolescence. For the most part still an antique form, these buildings perform as rabbit warrens, with fixed space options and severe regimentation of movements. Even the occasional use of overhead projectors and other media aides only serves to intensify the enclosed and static experience presented by the classroom.[43] Spatial inflexibility generates an inflexibility about the processes of time, concretized by rigid scheduling, and contradicts a fundamental truth that "the same environment is not necessarily experienced in the same way by different individuals or, extending the argument, by different groups." [44]

Given a world wherein we can experience events instantaneously, we still cling to the belief that crucial processes such as education must occur as sanctioned in a fixed physical location. The fact that our private experiences evermore outstrip our public experiences in range, quality, and intensity causes considerable sensorial confusion and leads to skepticism about the worth of institutional life. Our point here is simply that environmental inadequacy is one of a series of factors in the emergence of a loss of energy and a need to escape, whether by studious withdrawal, as in the erosion of commitment, or more dramatically by the use of drugs or participation in the renascence of the occult and other counterculture fringe groups.

Certainly men of medicine should not function as the police department or as an extension of the clergy. On the other hand, they should leave no stone unturned in the effort to ameliorate human illness, whether it be of an explicit kind, as a result of epidemics, violence, or drugs, or of the more subtle type, brought on by a developing alienation from our work, our community, and even from ourselves. The local doctor has his hand on a barrage of symptoms and complaints. If he digs deep enough, he will find that environmental malaise plays a large role in developing and spreading social afflictions. In our society, the physician's role is extremely prestigious. Whether it should remain so is open to serious question, but so long as it does, this role should be put to better advantage. As diagnosticians of environmental sensibility, in concert with other socially sensitive agencies and individuals, the medical profession should lend its authority and wisdom to the urgent demand for creating environments which are continuous, supportive, and fertile for the very best of human living. In commenting on the relevance of the Hippocratic oath, René Dubos makes the following point:

> The well-being of man is influenced by all environmental factors: the quality of the air, water, and food; the winds and topography of the land; and the general living habits. Understanding the effects of environmental forces on man is thus the fundamental basis of the physician's art.[45]

If the affective quality of an environment is a crucial factor in human well-being, and I believe that it is, then that aspect of medicine known as preventive medicine must attend to it, even if it is at the partial expense of those startling breakthroughs which affect the isolated few. American society is now in a bizarre situation where we have reached dizzying heights of scientific and technical achievement while we simultaneously experience an increase in violence, disaffections, and social disease. The call to education and government is to reorder priorities. Medicine should do likewise.

NOTES

1. John Clendenning, ed., *The Letters of Josiah Royce* (Chicago: The University of Chicago Press, 1970), p. 586.
2. Cf. Mervyn Susser, *Community Psychiatry: Epidemiologic*

and Social Themes (New York: Random House, 1968), p. 355. "For instance, in New York City rates of perinatal, infant and maternal mortality that mortify conscientious health officials exist side by side with enormous medical virtuosity. The virtuoso performance of medicine is at the nub of the problem. In the great medical centers the effectiveness of care is likely to be measured, as we have noted, by its quality in an episode of illness at the point of delivery. In the twentieth century a more appropriate measure of accomplishment is the impact of a system of medical care on the health of a defined population."

3. Fritz Heider, "Consciousness, the Perceptual World, and Communications With Others," in Renato Tagiuri and Luigi Petrullo, eds., *Person, Perception and Interpersonal Behavior* (Stanford: Stanford University Press, 1958), p. 31.

4. Erich Lindenmann, Foreword, in Herbert Gans, *The Urban Villagers* (Glencoe: The Free Press, 1962), p. v. For extensive support of Lindenmann's judgment, cf. Marc Fried, "Grieving for a Lost Home;" in Leonard J. Duhl, ed., *The Urban Condition* (New York: Basic Books, 1963), pp. 151-171.

5. Cf. R. D. Laing, *The Divided Self* (Baltimore: Penguin Books, Inc., 1965), pp. 27-38, for penetrating remarks on the reduction of the patients' experiences to those proscribed by the doctor.

6. Richard Sennett, *The Uses of Disorder—Personal Identity and City Life* (New York: Alfred A. Knopf, 1970), p. 9.

7. *Ibid.*, pp. 9-10.

8. Cf. William James, *A Pluralistic Universe* (New York: Longmans, Green and Co., 1909), p. 60. "The treating of a name as excluding from the fact named what the name's definition fails positively to include, is what I call 'vicious intellectualism.' "

9. Martin Buber, "Education," *Between Man and Man* (London: Routledge and Kegan Paul, 1947), p. 97.

10. Cf. John J. McDermott, "Privacy and Social Therapy," *Soundings*, vol. 3, no. 3 (Fall 1968), 346-357, for a discus-

sion and evaluation of some new approaches to "interviews."

11. Robert Sommer, *Personal Space—The Behavioral Basis of Design* (New York: Prentice-Hall, 1969), p. 91.

12. David Mechanic, "Community Psychiatry: Some Sociological Perspectives and Implications," in Leigh Roberts *et al.*, eds., *Community Psychiatry* (New York: Anchor Books, 1969), p. 231.

13. Michael Harrington, *The Other America—Poverty in the United States* (New York: The Macmillan Co., 1963), p. 4.

14. For a similar story, cf. Genevieve Ray, "An Anglo's Barrio," in Susan Cahill and Michele Cooper, eds., *The Urban Reader* (Englewood Cliffs, N.J.: Prentice Hall, 1971), p. 34, where a welfare mother chides a Vista volunteer. "You kids come into our communities and are shocked by the garbage and rats. You want to start clean-up campaigns and get rid of the rats. I have lived with them for 40 years, and unless one bites my daughter, rats are the least of my problems. You find out what *I* am concerned about, even if it is a broken door hinge, and start to work on that."

15. Cf. William James, *Psychology—The Briefer Course* (New York: Henry Holt and Co., 1892), p. 165. Long ago, William James wrote that "it is, the reader will see, the reinstatement of the vague and inarticulate to its proper place in our mental life which I am so anxious to press on the attention." Cf. also Gardner Murphy, *Human Potentialities* (New York: Basic Books, 1958), pp. 302-329, for a discussion of novelty in human experience, and especially pp. 312-313, where he considers the vast range of methods of articulation which differentiate cultures.

16. Witness the hatred of project living as expressed by Juan Gonzales, in Charlotte Leon Mayerson, "Two Blocks Apart," Cahill and Cooper, *op. cit.* Some discussion of the urgent reasons behind such hostility are to be found in Fried, *op. cit.,* and John J. McDermott, "Deprivation and Celebration: Suggestions for an Aesthetic Ecology," in James M. Edie, ed., *New Essays in Phenomenology* (Chi-

cago: Quadrangle Books, 1969), pp. 116-130. And John J. McDermott, "Nature Nostalgia and the City: An American Dilemma," *Soundings*, vol. 4, no. 1 (Spring 1972).

17. William Moore, Jr., *The Vertical Ghetto—Everyday Life in an Urban Project* (New York: Random House, 1969), pp. 31-32n. A specific case of social-medical pathology caused by an absence of complaint is reported. "In one case of acrophobia, a tenant and his family had been reassigned an eleventh-floor apartment from one that they had been assigned on the second floor. Although the man was a good tenant and appeared to be a good family man, he suddenly began to stay away from home for long periods of time, sometimes for days. Because his wife was concerned, she related the new behavior to a social worker, whom the husband agreed to see. After several discussions, it was revealed that the tenant was deathly afraid of height. Moreover, he could never ride the elevator. He would walk eleven floors."

18. Luigi Pirandello, "Six Characters in Search of an Author," in Eric Bentley, ed., *Naked Masks* (New York: E. P. Dutton and Co., Inc., 1952), p. 224.

19. Cf. the extensive collection of materials by Harold M. Proshansky, *et al.*, eds., *Environmental Psychology—Man and His Physical Setting* (New York: Holt, Rinehart and Winston, 1970). A number of these essays are directly pertinent to the problems of social medicine.

20. Cf. Stuart F. Spicker, ed., *The Philosophy of the Body—Rejections of Cartesian Dualism* (Chicago: Quadrangle Books, 1970), for historical perspective on this problem.

21. Henri Bergson, *Matter and Memory* (New York: Doubleday and Co., 1959) (1896), p. 1.

22. *Ibid.*, p. 4.

23. William James, "The Experience of Activity," in John J. McDermott, ed., *The Writings of William James* (New York: Random House, 1967), p. 284, n. 180.

24. Ian W. Alexander, *Bergson—Philosopher of Reflection* (New York: Hillary House, 1957), p. 31.

25. John E. Smith, "Radical Empiricism," *Proceedings of the Aristotelian Society,* vol. 55 (March 1965), 205-218.

26. William James, "The Stream of Thought," *Writings,* p. 70.

27. Bergson, *op. cit.,* p. 23.

28. *Ibid.,* p. 55.

29. Michael Polanyi, *The Tacit Dimension* (New York: Anchor Books, 1967), p. 16.

30. William James, *The Principles of Psychology,* 2 vols. (New York: Henry Holt and Co., 1890), I, 8.

31. Robert Jay Lifton, "Protean Man," *Partisan Review,* vol. 35, no. 1 (Winter 1968), 13.

32. From "The Vanilla Fudge," cited in Edmund Carpenter, *They Became What They Beheld* (New York: Ballantine Books, 1970).

33. Gordon Allport, *Becoming* (New Haven: Yale University Press, 1955), p. 51. We should pay heed to the comment of the painter William de Kooning who remarked that "the past does not influence me; I influence it." Cited in John Cage, *Silence* (Cambridge: M.I.T. Press, 1966), p. 67.

34. Cf. Richard L. Meier, "Living with the Coming Urban Technology," in Elizabeth Geen, *et al.,* eds., *Man and the Modern City* (Pittsburgh: University of Pittsburgh Press, 1963), pp. 59-70, for a discussion of the sensorial overload and the increase of harassment brought on by the expansion of mass media communications.

35. James Marston Fitch, "Experiential Bases for Aesthetic Decision," in Proshansky, *op. cit.,* p. 76.

36. John Dewey, *Art as Experience* (New York: Capricorn Books, 1958) (1934), p. 40.

37. *Ibid.,* p. 40.

38. Cited in Serge Chermayeff and Christopher Alexander, *Community and Privacy* (New York: Anchor Books, 1965), p. 29.

39. Cf. Sheila Berkley, who makes urban play sculptures, in *New York,* September 6, 1971, p. 52. She comments: "Practically everything people touch in this city is rigid.

With my things, they can feel, smell, pull, stretch, hit, punch and make noises. They are participants as well as viewers." A student in my seminar on "Urban Aesthetics," Miss Jane Donenfeld, made a film of more than one hundred city signs. All but one said *No* or revealed some other form of prohibition. The one positive sign was a welcome to the city, which was followed by a series of prohibitions.

40. We should take notice that tedium has entered even monumental achievements. What could be more anaesthetic than the simple jutting up of the formless twin towers of the World Trade Center in New York City and what are we to make of the 747 airplane, which has removed from us the experience of flying?

41. Cf. Jane Jacobs, *The Death and Life of Great American Cities* (New York: Vintage Books, 1961), p. 13. Jane Jacobs, for one, criticizes the unreal character of city planning and design, comparing it at one point, to the stage of "bloodletting" in medicine. She calls for an embarkation "upon the adventure of probing the real world."

42. Chermayeff and Alexander, *op. cit.*, pp. 78-79.

43. James Marston Fitch, "Experiential Bases for Aesthetic Decision," in Proshansky, *op. cit.*, p. 79. He holds of "good architecture" that "far from offering solid, impermeable barriers to the natural environment, its outer surfaces come more and more closely to resemble permeable membranes which can accept or reject any environmental force. Again the uterine analogy; and not accidentally, for with such convertibility in the container's walls, man can modulate the play of environmental forces upon himself and his processes, to guarantee their uninterrupted development, in very much the same way as the mother's body protects the embryo." A recent example of this approach is to be found in the rectractable rooves and membrane dams of the German architect, Frei Otto.

44. Asa Briggs, "The Sense of Place," in *The Fitness of Man's Environment* (Washington, D.C.: Smithsonian Institution Press, 1968), p. 79.
45. René Dubos, *Man, Medicine and Environment* (New York: Mentor Books, 1968), p. 74.

CHAPTER SEVEN

Nature Nostalgia and the City:
An American Dilemma

... that men shall say of succeeding plantacions: the lord make it like that of New England: for we must Consider that wee shall be as a Citty upon a Hill, the eies of all people are uppon us; ...

—John Winthrop

The only room in Boston which I visit with alacrity is the Gentlemen's Room at the Fitchburg Depot, whee I wait for cars sometimes for two hours, in order to get out of town.—

Thoreau

Generalizations about national cultures are notoriously inexact, for exceptions abound. The judgments of a single perceiver, however imaginative, are often narrowing. This is especially true of interpretations of a culture as vast and as complex as America. Nonetheless, cultures often subsequently live out these

179

generalizations, for they are frequently articulations of deeply held images, projected onto the stream of history. In many instances, whatever the paucity of facts at the origin of the generalization, its power soon engenders the sustaining empirical support.[1] So true is this of analyses of American culture that one recent commentator, Daniel Boorstin, can hold that we live in terms of "pseudo-events," [2] make-ups which take their place in our consciousness as reality.

Despite the methodological problems [3] and the warning of Boorstin, and while not oblivious to the risk of self-deception, I offer that the following generalization has uncommonly profound and expansive empirical roots: American urban man has been seduced by nature. By this I mean that at the deepest level of his consciousness urban man functions on behalf of nature metaphors, nature expectancies, and a nostalgia for an experience of nature which neither he nor his forbearers actually underwent. For contemporary America, the implications of this situation are significant. In the first place, we are blocked off from understanding the dramatic and necessary conflict with nature, which characterized American life until recently. Indeed, we have become naive and ahistorically sentimental about that conflict. Second, we have often failed to diagnose the limitations and strengths of our present urban context on its own terms, rather than as a function of the absence of nature.

I am not, of course, claiming that this contention about the role of nature is the only or even the major key to the solution of the American urban crisis. On the other hand, I do hold that much contemporary diagnosis, whether of ecology, youth culture, or alienation, is woefully out of context without some grasp of the significance of this theme in the development of American consciousness. The basic problem is not one of general inattention, for we have a rich and long-standing literature on the meaning of nature and, of more recent vintage, an escalating literature on the city. We do not, however, have a broad tradition of analysis which focuses on their interrelationship, especially as written from the side of the urban experience. So as not to be waylaid by the vastness of our theme, let us consider the fundamental meaning of nature in American culture and its import for our understanding of time and the related possibilities for institutional transformation. If we then contrast this analysis with similar themes at work in urban consciousness, we should have some insight to the subtle but powerful role of nature in our present urban difficulties.

NATURE AS CONTEXT

For it is the wilderness that is the mother of that nation, it was in the wilderness that the strange and lonely people who have not yet spoken but who inhabit that immense and terrible land from East to West, first knew themselves, it was in the living wilderness that they faced one another at ten paces and shot one another down, and it is in the wilderness that they still live.
—Thomas Wolfe, *Men of Old Catawba*

Even the slightest familiarity with the history of American culture, especially its literary stand, will yield an awareness of the extraordinary importance of the nature motif. The philosophical dimensions of the meaning of nature are deeply rooted in European thought, beginning with the notion of *phusis* in Greek culture and reconstituted subsequently as *natura* in medieval and early modern philosophy. The complexities of the development of this notion are endless, as an analysis of that aspect called "natural law" will readily reveal. This tradition does not account, however, for the meaning of nature in American culture.

In America there was an originating clarity to the experience and understanding of nature; it meant land, ferocious but untrammeled and free. The experience of nature in the early history of American culture was set in a dialectical tension between wilderness and paradise, or perhaps more accurately, a dialectic *inside* wilderness between desert and garden, between terror and salvation.[4] The odyssey of the Puritan is instructive in this regard. The Puritan had a profound sense of unregeneracy built into the very fabric of his being, as if the struggle between wilderness and paradise were being played out within his own autobiography.[5] On the American scene, the Puritan confronted wilderness as an external phenomenon, and its presence within his own soul slowly became eroded. In time, American man saw himself, his very presence, as the salvific factor in an unregenerate wilderness; paradise as the planting of a garden in the wild. Change these terms to the language of the expanding frontier and you have an intriguing insight into the American drive to conquer nature.[6]

From the time of the Puritans to the beginning of our century, despite vast geographical differentiae, nature experienced as land was held to be the fundamental locus for symbolic formulations of our cultural and religious life. The struggle for survival in a physical sense was undoubtedly an irreducible matrix in this confrontation with the land. Morton and Lucia White write that "land ruled supreme, and seemingly limitless untamed nature, rather than the city, was the gigantic obstacle that confronted the five million people who populated the United States of America in 1800."[7] Beginning with the Puritans, however, there was another and deeper sense of that obstacle: one which saw the land as nothing less than the New Jerusalem. For the Puritans, if the kingdom is to come, it will come upon the land and show itself as continuous with the rhythms of nature. At the close of a moving paragraph on the correspondence of nature to salvation, Samuel Sewall writes in his "Phaenomena" (1697):

> As long as nature shall not grow old and dote but shall constantly remember to give the rows of Indian Corn their education, by Pairs: So long shall Christians be born there; and being first made meet, shall from thence be Translated, to be made partakers of the Inheritance of the Saints in Light.[8]

The role of nature in personal regeneration becomes tremendously intensified on the American scene. It is a dominant theme in the life and conversion experiences of Jonathan Edwards, for whom the "doctrines of the gospel" were to his soul as "green pastures." [9] And in the nineteenth-century revisiting of the paradise theme, we witness the harrowing journey of the Mormons from Nauvoo, Illinois, to the Great Salt Lake as quest for salvation, "a stake in Zion," played out against the backdrop of an alternating violence and beneficence of the land. In 1835, James Brooks sees Nature as the guarantor of our salvation.

> God has promised us a renowned existence, if we will but deserve it. He speaks this promise in the sublimity of Nature. It resounds all along the crags of the Alleghanies. It is uttered in the thunder of Niagara. It is heard in the war of two oceans, from the great Pacific to the rocky ramparts of the Bay of Fundy.... The august TEMPLE in which we dwell was built for lofty purposes. Oh! that we may consecrate it to LIBERTY and CONCORD, and be found fit worshippers within its holy wall.[10]

In commenting on this and similar assertions, Perry Miller writes: "so then—because America, beyond all nations, is in perpetual touch with Nature, it need not fear the debauchery of the artificial, the urban, the civilized." And, he adds, that nature "had effectually taken the place of the Bible." [11] Closer to our time, at the beginning of this century, John Muir, under the rubric of conservationist language, sees salvation as tied to the preservation of wilderness and the American struggle as one "between landscape righteousness and the Devil." [12] Muir had also written about "thouands of nerve-shaken, over-civilized people are beginning to find out that going to the mountains is going home; that wildness is a necessity; and that mountain parks and reservations are useful not only as fountains of timber and irrigating rivers, but as fountains of life." [13]

The messianic interpretation of the land was not always cast in biblical or even religious language. In a parallel development, the history of American thought also brought forth a tradition which understood the land as an ethical and political resource able to transform human nature for the better. Nowhere is this more obvious than in the early writings of Thomas Jefferson. In his *Notes on the State of Virginia*, Jefferson offers that "those who labor in the earth are the chosen people of God. . . . While we have land to labor then, let us never wish to see our citizens occupied at a work bench, or twirling a distaff." [14] Jefferson sees the workshop as associated with cities, and it is thereby better to have them remain in Europe, for "the mobs of great cities add just so much to the support of pure government as sores do to the strength of the human body. It is the manners and spirit of a people which preserve a republic in vigor. A degeneracy in these is a canker which soon eats to the heart of its laws and constitution." [15]

In a strain anticipatory of much of later American thought,[16] Jefferson sees the commitment to the land as passionate and moral. John Anderson, in his book on *The Individual and the New World*, writes that

> Jefferson found in his American experience a faith that man's egoism might disappear under some conditions of human commitment to the new land.
>
> In his conception that man's commitment to the New World might contain the principle for the control of man's natural egoism, Jefferson not only re-directed attention to the environment of the American continent, he suggested that man's true nature emerged fom this reference. Jefferson sought thus to formulate those conditions of human acceptance of the New World under which man's moral nature might emerge and effectively control his egoism.[17]

The experience of the land as a basis for a democratic ethos, as articulated by Jefferson, remained a deep characteristic of American political literature throughout the nineteenth century, but it did not negate completely the earlier biblical dimension which saw the land as the readiness for the coming of the kingdom of time. The convergence of these attitudes toward the land are found not only in the evangelical interpretation of frontier experience but in the symbolic versions of man's place in nature as found in Emerson and Thoreau. Writing in 1927, Lucy Lockwood Hazard in her book on *The American Frontier and American Literature* stated that "it is time to strip from the Emersonian hero the decorous toga and conventional mask with which rhetoric and philosophy have disguised him, and show that 'the American Scholar' and Davy Crockett are brothers. . . ." [18] It was, after all, in the address on "The American Scholar" that Emerson told us "so much only of life as I know by experience, so much of the wilderness have I vanquished and planted, or so far have I extended my being, my dominion." [19]

Emerson has a deep feeling for what Leo Marx refers to as the "metaphysical powers of landscape." [20] And this sensibility lends him to an abiding hostility against the city. In his essay on "Culture" Emerson writes,

> Whilst we want cities as the centres where the best things are found, cities degrade us by magnifying trifles, the country man finds the town a chop-house, a barber's shop. He has lost the lines of grandeur of the horizon hills and plains, and with them sobriety and elevation. He has come among a supple, glib-tongued tribe, who live for show, servile to public opinion. Life is dragged down to a fracas of pitiful cares and disasters. You say that God ought to respect a life whose objects are their own; but in cities they have betrayed you to a cloud of insignificant annoyances.[21]

In a note to that text, Emerson is cited as having commented that on his passing the woods on Walden Ledge, "on the way to the city, how they reproach me!" [22] The land, then, was more than open space and sylvan woods; it was a spiritual resource and a moral challenge. Thoreau offers us the most perceptive phrasing of this power of the land:

All things invite this earth's inhabitants
To rear their lives to an unheard of height
And meet the expectation of the land: . . . .[23]

It is the "expectation of the land" which has driven us, notwithstanding repeated disappointments in the realization of these expectations. In Perry Miller's phrase, we are "nature's nation." [24] And for John Anderson, our visions about the possibility of the land "express an intuition of the reflexive direction of human energy necessary to freedom. In such intuitions, Americans have seen themselves as marching across the wilderness and with more or less clarity have conceived of themselves as representative of mankind's ultimate place in the unknown universe." [25] The empirical basis for these mythic interpolations of our experiencing the land was the sheer prodigality of space and the related reconstituting of our experience of time. The importance of this interrelationship of space and time within the context of our experience of nature cannot be overestimated, for the experience of time is a crucially distinctive characteristic of any culture, and as we replaced nature experience with urban experience we failed to reorient our sense of space and time in a way consistent with this shift in context.

In specific terms, the experience of nature as open and free space generated for Americans a sense of time as option, as possibility. In an essay on "The American People: Their Space, Time and Religion," Sidney Mead comments that

Americans never had time to spare. What they did have during all their formative years was space—organic, pragmatic space—the space of action. And perhaps this made the real difference in the formation of "this new man." [26]

Space, however, is time undergone. The absence of "time to spare" really means the absence of time as introverted experience, that is, the absence of the struggle to achieve identity while subject to the contours of fixed options. Spatial claustrophobia turns us in on ourselves, interiorizing the landscape so that it is continuous with our imagination rather than with our vision. Over against this, in a context of open space, there is the possibility of projecting oneself outward and achieving identity as subject to the emerging novelties of the space of action. The presence of options gave dignity to events, for they were chosen rather than inherited. Put otherwise, a man could come to himself by relocating. The "space of action" was the locus of novelty and, paradoxically, the locus of self-awareness. Growth was inseparable from shifts in spatial contours, thereby indirectly transforming our experience of time from that of waiting, backing, and filling, to that of anticipating and the structuring of possibility. The shift in the word "trip" is instructive here, for its present meaning of a hallucinogenic visit to our inner landscape contrasts starkly with its open-ended spatial exploration in the vernacular of naure language.[27] Nature experienced as open space was not a nature in which man sat, derivative and self-preening. On the contrary, the undergoing of nature of which I speak found man grappling and reaching, fed always by shifts in location, even when such shifts came to him vicariously, as in the influence of the legendary evocations of the "mountain men" on the consciousness of the eastern seaboard.[28]

It is important to realize that the space of which I speak was riddled with drama, not only of natural origins—mountains, forests, and great rivers—but of sociopolitical origin—the presence of Indians and the struggles over territory and gold. Space, flat and boxed, is not a sufficiently humanizing context for man's situation. The drama of space is proportionate to its capacity for novelty. In the experience of nature, movement is necessary whether it be real or vicarious, the assumption being that something new, different, better is out there, just over the next ridge. In that tradition we are riven with the need of beginning again and again. Commenting on Emerson's oracular text, "why should not we also enjoy an original relation to the universe?'[29] Frederick Jackson Turner asks, "Let us believe in the eternal genesis, the freshness and value of things present, act as though, just created, we stood looking a new world in the face and investigate for ourselves and act regardless of past ideas." [30] It is this quest for novelty, expressed while he was still a young man, that we should read into Turner's later designation of the meaning of American space as a frontier, namely, as a series of options.

When events are framed against novel occurrences, the experience of ordinary living takes on the hue of an imaginative reconstruction of life. William James, for example, has written that "according to my view, experience as a whole is a process in time...." [31] but if the setting for this process, relative to each life lived, is characterized by repetition and by the plodding dullness of a context that rarely, if ever, is broken into by basic shifts in direction and possibility, then however eschatologically viable, our lives experience little of import in immediate terms.[32] The sense of option, as created by the novelties of open space, enabled American man to ground a deeply felt but rarely sustained religious belief, namely that the passing of time was a healing and liberating experience.

By way of specifying this contention, let us take as example from one of America's most profound although unappreciated philosophers, Josiah Royce. A Californian and a child of the frontier, Royce was born in the mining camp of Grass Valley, high in the Sierras. His early experience bequeathed to him a fascination with the evolution of American communities, especially their combination of moral imagination and novel physical settings. Royce believed that landscape and climate were constitutive of consciousness, and given man's efforts time was a healing force. In his *History of California,* Royce describes the evolution of a mining community in a section he entitles "The Struggle for Order: Self-Government, Good Humor and Violence in the Mines." Royce's conclusion to this chapter illustrates the earlier commitment to a salvific future as witnessed and sustained by the possibilities inherent in an open and fecund nature (though the last line of this text is depressing, for, as we too well know, rivers no longer purify themselves):

The lesson of the whole matter is as simple and plain as it is persistently denied by a romantic pioneer vanity; and our true pride, as we look back to those days of sturdy and sinful life, must be, not that the pioneers could so successfully show by their popular justice their undoubted instinctive skill in self-government—although indeed, despite all their sins, they showed such a skill also; but that the moral elasticity of our people is so great, their social vitality so marvelous, that a community of Americans could sin as fearfully as, in the early years, the mining community did sin, and could yet live to purify itself within so short a time, not by a revolution, but by a simple progress from social foolishness to social steadfastness. Even thus a great river, for an hour defiled by some corrupting disturbance, purifies itself, merely through its own flow, over its sandy bed, beneath the wide and sunny heavens.[33]

Now the history of Royce's California is the history of relocated Americans, pulled by the land and the chance of a fresh start. Whatever the persuasion (and the spectrum embraced a wide number of social, political, and religious convictions), the assumption operative was an acceptance of the dramatic enhancement of one's possibilities by the presence of uncommitted land and a variety of nature experiences. Such an assumption was operative earlier in the century on the eastern frontier, as witnessed by a text on the comparatively simple move from old Virginia to western Virginia. What greater testament to the moral and political liberation which results from the experience of nature than at the Virginia Convention in 1830, when a Western Virginia delegate was heard to say:

But sir, it is not the increase of population in the West which this gentleman ought to fear. It is the energy which the mountain breeze and western habits import to these emigrants. They are regenerated, politically I mean, sir. They soon become *working politicians;* and the difference, sir, between a *talking* and a *working* politician is immense. The Old Dominion has long been celebrated for producing great orators; the ablest metaphysicians in policy; men that can split hairs in all abstruse questions of political economy. But at home, or when they return from Congress, they have negroes to fan them asleep. But a Pennsylvania, a New York, an Ohio or a western Viginia statesman, though far inferior in logic, metaphysics, and rhetoric to an old Virginia statesman, has this advantage, that when he returns home he takes off his coat and takes hold of the plow. This gives him bone and muscle, sir, and preserves his republican principles pure and uncontaminated.[34]

The theme of "regeneration," spurred on by land, uttered here in a traditional political setting, reached its zenith of intensity in the hundreds of nineteenth-century American experimental communities. What had been European visions, festering with frustration, found their way into American life as communities capable of covenanting on available land, often free. These communities, most often extremely critical of American society, had the possibility of working out a range of beliefs relative to free love, socialism, or the mysteries of diet. The availability of land enabled a fair test [35] to be made of the claims for viability of these life-styles. Furthermore, the ensuing relevance of certain aspects of their vision was made possible by the stretch of time, in some cases several generations, during which they could maintain the original character of their communities.

Given the opportunities of land and the extensive time in which to operate, the failure of a new community, experimental or otherwise, was not a crushing blow. Failure was not due to repression or the absence of opportunity but rather to the inadequacy of the idea and its implementation before the test of time. Even as late as the depression of the thirties in our century, Americans were not prone to the experience of alienation and cynicism, now so deeply rooted in American life.[36] But the erosion of belief in endless options, generated by nature, and in the passing of time as liberating has now become a major touchstone of contemporary American society. This development is not unrelated to the fantastic growth of the American city and the begrudged emergence of urban man.

In a word, we have lost our access to experimental space. This is true not only of the great cities, where the vast majority of us now live, but of Butte, Montana, or Burlington, Iowa, or Zuñi Pueblo, New Mexico, where the disenfranchised huddle together under the ironically cruel aegis of an extraordinary yet private natural setting managed by absentee ownership. The revisionist historians notwithstanding, Frederick Jackson Turner was correct; the closing of the frontier however symbolic rather than statistical it may have been at the turn of the century, was to spell the inevitable end of a deeply ingrained style. The deeper problem is whether the loss of experimental space will spell also the loss of the experimental temper in America. To put it idiomatically, can rehabilitation replace relocation as the locus for prophetic vision and even more broadly based experimental communities? Or must we accede to those culture prophets, powerful and incisive in their own way, like N. O. Brown, for whom the city is already an Armageddon from which we must take nomadic flights, or Charles Reich, who offers us a quasi-revolutionary re-Greening of America.

The new rhetoric is often fed from two sources, nature nostalgia and a long-standing corollary, the conviction that the city is a trap. So long as our image of the city is a function of our image of nature, we shall intensify our hostility to urban life and our negative judgment will be self-fulfilling. As the actuality of nature recedes in our life, our nostalgia for it becomes increasingly riddled with unreality and innocence about its complexity and dangers. Only a radically reconstituted image of the city will provide us with a new resource for structuring once again a sense of option and experiment as continuous with everyday life. Let us sketch some of the obstacles to such a reconstitution.

THE CITY AS CONTEXT

And the critical rhythm of a city is the sequence of closing
hours, the city's play with the order of the eternal sun.
                                                    —Robert Kelly

I isolate several characteristics of our image of the city, which,
by no means exhaustive, are nonetheless revealing. Even a brief
analysis of these characteristics will provide us with a different
perspective from which to view both the plight of urban man
and some of the direction necessary for the amelioration of his
future.

The first characteristic is double-pronged, with the interacting
resonance of a tuning fork. On the one hand, we lament the city
as being without nature. On the other hand, the nature we have
in mind in such a lamentation and about which we are nostalgic
is stripped of its most forbidding qualities: loneliness, unpredic-
tability, and the terrors of the uninhabitable. Witness the
innocence of this comment from Dallas Lore Sharp, a turn-of-
the-century commuter from a suburb just outside of Boston.

> And this our life, exempt from public haunts and those
> swift currents that carry the city-dweller resistlessly into the
> movie show, leaves us caught in the quiet eddy of little
> unimportant things—digging among the rutabagas, playing
> the hose at night.[37]

For the most part, the nature envisioned by urban and
suburban man is one that has been domesticated by the very
qualities of the city which we take to be unnatural. Commenting
on an earlier form of nature nostalgia, Lewis Mumford points to
the too often overlooked grubbiness of the open road. He writes
in *The Golden Day:*

> The vast gap between the hope of the Romantic Move-
> ment and the reality of the pioneer period is one of the

sardonic jests of history. On one side the bucolic innocence of the Eighteenth Century, its belief in a fresh start, and its attempt to achieve a new culture. And over against it, the epic march of the covered wagon, leaving behind it deserted villages, bleak cities, depleted soils, and the sick and exhausted souls that engraved their epitaphs in Mr. Masters' Spoon River Anthology.[38]

And recall Van Wyck Brooks' description of the America of Emerson's time: "Alas for America! An air loaded with poppy and all running to leaves, to suckers, to tendrils, to miscellany, dispersion and sloth. A wilderness of capabilities, of a many-turning Ulyssean culture; an irresistibility like Nature's, and, like Nature, without conscience." [39]

I make no attempt here to deprecate the majesty of nature nor, as I tried to make clear above, to deny its real capacity as a setting for distinctive social and political growth. Under the press of nostalgia, however, we strip both nature and city of ambivalence, in a bizarre reversal of the wilderness and paradise theme. We now name the city a jungle and ascribe habitability in proportion to our distance away from it. Indeed, we often seem to give the city credence only to the extent that we are able to import nature, to "green" it. Vest-pocket parks and isolated city trees receive our affection while we allow public conveyances, building facades, and other urban artifacts to deteriorate. We seem oblivious to the fact that efforts at "greening" such as Golden Gate Park in San Francisco are often masterpieces of artifact and directly attributable to urban man's management of nature.

As a matter of fact, in our time artifacts shape the entire context of nature. Our American culture has long succumbed to the principle of accessibility on demand, and as heightened by modern technology, particularly the automobile and the airplane, has successfully driven out nature in the sense of "wilderness," which, *a fortiori,* denies accessibility. We resist facing up to the loss of wilderness in America. In the more than two hundred photographs accompanying Freeman Tilden's

aforementioned book on *The National Parks,* hardly an automobile is to be seen, but for those of us who have visited those
parks and natural monuments, automobiles are omnipresent
along with the roads, souvenir stands, and the apparently self-
propagating beer can.[40] Turning a wilderness into a park is, after
all, a gentle form of urbanization.

Our innocence about the artifactuality of our experience of
nature interacts with our failure to form any better image of the
city. On one side, we harbor a deep conviction (perhaps
prejudice is a better word) of the superiority of the organic over
the inorganic, of the natural over the artifactual. Nonorganic
material becomes at best functional and at worst dehumanizing,
saved only by the arbiters of the asthetics of high culture as it is
present in acceptable architecture, museums, and outdoor
sculpture. The latter become for many critics of the city the only
redeeming features of urban life. Peter L. Marks, for example, in
an essay on "A Vision of Environment," tells us that New York
is "far too large" but that one should have a city the size of
Minneapolis so as to preserve the "urban amenities," which he
lists as "museums, galleries, theaters, opera, etc." [41] Such
amenities are sought by a very small percentage of city people,
and they in no way represent the marvels of urban design, the
intensity of urban interaction, or the complexity of urban
possibility. Many critics of the city have no sense of the pulse of
city life except that prescribed by those cultural canons continuous with the lives of the critics.[42] Given such an interpretive
context, as we move through the alleged travail of everyday
experience, we seem reduced to the impropriety and therefore
the social inability to generate nonorganic aesthetic metaphors
able to provide the security and affection nostalgically traceable
to nature metaphors.[43]

The contrasts between "naturals" and urban materials are
inevitably invidious. Grass is soft whereas wood and metal are
hard. The sense of touch has either eroded, as with regard to
cloth and wood, or never developed as with regard to aluminum,
plastics, and the vast range of synthetics. Woodland light is
diaphanous and playful, but city light as refracted from giant

slabs of glass is arching and brittle. Dung is earthy and a sign of life, whereas axle grease is dirty and a necessary burden. Many of us were taught as children to distinguish between the clean dirt of nature and the dirty dirt of the playground and the street. Why is it that "swinging on birches" is affectionate and wistful but sitting on curbs is pouty and "hanging out"? Such contrasts are endless and they are maddening because they distort and repress one entire side of our experience—or, more accurately, if we are honest with ourselves, for most of us our *only* direct experience.

The source of this prejudice is only partially nature nostalgia and the historical seduction of its metaphors. From another vantage point, a more decisive characteristic emerges, namely, that we have failed to articulate our distinctively city experience in aesthetic terms. Just as for decades we have taught multiracial, multiethnic children in the context of a bland WASPish world, so too have we taught children in a vague combination of a gentle nature setting and appeals to the value of high culture. Such a pedagogy continues to be oblivious to the teeming relational fabric of urban experience and to the rich nutrients of technological style which children would soak up, as if to the "manor" born, if so encouraged. Unfortunately, we have held fast to the style and language of traditional pedagogy and, as such, have missed the startling idiomatic evolution from nature language to industrial language, to say nothing of the recent emergence of electronic language.

Urban alienation proceeds from the bifurcation of lived experience and institutional formulation, particularly on the part of the schools, churches, and social-political agencies. The truth is that for hordes of urban children, the argot of street language provides their fundamental education, their coming to consciousness. Unsanctioned as experiences, these sensibilities and insights ride beneath the surface of personal life, unable to bring the person into an acceptable creative life. Our task is to sanction and celebrate these processes of urban living, within the confines of urban institutions. Speaking only of the schools, we must learn, for example, how to integrate the powerful message of jazz, with its emphasis on improvisation, processive unity, and indirect communication (each an urban style). We must learn of the vast array of city materials and generate novel nonnature metaphors to describe our ways of experiencing them. We must learn how to personalize our evaluations of ordinary experiences to render them aesthetic, commensurate with new materials, new techniques, and new anticipations. Could not our watchword be the penetrating remark of John Dewey: "Even a crude experience, if authentically an experience, is more fit to give a clue to the intrinsic nature of esthetic experience than is an object already set apart from any other mode of experience."? [44] These strategies will aid in overcoming one of the deepest and most pervasive sources of our alienation, the separation of the affective life from the processes of urban experience. As strategies they assume, however, a turning back of still another characteristic of our image of the city, that is, our sense of space.

City space is enclosed space, and therein we find a crisis for urban man. As we have attempted to show above, the primary meaning of nature for America was the presence of open space, with its corollary, a sense of time as prospective and fruitful. In the last twenty years, as the diagnosis of the city has become increasingly negative, we have made attempts to restructure it subtly but powerfully under the rubric of urban reclamation and renewal we have reembodied this hankering for open space. We failed to realize that people brought to consciousness in enclosed space had interiorized their sense of time and endowed the immedate environment with the drama of landmarks, whether they be funeral parlors, candy stores, playgrounds, or street processes. Largely unarticulated, this sense of time was a way of protecting the city-dweller from the rapid but pyramidal pace. Experience in the city was hectic, intensive, and escalatory, but not spatially expansive. Entire lives, even generations, were lived out on a single street, known affectionately as the "block." [45] In such an environment it was necessary to structure "stabiles," moments of security and repetition, as a base from which to participate in activities which far outstripped the natural sense of pace and which multiplied novelties at a rate quite beyond personal absorption, let alone comprehension.

Many years ago, the building of the then great apartments on Riverside Drive in New York City occasioned Henry James's comment that they were merely holding the spot for whatever was to replace it.[46] As the pace quickened, each city dweller structured his or her own version of the environment, developing in either personal terms or in closely knit communal terms what Kevin Lynch has called nodal points, ways of comfortably and knowingly experiencing the environment. Nodes are points, "the strategic spots in a city into which an observer can enter and which are the intensive foci to and from which he is traveling." [47] These nodal points, not to be confused with landmarks, are too often assumed to be large and obvious, as squares, powerful buildings, or boulevards; more often they are intensive refinements of one's movement through city-space, the feel of a small street, a lobby, a stoop, a bar, a subway stop, refined even to the north or south entrance. In effect, they are embodiments of intimacy, urban style. They are ways of domesticating the rush of city life. They are sources of affection. Listen to a young black student at Queens College conclude his poem of praise to Harlem.

> 'Cause we own the night
> And the streets and the sounds and the air itself
> And the life is there
> And the movement is there
> And all of our energy
> And the spirit is there
> On through the night
> And right through the dawn
> Through those wide/funky/
> Bad/
>   Black/
>   Streets [48]

Any attempt at massive urban transformation which fails to

take into account the deep feeling that people have for their environment, however objectively inadequate, is doomed to failure. The difficulty with extensive relocation is not simply the wait to enter a new home, although that wait is often cruel and abortive. Nor is it simply the loss of an apartment or dwelling. It is the destruction of those nodal points which not only took generations to web into the seam of personal experience but acted as a subtle resource for coping with the massive energy of the city at large.[49] Home, then, is not simply the apartment or even the building. Rather it is correlative with a wider range of experience, including neighborhood and city region or just accessibility to the familiar. In his profound essay "Grieving for a Lost Home," Marc Fried [50] evokes the sadness of those residents who were bullied out of their homes in the West End of Boston. Although many interpersonal relations could be kept in the new location, it was the loss of spatial identity for which they grieved. What is striking about Fried's findings is the extensive presence of bodily responses to the loss. Many persons reported serious depression, nausea, and weeping. Deep in our psyche we are profoundly attached to the allegedly lifeless forms of the urban scene, our streets, lights, and sounds.

The need would seem to be to learn the techniques of rehabilitation rather than fall prey to the precipitous use of the scissoring of spatial relocation. We have some small signs of an increased sensitivity to this need. In New York City, fifty-nine residents of a neighborhood called Corona, led by the urban rhetoric of Jimmy Breslin, staved off relocation and are now **struggling to maintain their community against the power of official policy. Even minor relocation was thought to be painful** and excessive, for as Francis X. Clines wrote in the *New York Times*, the relationships were, after all, "structural as well as human."

The job of relocating houses could prove as delicate as heart surgery, for there is an attractive crazy-quilt of structural and human relationships present. For example, Mrs. Thomas •Manfre has a house, marked by a lawn madonna, that looks to the rear unto her husband's boyhood home, where a niece now lives. Her 70 year old mother lives off to the side in a separate home, small and brown with a pigeon coop on the roof.

All three are as one in her family's diary, Mrs. Manfre explained, "There have been deaths here and my brother Joey was born here," she said.[51]

We are under obligation to develop an enriched understanding of the relationship between urban structure and urban person. We must develop insight into the time of city-space and the space of city-time. And we must search for a way to render our bodies as continuous with technological artifact as they were with the environs of nature. We have to celebrate this continuity and build accordingly.

If we fail in these tasks, contemporary urban man will simply be in place and as such detached from the processes of living. But, as Royce [52] warns us, the detached individual without deep feeling for his environment dilutes the energies necessary to build communities. And when under duress, the detached individual abandons restraint and, out of disrespect for the variety of life styles, moves to suppress them. We should be warned that nature nostalgia detaches us from the urban present and promulgates condescension, disinterest, and eventually hostility. For better or worse, American man is now urban man, or at the least, megapolitan man. Nature nostalgia, no matter how subtle, does not serve him well. It is time for a turning and a celebrating of the dazzling experiences we have but do not witness for all to share. The city is now our home; in the most traditional and profound sense of the word, it is our land.

NOTES

1. A cardinal example of generalizations creating their own evidence is to be found in David Riesman, Nathan Glazer, and Reuel Denney, *The Lonely Crowd* (New Haven: Yale

University Press, 1950). Our deep contemporary self-consciousness about directedness and manipulation dates from that book.

2. Cf. Daniel Boorstin, *The Image: A Guide to the Pseudo-Events in America* (New York: Harper Colophon Books, 1964).

3. Cf. Leo Marx, "Pastoral Ideals and City Troubles," *The Fitness of Man's Environment* (Washington: Smithsonian Institution Press, 1968), pp. 142-143. Marx claims that the contention of an antiurban bias as existent in American literature is a misreading of the metaphoric intention of that tradition. He may be correct about the "intention," but the fact is that the popular interpretation of American literature has sustained a nature romanticism and a distrust of the city.

4. Cf. George H. Williams, "The Enclosed Garden in the Wilderness of the New World," *Wilderness and Paradise* (New York: Harper and Bros., 1962), pp. 98-131. Cf. also Roderick Nash, *Wilderness and the American Mind* (New Haven: Yale Universty Press, 1967).

5. Cf. Edward L. Morgan, *Visible Saints* (Ithaca, N.Y.: Cornell University Press, 1962), pp. 67-73, and Daniel B. Shea, Jr., *Spiritual Autobiography in Early America* (Princeton, N.J.: Princeton University Press, 1968).

6. For a brilliant analysis of the edenic theme in America, cf. Charles L. Sanford, *The Quest for Paradise: Europe and the American Moral Imagination* (Urbana, Ill.: University of Illinois Press, 1961).

7. Morton and Lucia White, *The Intellectual Versus the City* (New York: New American Library, 1962), p. 19.

8. Samuel Sewall, "Phaenomena," in Perry Miller and Thomas H. Johnson, *The Puritans*, vol. I (New York: Harper Torchbooks, 1963), p. 377.

9. Jonathan Edwards, "Personal Narrative," in Clarence H. Faust and Thomas H. Johnson, eds., *Jonathan Edwards* (New York: Hill and Wang, Inc., 1962), p. 67.

10. Cited in Perry Miller, "Nature and the National Ego,"

Errand into the Wilderness (New York: Harper Torchbooks, 1956), p. 210.

11. Miller, *art. cit.,* p. 211.

12. Cited in Williams, *op. cit.,* p. 130.

13. Cited in Freeman Tilden, *The National Parks* (New York: Alfred A. Knopf, 1970), p. 22.

14. Thomas Jefferson, *Notes on the State of Virginia* (New York: Harper Torchbooks, 1964), query 414, pp. 157-158.

15. Jefferson, *op. cit.,* p. 158.

16. Cf. Morton and Lucia White, *op. cit.,* for an excellent survey of the deep-seated animus against the city that pervades American thought. The Whites, however, seriously underplay the spiritual significance of the land in American life.

17. John M. Anderson, *The Individual and the New World* (State College, Pa.: Bald Eagle Press, 1955), p. 12.

18. Lucy Lockwood Hazard, *The Frontier in American Literature* (New York: Frederick Ungar Publishing Co., 1927), p. 152.

19. Ralph Waldo Emerson, "The American Scholar," *The Complete Works of Ralph Waldo Emerson,* vol. I (Boston: Houghton, Mifflin and Co., 1904), p. 95.

20. Leo Marx, *The Machine in the Garden: Technology and the Pastoral Idea in America* (New York: Oxford University Press, 1967), p. 232.

21. Emerson, "Culture," *Works,* VI, 153.

22. *Ibid.*

23. Carl Bode, ed., *Collected Poems of Henry Thoreau* (Baltimore: The John Hopkins Press, 1964), p. 135.

24. Perry Miller, *Nature's Nation* (Cambridge: Harvard University Press, 1967).

25. Anderson, *op. cit.,* p. 41.

26. Sidney E. Mead, *The Lively Experiment* (New York: Harper and Row, 1963), p. 5.

27. Cf. Leslie Fiedler, *The Return of the Vanishing American* (New York: Stein and Day, 1969), p. 187, for a similar remark.

28. Cf. the excellent chapter on "The Mountain Man," in Henry Nash Smith, *Virgin Land: The American West as Symbol and Myth* (New York: Vintage Books, 1957), pp. 88-89.

29. Emerson, Introduction to "Nature," *Works,* I, 3.

30. Cited in Smith, *op. cit.,* p. 296, n. 4.

31. William James, *The Meaning of Truth* (New York: Longmans, Green and Co., 1909), p. 111.

32. This passage, with slight changes, is taken from an earlier effort to ground an American metaphysics of history. Cf. John J. McDermott, *The Amercan Angle of Vision* (West Nyack: Cross Currents Paperback, 1966).

33. Josiah Royce, *Basic Writings of Josiah Royce,* John J. McDermott, ed., vol. I (Chicago: University of Chicago Press, 1969), p. 117. Cf. also the chapter on "The Temper of the West" by James Bryce in *The American Commonwealth,* vol. I (London: Macmillan and Co., 1891), pp. 696-706, for a vivid description of open land from a European point of view.

34. Cited in Frederick Jackson Turner, "The Significance of the Frontier in American History," Ray Allen Billington, ed., *Frontier and Section* (New York: Prentice-Hall, 1961), p. 57.

35. Out of an extensive literature, I will mention only William Hinds, *American Communities,* first published 1875 (reprinted, New York: Corinth Books, 1961).

36. Compare contemporary social diagnosis with the reports of the depression as found in *The Great Depression,* ed. David A. Shannon (New York: Prentice-Hall, 1960) and Studs Terkel, *Hard Times* (New York: Pantheon Books, 1970).

37. Cited in Peter J. Schmitt, *Back to Nature—The Arcadian Myth in Urban America* (New York: Oxford University Press, 1969), p. 20. For many further instances of such nostalgia cf. Samuel R. Ogden, ed., *America the Vanishing—Rural Life and the Promise of Progress* (Brattleboro, Vt.: The Stephen Greene Press, 1969).

38. Lewis Mumford, *The Golden Day* (Boston: Beacon Press, 1957), p. 38.

39. Van Wyck Brooks, "Emerson at Sea," in Carl Bode, ed., *Ralph Waldo Emerson* (New York: Hill and Wang, 1968), p. 68.

40. By contrast, see the stark reality in instances of urban photography, cf. e.g. the remarkable set of photographs in Susan Cahill and Michele F. Cooper, eds., *The Urban Reader* (New York: Prentice-Hall, 1971).

41. Peter L. Marks, "A Vision of Environment," *The American Scholar*, vol. 40 no. 3 (Summer 1971), 426. This essay is a utilizaton, albeit imaginative, of nature nostalgia, revealing contempt for city life, which he describes by reference to the cliché, "urban anonymity."

42. What, for example, are we to make of this broadside from the landscape architect Ian McHarg?" "I contend that . . . the modern city inhibits life, that it inhibits man as an organism, man as a social being, man as a spiritual being, and that it does not even offer adequate minimum conditions for physiological man; that indeed the modern city offers the least humane physical environment known to history" ("Man and Environment," in Leonard J. Duhl, *The Urban Condition* [New York: Simon and Schuster, 1969], p. 49).

43. For a discussion of urban aesthetic metaphors, cf. John J. McDermott, "Deprivation and Celebration: Suggestions for an Aesthetic Ecology," in James Edie, ed., *New Essays in Phenomenology* (Chicago: Quadrangle Books, 1969), pp. 116-130.

44. John Dewey, *Art as Experience* (New York: Capricorn Books, 1950), p. 11.

45. Even in a terribly afflicted neighborhood, the "block" maintained a deep spirital hold on its residence. Cf. the extraordinary photographic essay by Herb Goro, *The Block* (New York: Random House, 1970).

46. Cited by Ray Ginger, *Modern American Cities* (Chicago: Modern American Cities, 1969), p. 3.

47. Kevin Lynch, *The Image of the City* (Cambridge: M.I.T. Press, 1959), p. 47. Cf. also the refreshing experimental

perspectives in Stanley Milgram, "The Experience of Living in Cities," *Science*, Vol. 167 (March 13, 1970), pp. 1461-1468. Some of these perspectives are taken into consideration in the exciting new work of Paolo Soleri. Cf. Donald Wall, *Visionary-Cities: The Archology of Paolo Soleri* (New York: Praeger Publishers, 1971).

48. Richie Orange, "Harlem," in Cahill and Cooper, *op. cit.*, p. 143.

49. For a poignant description by young Juan Gonzales of "his being renewed" into a project, cf. Charlotte Leon Mayerson, "Two Blocks Apart," in Cahill and Cooper, *op. cit.*, pp. 76-81. Cf. also the review article by Roger Sale, "Cities and the City," *New York Review of Books*, January 28, 1971, p. 40, where he tells of the ramifications in the taking down of a basketball hoop on a city block.

50. Cf. Marc Fried, "Grieving for a Lost Home," in Duhl, *op. cit.*, pp. 151-171.

51. Francis X. Clines in *The New York Times*, December 2, 1970, p. 43.

52. Cf. Josiah Royce, "The Hope of the Great Community," in *Basic Writings*, p. 1156.

CHAPTER EIGHT

Space, Time, and Touch: Philosophical Dimensions of Urban Consciousness

As man is a responsible constructor of the environment he is unavoidably influencing his own genetic structure.[1]

Urban experience is a vast and complex process of interwoven institutions, events, and perceptions. It can be subjected to analysis only from a wide range of perspectives and disciplines, each of them limping in turn from an unavoidable narrowness, although each providing necessary data and, hopefully, vision. Urban studies, itself a comparatively new endeavor, seems to have no methodological uniqueness or consistency, borrowing from one or another of the social and applied natural sciences. In this present essay, we do not attempt to resolve that difficulty in any detail, although our approach hints at the direction such a methodology would take, namely, treat the city as an interdisciplinary phenomenon, yielding to no single discipline or to a gathered potpourri of several disciplines, but rather as the source of an entirely new language and set of assumptions and criteria. Such a need calls for philosophical contributions, to this point starkly absent.[2] By way of a context for our present discussion, I offer the following generalized attitudes as operative in our approach to urban experience.

CONSCIOUSNESS-RAISING AND DISAFFECTION

The major difference between consciousness-raising and coming-to-consciousness or awareness is that the former pertains to experiences long undergone but unappreciated or repressed, whereas the latter connotes novelty of perception. In the past decade the poor (unsuccessfully), and black Americans and women (each with some success), have participated in the experience of consciousness-raising. One of the dramatic and salutary characteristics of such efforts at consciousness-raising is the upending of stereotypes and the concomitant revolution in self-image and sense of worth. Central to this endeavor is the significance of the aesthetic dimension, understood as both environmental and as embodied in personal style. Indeed, it can be argued that the strategy which engenders a transformation of aesthetic sensibility is more praiseworthy and long-lasting than one which effects a change in political sensibility, as witness the debate between Norman O. Brown and Herbert Marcuse on precisely this issue.[3]

More specifically, I offer here that a necessary and even crucial addition to the recent occasions of consciousness-raising has to do with our response to urban experience. Stated simply, urban consciousness in America is usually secondhand consciousness, derivative from a defensive attitude and lacking in deeply rooted patterns of pride, responsibility, and distinctive sensibility. Of particular concern in this regard is the absence of an articulated urban aesthetic and the bizarre domination of a high-culture aesthetic by which cities become known and evaluated by their museums, monuments, and other replications of an aesthetic past.

It is true, of course, that to avoid the perils of self-deception, consciousness-raising of any sort has to be accompanied by an ongoing internal critique, especially of pretense and false claims. We are not about to hide from view, therefore, the painful awareness of what few or any would deny, the extensive afflictions found in the contemporary American city. In fact, one of the most severe and pressing social problems of contemporary America is the deep discontent pervasive of urban life, especially as it is expressed in the apparent opposites of boredom and violence. Regarded by many [4] as a pathological situation of epidemic proportions, urban discontent is fostered by schools and by social agencies, remains unameliorated in hospitals, let alone prisons, and has been largely ignored as a problem by traditional religious and political institutions. In keeping with the sociology of the vicious circle, this urban discontent festers and generates hostility and violence, which in turn escalates fear and promotes still wider patterns of alienation and anomie. In New York City at the present time, one of the most distinctive urban artifacts is the fox-lock, a metal rod from door to floor signaling that others are locked out but symbolizing as well that we are locked in. Recent events in the city of Boston, mindless stonings and burnings of persons, remind us again of the message delivered in the 1960s, showing us how close to the surface rides the explosive and destructive response of the often bitter and repressed urban mass. That message rings loud: if we loathe our environment, in time we shall destroy it.[5] The underlying questions, then, are why we have allowed our cities to be objects of hate and sources of alienation and what are the means by which we can turn that situation around so that celebration and affection become the governing attitudes.[6]

It is obvious that such a major undertaking as the reconstituting of urban life cannot yield to a single nostrum, no matter what its potential or the commitment of its supporters. An integration of basic political, social, educational, economic, and ecological strategies is necessary if the city is to be healed. What strikes us as odd, however, is that little attention has been given to how urban people actually "feel" [7] about the city. When they leave, what do they miss? Do they stay out of necessity, or do they stay out of affection? For the most part, do urban people share those variable approaches of urbanologists who see the city as being viable if it were cleaner, or less noisy, or less polluted, or less crowded? Do flamboyant buildings, trade and culture centers, bypass expressways, penetrate to the core of perceptions held by urban people about their city? Are the tangles over neighborhood schools and community control explicable in racial or even educational terms, or do they reveal other, distinctively urban needs? Does urban transportation perform basically as a "people mover" or does it serve other fundamental human dimensions, such as social and aesthetic? More such questions abound, which, if posed in the right vein to urban people themselves, would in my judgment elicit some surprising responses.[8] The fundamental problem has to do with those who see themselves as responsible for curing the ills of the city, for even when genuinely concerned they tend to proceed from perceptions other than those of the people affected. We point, then, to an unfortunate gap between the urban experience and its articulation and again between the articulation and how it is heard by those with the power of decision. That gap spawns distrust, an erosion of confidence, and an abandonment of commitment by all concerned. More care must be addressed to the area where that gap most occurs, in the affective dimension of experience which more often is referred to philosophically as the aesthetic.

THE URBAN AESTHETIC AND NATURE NOSTALGIA

The meaning of the aesthetic in its widest and most general sense has to do with human feeling as enhanced by transaction with nature, an event, or an artifact. In its more restricted sense the aesthetic has reference to matters of taste, works of art, and art-events such as theater and dance. One of the more creative implications of the development of "modern art" over the last seventy-five years was the shattering of a constricted and proprietary approach to art and to the aesthetic. Endowed with the riches of new materials and techniques, largely due to advances in technology, the forms that art may take now are virtually as extensive as the number of participants. Of even more importance in this development is the stress given to the aesthetic significance of ordinary experience and to the artifacts of everyday life, thereby giving rise to an appreciation of the enormous increase in our own experience of shapes, sounds, colors, textures, and patterns of mediation. Nowhere is this development more apparent than in the experience of our cities, which can be described, in contemporary terms, as a vast assemblage, undergone kinetically, laced throughout with the tensions, mishaps, celebrations, and fulfillments worthy of any rich assemblage.

In my judgment, then, the scope of an urban aesthetic is nothing less than all the affective transactions experienced in urban life, and the task of an urban aesthetic is to articulate those transactions in a language as close to the quality of urban experience as spoken and written discourse will allow. Grady Clay states this task as follows:

> Most Americans are captives of an object-ridden language which they must awkwardly manipulate to deal with a changeable, processful thing called city. They speak of "downtown" as a place, but it is many places, scenes of overlapping actions, games, competitions, movements. There are many towns: downtown, uptown, crosstown, in town, out-of-town, old and new town, smoketown, honkytown, shantytown. A city is not as we perceive it to be by vision alone, but by insight, memory, movement, emotion, and language. A city is also what we call it and becomes as we describe it.[9]

While this approach does not preclude the possible importance of the arts and of the urban centers for the arts, an urban aesthetic is both a more extensive and a more fundamental response to urban life. It can be argued that concentration on the role of the arts as equivalent to the aesthetic character and quality of a city has worked to the disdvantage of urban sensibilities, in funding, for example, or in the frequent generating of attitudes of condescension to more "proletarian" aesthetic needs. Concretely, in aesthetic terms, I find the refurbishing of Yankee Stadium as equal to the construction of Lincoln Center.

Before proceeding to the main theme of this essay, on the experience of urban time and space, one further methodological caution should be flagged. While it is simple to urge, as being essential to the development of an urban aesthetic, that we utilize a distinctively urban language, the undertaking is more difficult than appears at first reading. A basic obstacle emerges when we realize that the American mind is overrun with nature metaphors and with a deep bias for the superiority of nature experience over urban, artifactual experience. There resides behind this fundamental American attitude a complex cultural, social, and intellectual history,[10] and we repeat here a previously stated generalization about the significance of American nature nostalgia for the development of a new urban consciousness.

American urban man as been seduced by nature. By this I mean that at the deepest level of his consciousness urban man functions on behalf of nature metaphors, nature expectancies, and a nostalgia for an experience of nature which neither he nor his forbearers actually underwent. For contemporary America, the implications of this situation are significant. In the first place, we are blocked off from understanding the dramatic and necessary conflict with nature, which characterized American life until recently. Indeed, we have become naive and ahistorically sentimental about that conflict. Second, we have often failed to diagnose the limitations and strengths of our present urban context on its own terms, rather than as a function of the absence of nature.[11]

Given this historical attitude in America, it is not, therefore, coincidental that two of the more discussed writers of the last five years, Theodore Roszak [12] and Charles Reich,[13] have incorporated antiurban, antitechnological attitudes into their blueprints for an ameliorated future. If, by the most cautious of statistics, more than 80 percent of Americans live on 10 percent of the land, what are urban dwellers to think of the relevance of a strategy for the future which calls for the "Greening of America," let alone the belief that cities should be abandoned. Even in incomparably more profound thought than that found in the commentators on the counterculture, we find a deep disquiet and even hostility to the city as over against nature. There is a direct and acknowledged reflective line from Emerson, who "shuddered when he approached New York," [14] to Norman O. Brown, who writes, "hence a city is itself, like money, crystallized guilt." [15]

Returning to the contention that nature nostalgia presents an obstacle to the development of an urban aesthetic, we may complain here not only of the obvious innocence of the belief that cities can become humanized and aesthetized in direct relation to their ability to "green" the environment, as in vest-pocket parks or sporadic splurges of tree-planting, but also of the much deeper difficulties which attend any attempt to articulate urban experiences from such an alien social-psychological context. Let us be quite specific at this point. If an effective and genuine urban aesthetic depends on the utilization of distinctive urban metaphors,[16] we have to cut deeper than the unreflective use of urban argot like "street rat," "corner boy," "kiosk," or "pushcart."

I contend, rather, that virtually all of our language is contexted by our urban setting and has a different implicitness when so grasped, as, for example, in the language of urban time and urban space. Indeed, I would point even to the language of urban nature, for we experience rain differently in a street than in a field, while slush is urban snow. Kansas sunlight differs obviously from the sunlight which arches off great slabs of glass or darts furtively through alleys and plays on parapets. *Mutatis mutandis,* the affairs of nature vary with the cities in which they are experienced. More helpful, however, to our effort to develop the language of an urban aesthetic are the fundamental contexts of experienced time and space, in terms of which we communicate our needs, anticipations, and generalized sensibilities. Timed bodies, we touch and are touched by the things of space, human artifacts. What are the originating qualities of this process when it dwells within the matrix of urban experience? We turn first to urban space and urban artifact.

URBAN SPACE AND URBAN ARTIFACT

Perhaps it would be helpful to begin with a brief summary of the meaning of nature space, a theme developed elsewhere.[17] In American experience, nature space is endowed with the character of the sacred, for salvation, historically and religiously, was thought to take place on the land. This judgment is true not only of the American Puritans of the seventeenth century but of, for example, James Brooks, who in 1835 tells us that "God has promised us a renowned existence, if we will but deserve it. He speaks the promise in the sublimity of nature." [18] In our own time the ecologist Eliot Porter is fond of citing Thoreau, "In Wildness is the preservation of the world." [19]

Dwellers in nature space have a deep and abiding sense of the continuity of the body with the environment. Such continuity creates, in turn, a confidence in the fertility of nature, elsewhere if not here, which was so often expressed in the decision to relocate rather than to rehabilitate. In personal terms, the experience of vision is preeminently physical, spatial, expansive; it is characterized by horizontality and evaluated by reach. While the environment of nature space is extraordinarily rich in stimuli, much of it is hidden from the ordinary patterns of response.[20] The more dramatic stimuli of nature space function at a distance, cutting the intimacy of tactile response, which more often reflects the ambience of wonder and awe, rather than of control. Although man dwells more or less comfortably in nature space, the overarching awareness is that the environment

preceded us and will outlast us. We can say of our experience of
nature space that it involves body continuity, cultivation skills,
and a paradoxical alternation between the disparate responses
of awe and boredom.

Our experience of urban space has a dramatically different
point of origin. Urban space is not found space but chosen
space, managed space, especially in the creation of a multiplicity
of spaces within space. The most frequent way to manage space
so as to create urban space is to move from horizontal
experiencing to vertical experiencing. While it is not an absolute
requisite for an environment to qualify as a city, verticality,
however modest, is the seminal spatial characteristic of most
cities. This is particularly true of American cities [21] and,
interestingly, it is rapidly becoming true of the American
suburb.

By virtue of tall buildings we have created layers of livable or
singly usable space which can simultaneously realize the needs
of multiple members of people while yet insuring spatial
proximity and even providing for intimacy or solitude. We focus
here not only on the prepossessing verticality of the skyscraper
but also on the more subtle versions seen in subways, elevated
trains, underground arcades, overhead walkways, elevated expressways, and multilayered bridges. Urban space as vertical
space is radically pluralized on a single site. Urban place often
cannot be identified with a single piece of land or with a single
function. Although many people journey each day to the same
urban building, they would not think of themselves as going to
the same place. An urban place is a placeholder for a multiplicity of functions, so that the source of identification is less
likely to be "where" than it is to be "what goes on." The event
replaces the place as having priority in our consciousness; in the
words of Kevin Lynch, "what time is this place?" [22] Despite the
apparent heaviness of concrete and stone, large urban buildings
are gatherers and dispatchers of urban personal processes, as
much creatures of time as of space.[23]

Further intriguing implications emerge from the experiential
dominance of verticality in city life. It becomes obvious, for

example, that cities should be walked to be experienced fully, for automobiles are horizontally oriented, making rear vision hazardous and entirely blocking upward vision. In this regard we should lament the passing of the double-decker, open-top bus, for it so aptly symbolized the focus of urban visual action. A more important implication of verticality is that it develops in us a shorter vision-reach, yet one that is more intense and one that tends to interiorize itself. Stone, brick, concrete, metal, and building glass are not vision-penetrable. Buildings are clustered together, and the most we can see, boulevards excepted, is a block or so ahead. Our eyes confront and bounce off these massive, impermeable buildings, turning our vision back in to ourselves, feeding imaginative relations. In effect, our eyes rarely "run on," wandering over great distances as they do in nature space. Significantly, in order to do that in urban space, we must climb to the top of the tallest building and look out and over. The shrinkage of horizon and the impenetrability of urban objects combine to intensify the significance of what we do see in urban sight.

Urban life, therefore, leans more to the working of the imagination and to the development of often inarticulated but complex patterns of symbolization. Frequently dwarfed by immense artifacts, urban man has a constant sense of something hovering over him. The response to this huge presence is not quite that of awe, for it is, after all, man-made. Nonetheless, in an effort to assure human responsibility for this environment and to enhance participation in even its most prepossessing of architectural creations, urban man "blocks" out small pockets of lived space and endows them with deep symbolic meaning.[24] They, rather than the famous or honorific, are the true urban landmarks. We speak here of newsstands, tiny restaurants, bars, fruit stands, vendor spots, funeral parlors, playgrounds, lobbies, public bathrooms, and certain street corners. Such "landmarks"[25] are anonymous and are described only by their location, which is only proximate to giant buildings or under bridges or eccentrically present in the midst of an urban complex devoted to more formal endeavors. Symbolically, to

meet someone at the pretzel vendor outside of the World Trade
Center serves as a hopeful reminder that, no matter how
awesome, the urban environment shall serve man and not the
reverse.[26]

A further contributing factor to the urban introverting of
spatial sensibility is the role of artifactual light. While it is true
that we are the first century for whom night and darkness are
not synonymous, we tend to forget the intervening array of
shadows which exists beween night and light. From the neon
brightness of the center city, through the speckled light of the
great apartments, those dozing day buildings, and along the
bejeweled bridges, night light finally plays itself out on side
streets, doorways, alcoves, stairwells, and alleys, only to break
out again in the stark glare of the all-night cafeterias. The light
we choose is the mood we seek, as we alternate between the
disparate needs of intimacy and anonymity, heightened by the
range of options which bear down upon us in urban life.

The response to artifactual light is only one of the multiple
ways in which our bodies resonate to the urban environment.
We may point to a widely held prejudice, that, in contrast to our
experience in nature space, our bodies are fundamentally alien
to the textures of urban space, that is, to technological artifact,
media, and material. The sources of this prejudice are complex
and varied, but in the main they can be traced to the deeply felt
commitment we have to the superiority of the natural over the
artifactual. This distinction, in keeping with our propensity for
philosophical dualism, sets one category over against another;
from such a method flows a series of invidious comparisons, the
organic versus the inorganic, life versus death, natural versus
artificial, and real versus ersatz. In turn these distinctions spill
over into aesthetic judgments having curious but revealing
emphases. For the most part the natural is associated with
salutary endowments, such as soft, fertile, rich, and blooming.
Even the apparently negative in nature, such as the bleakness of
the moor or the mystery of the desert, is transformed in our
affectionate version. With technological artifacts, on the other
hand, the descriptive language is either prosaic, as in character-

izations like interesting, clean, necessary, functional, or it is negative, as in drab, shabby, dehumanizing, noxious; or again, if it is in praise, then it is not technology of which we speak but "art," as in a beautiful building, bridge, or monument. The operative assumption here is that we honor a hierarchy of favored materials, arranged according to their proximity to the organic, that is, the natural, as witness, in descending order, cloth, wood, stone, brick, aluminum, and plastic. In effect, we *render* our bodies alien to nonorganic materials.

Now this situation cuts deeper than it appears; it can only be attributed partially to nature nostalgia, or for that matter to a twentieth-century version of the ever present temptations of a Neoplatonic hierarchy of forms.[27] The underlying question is whether man can be as continuous with urban artifact as he is with the affairs and creatures of nature. I believe that such continuity is both possible and desirable. In that vein I would hold, for example, that the Mississippi River and the Bitterroot Mountain Range are no more or less "alive" than Wrigley Field or Scollay Square, for they all "live" off the endowments of human history, although the latter pair owe their existence to us as well. It has to be admitted that this sort of statement runs against the grain of long nurtured assumptions in common parlance. This is not to say that we do not feel affectionately about artifacts, but it is to say that we do not, in general, speak such affection. What is it, then, that prevents us from acknowledging, developing, and celebrating our intimate tactile relations with artifacts? Is it that we have defined our bodies too narrowly, too unimaginatively? Is it that we have underestimated the multiple ways in which we penetrate and are penetrated by the physical environment, taken in all of its artifactual manifestations, in contrast to the activites of nature? Is it that we have made too much of the eyes and not enough of the hands? [28]

No doubt each of these operative attitudes figures significantly in diluting our potential for developing richer relations with the world of artifacts. More extensive examination would most likely turn up other obstacles of similar character and importance. A continuation of such a list of obstacles does not, however, go to the heart of the matter; in a way somewhat reminiscent of the chiding given to Meno by Socrates, we should try to locate the fundamental source from which these obstacles proceed. In my judgment this search leads to a set of metaphysical assumptions which, despite more than two thousand years of turbulent philosophical history, still undergirds much of our consciousness. Put obviously and polemically, when discussing and analyzing the human condition we have not integrated adequately into the language of description and response the shift from a metaphysics of substance, thing, and place to one of process, relations, and field. Nor have we absorbed significantly the evolution of the meaning of inquiry from primarily that of "looking at" to primarily that of constituting. Whether the source be existential, phenomenological, depth psychological, or "future shock" jargon, abundant testimonies acknowledge and even take for granted this shift in consciousness. Yet, despite this flamboyant rhetoric of the twentieth century, celebrating, as it does, "Protean man" and the endless possibilities of human creativity, it remains painfully true that contemporary institutions still sustain themselves on a jejune anthropology, characterizing and "dealing" with man in terms of obviousness and sameness. Our options seem pared to a virtual Scylla and Charybdis: either to celebrate our own ordinary experience and be rendered idiosyncratic, or to "get with it" and thereby abandon the originating qualities of our own perceptions. We have many incisive diagnosticians [29] of this contemporary affront, and we do not have to accept their remedies in order to share their warning that, no matter how developed and confident in his self-consciousness, Protean man, self-making man, is not liberated if the world in which he lives is alien.

Expanding the phrase "works of art" to mean the making of artifacts, the making of the city, the making of the world, we may accept John Dewey's judgment that the "task is to restore continuity between the refined and intensified forms of experience that are works of art and the everyday events, doings and sufferings that are universally recognized to constitute experience." [30] While undertaking this task, we should take heart from the fact that the recent revolution in modern art and modern design has pressed upon us a new realization of the aesthetic dimensions of ordinary experience, especially the impact of new materials and techniques inseparable from technological artifacts, and consequently holds out new options for the enhancement of the human condition. But as we have indicated earlier, because of philosophical presuppositions of long-standing, the transformation of aesthetic sensibility with regard to artifacts has not received the wide endorsement necessary if it is to function within the fabric of common consciousness. On the contrary, such an awareness seems, ironically, to be the preserve of the devotees of high culture, for whom in general the urban artifact appears in museums, honored under the rubric of the latest art movement rather than as a living presence in their lives. This development is not what I had in mind when I echoed Dewey's call for celebration of the things of ordinary experience.[31] Perhaps even a brief excursion into the thought of William James and John Dewey will provide some direction for a richer philosophical inquiry into the meaning of artifact.

ARTIFACT AS RELATIONAL[32]

In 1951, at the age of ninety-two, John Dewey, in one of his last written comments, stated presciently the task of a contemporary philosophy of inquiry. "If I ever get the needed strength, I want to write on *knowing* as the way of behaving in which linguistic artifacts transact business with physical artifacts, tools, implements, apparatus, both kinds being planned for the purpose and rendering *inquiry* of necessity an *experimental transaction.*"[33] Such a relation-oriented or transactional epistemology depends on a very different metaphysical underpinning than that dominated by the notion of substance in the history of Western philosophy.

Thinkers as diverse as James, Bergson, Whitehead, and Dewey have emphasized the move from substance to process as the basic metaphor in a metaphysics. Of these, James's thought was the most decisive, for he offered both the first and the most explicit statement that the most fundamental characteristic of reality is not substance, essence, or thing but a relational manifold. James held that things were nothing "but special groups of sensible qualities, which happen practically or aesthetically to interest us, to which we therefore give substantive names, and which we exalt to this exclusive status of independence and dignity." [34] And later on he tells us that "there is no property *absolutely* essential to any one thing." [35]

Implicitly with James and explicitly with Dewey, inquiry becomes a transaction between the knowing self and the transactions carried on within the affairs of nature and culture. "Knowledge" then is a knowing of processes rather than of objects, the latter being definitional loci, pragmatically constructed to effect optimum management of the transactional relationship between awareness and decision. Put differently, James contends that "Perception and thinking are only there for behavior's sake." [36] Rather than being set over against the world, we find ourselves within its concatenated fabric, having to hook onto its flow so as not to be bypassed, while yet structuring a self-presence for purpose of evaluation and identity. Known as radical empiricism, this philosophical approach proceeds from what he refers to as "a statement of fact," [37] namely that we affectively experience relations equivalent to our experience of things. He writes, "If there be such things as feelings at all, *then so surely as relations between objects exist* in rerum natura, *so surely and more surely, do feelings exist to which these relations are known.*" [38]

Following his affirmation that consciousness is a relational stream, affectively continuous, and that objects are human constructs or perches, insulated within the stream by conceptual schema, James proceeds in a series of essays to an even more controversial assertion that matter and mind are not ontologically but only functionally or behaviorally different. Without our stopping here to comment on the difficulties involved in his underlying notion of "pure experience," [39] James, in denying an ontological division between matter and mind, points to the extraordinary quality of the human being who has experience in both ways, simultaneously. Just as there is no ontological dualism within the self, classically known as body and soul, so too there is no ontological dualism between the self and the world. Now the startling consequence of this view for the present context is that if man and the world are made of the same reality and only function differently, then the things of reality as made by man are ontologically similar. Artifacts, then, are human versions of the world acting as transactional mediations, representing human endeavor in relational accordance with the resistance and possibility endemic to both nature and culture.

So long as artifacts remained as obvious "utiles," enhancing human activity by virtue of increased leverage, strength, durability, or accessibility, the man-world polarity held firm as an exhaustive description. We can refer to this centuries-long tradition in terms of the human use of tools. Regarded for the most part as necessities, unless occasionally bestowed with something more by the aesthetic criteria of specific cultures, as, for example, culinary utensils, the presence of such artifacts rarely gave rise to philosophical discussions. Perhaps this is due in part to the fact that Western philosophy has been concerned far more with the eyes than with the hands and speaks of vision rather than of touch. It is noteworthy that the two most remarkable inventions of the early modern period, the telescope (1590) and the microscope (1608), both have to do with vision. And despite the enthusiastic response to the marvels revealed by these super-eyes, the epistemology remained the same, that is, man the viewer "unhiding" layers and outer reaches of the external world. Until the twentieth century it did not occur to us to realize that not only did we see "more" but that the viewer became profoundly transformed at the level of consciousness. If, as I believe, Kant is correct in his assertion that consciousness informs the world "sensuously," prior to its being known specifically, then transformations of consciousness, are, in effect, transformations of the world. Taking artifacts as "relatings" in the Jamesian sense gives us the history of artifact as a major strand in the history of the formulation of the meaning of the world.

The significance of James's rational metaphysics for an understanding of artifact becomes much clearer when we cite the move from industrial, machine-oriented technology to electronic technology which has occurred within the past century, and which is essential to' contemporary urban life. Electronic technological artifacts such as the telephone, radio, television, and computer terminals are "things" in the Jamesian sense, that is, perches or gathering places for ongoing relational processes. As perches they exist in time and space, classically understood relative to motion and dimension, but as activities they defy those limitations and create for us entirely novel sense relations to the world. What James regarded as the fringe of consciousness, or the wider range of consciousness, becomes concretized by the presence of electronic media, with Telstar performing as a global cerebral cortex.

At this point in our discussion we should remind ourselves of the problem which led to this brief exploration of a different philosophical approach, that is, the alleged inferiority of man's relationship to artifacts when contrasted with his relationship to nature. Put differently, the point at issue is whether human artifacts, as they come to resemble less and less the natural environment as experienced originally, are an alienating factor in human life. I have referred here to the evolution from the age of tools to the age of the machine, the combustion engine, and on to highly novel contemporary forms such as electronic media and the computer. My position is that this development of technology, far from being alienating, is in fact the most distinctively human activity, offering an originating aesthetic quality to our lives.[40] The significance of the natural environment as "natural" has been affirmed by contrast with the artifactual environment. It is, then, not at all surprising that, in our age of technological domination of the environment, a tremendous increase in the concern for the quality of the natural environment should come to the fore, although such concern should not lead to the now frequent disparaging of the artifactual environment. While it is a truism that man's history is inseparable from nature, it does not follow that man's history is explicable solely or even mainly in terms of nature. Furthermore, the uniqueness of the human organism, and of the human endeavor could never be experienced if an absolute continuity of man with the affairs of nature were honored. In my judgment, technological artifacts served not only to manage nature as problem-solving devices but served also to distance man from nature, thereby allowing the development of human history within a context which was *sui generis.* The most dramatic version of that uniquely human context was the creation of the supreme artifact thus far, the city, with which, we contend, our bodies are potentially as intimate as they are with the affairs of nature.

URBAN TIME

Having considered in some detail the experiencing of urban space and artifact as a context for human life, we turn now to a beginning analysis of some characteristics of urban time. Once again we must forgo a full discussion of the contrasting experience of nature time, offering only some contentions gleaned from previous consideration. Nature time can be described as fat time, running in seasons, even in years and decades. To a young city boy the prognostications of the *Farmer's Almanac* were as strange and alien as if they were made for a millennium hence. Nature times gives room to regroup, to reassess, featuring a pace and a rhythm tuned to the long-standing, even ancient responsive habits of our bodies. Feeding off the confidence in the regenerative powers of nature, time is regarded as realizing, liberating, a source of growth.[41] The rhythm of nature time shares with nature space a sense of expansiveness such that in nature we believe that we "have time" and that "in time" we too shall be regenerated. As exemplified by the extraordinary journey of the nineteenth-century Mormons, their "trek," a distinctive nature phenomenon, points to salvation "in time." Space is the context for "in time," both taken as a long period of time, walking from Nauvoo, Illinois, to the Great Salt Lake, Utah, and being saved "in the nick of time." In nature time, undergoing, doing, and reflection function simultaneously, thereby providing little need for "high culture," chunks of reflection taken out of the flow of experience. Perhaps the most obvious way to describe nature time is to call it baseball time, referring to a game in which the clock technically plays no role and which conceivably could last to infinity, tied to the end.

By contrast, urban time is thin time, tense, transparent, yielding no place to hide. Urban time is clock time, jagged, self-announcing time, bearing in on us from a variety of mediated sources, so often omnipresent and obtrusive that many people refuse to wear watches in an effort to ward off its domination. Why are clocks when worn on our bodies called watches? The first meaning of "watch" was to go without sleep, that is, to beat nature. Is the urban "watch" to "watch" time passing or is it to make sure that no one steals our time, as when we hoard time by saying that we have no time?

Clock time, like clock games, carries with it the threat of sudden death, an increasing urban phenomenon. But sudden death can be averted with but "seconds" to go. Urban time is "second" time, which may very well mean second chance or surprise time. We now have clocks which tell time in hundredths and even thousandths of seconds, reminding us how much faster we must go if we are not to be obsoleted, left behind, for cities have little patience with the past. Some people in the urban environment like to think that they live by nature time, but this assumption is self-deceptive, for such claims are relative only to the frantic urban pace. Clock time, after all, overrides nature time, as, for example, when at one second after midnight, in the pitch dark, your radio announcer says good morning and describes the events of your life that day as having happened yesterday.[42]

Beneath this somewhat anecdotal discussion of urban time there reside some significant implications. The rapid pace of urban time radically transforms the experience of our bodies, which often seem to lag behind. The network of communication media, which blankets a city like a giant octopus, constantly tunes us in to sensorially multiple experience, even if vicariously undergone. In a broad sense, when the setting is urban we experience less identity in spatial terms than proximity to events; rather than having a place, we identify ourselves relative to events taking place. In a city, when giving directions, the question as to "how long it will take" is not answered by the spatial distance traversed; rather the allotted time is a function of potential interventions, for the time of city-space is activity measured. Our imagination, fed at all times by the messaging of electronic intrusions,[43] races far ahead of our body, which we often claim to drag around. Yet, despite the pace, the apparent garrulousness and noise, urban life is extraordinarily introspective, enabling us to carve out inner redoubts of personal space. The urban person must protect himself against the rampaging activity of time, which dismantles our environment with alarming speed. It is a cliché that you can't go home again, for the spiritual and psychological experiences of childhood are unrepeatable; but further, for one seeking his urban childhood there is added the almost inevitable burden of having his physical environment obliterated. The urban past is notoriously unstable, so that in urban experience we often outlive our environment.

Just as the prepossessing verticality of urban space encourages us to endow body-scale places as experiential landmarks, so too in the rush of urban time is it necessary to further endow such loci with the ability to act as functional clots in the flow of time, in short, to stop time for a time. In urban argot we call this "hanging out," and we might reflect on how it differs from a new version, oriented toward nature and called "dropping out."

The verticality of urban space turns vision inward, and the speed of urban time revs up our capacity for multiple experiences, thereby intensifying the need for inner personal space to play out the experiences subsequently in our own "good" time. More often than is supposed, urban man does attain management of his inner personal space, and, contrary to the offensive cliché of antiurban critics, anonymity is *not* a major urban problem. As a matter of fact, urban life is crisscrossed with rich interpersonal relations, brought about by the extraordinary shortcuts to interpersonal intimacy which flourish in the type of situation we have been describing, namely, a welter of experiences, rapidly undergone, yet transacted by the ability of the person to impact some of them in both space and time and convert them to sources of emotional nutrition. Having cut to a bare minimum the time-span required to forge urban interpersonal relationships, in general one does not expect that longevity be a significant quality of these relationships. The pace of urban time, coupled with the people density of urban space, churns up tremendous possibilities for interpersonal life, for the multiplicity of relations widens considerably the range and quality of the intersections and transactions operative in our daily lives. As we see it, then, the major problem in urban life centers not in the relations between persons but rather in the relations of persons to the urban environment and in the studied institutional insensitivity to the aesthetic qualities germane to the processes of urban space and urban time.[44]

If we come full circle and remind ourselves of the need for urban consciousness-raising, a warning is in order. The healing and amelioration of the contemporary American city will be stymied if our efforts betray an ignorance or insensitivity to the experiential demands of the original qualities of being human in urban space and in urban time. As in most human situations, the caution of William James is relevant here:

Woe to him whose beliefs play fast and loose with the order which realities follow in his experience. They will lead him nowhere or else make false connexions.[45]

NOTES

1. Paolo Soleri, *The Arcology of Paolo Soleri* (New York: Anchor Books, 1973), p. xv.
2. One recent effort in this behalf has been made by A. K. Bierman, *The Philosophy of Urban Existence* (Athens: Ohio

University Press, 1973). It is highly idiosyncratic and is more a sociology of persons than an analysis of cities.

3. Cf. Herbert Marcuse, "Love Mystified: A Critique of Norman O. Brown," and "A Reply to Herbert Marcuse by Norman O. Brown," *Negations* (Boston: Beacon Press, 1969), pp. 227-247.

4. For two examples of urban jeremiads cf. Mitchell Gordon, *Sick Cities* (Baltimore: Penguin Books, 1965), and Nathan Glazer, ed., *Cities in Trouble* (Chicago: Quadrangle Books, 1970).

5. A recent verbal contention from some who are responsible for the care of urban parks is of interest here. Vandalism unanswered begets further vandalism, whereas vandalism to which there is an immediate response of repair and renewal tends to cure.

6. For the significance of "modern art" in this "turning" cf. John J. McDermott, "Deprivation and Celebration: Suggestions for an Aesthetic Ecology," *New Essays in Phenomenology,* ed. James Edie (Chicago: Quadrangle Books, 1969), pp. 116-130.

7. We add "feel" to that list of words begun by William James and supplemented by John Dewey, namely, experience, life, and history, as words which are double-barreled, connoting that which we do as well as that which we undergo. To "feel about" is not only to have feelings but also to touch, as when one goes on hands and knees or follows sounds and smells—that is, to be up and around. Cf. John Dewey, *Experience and Nature* (LaSalle: Open Court, 1929), p. 10.

8. For a discussion of the gap between how we actually feel about our environment and how we are assumed to feel, cf. John J. McDermott, "Feeling as Insight: The Affective Dimension in Social Diagnosis," *Hippocrates Revisited,* ed. R. J. Bulger (New York: Medcom Press, 1973), pp. 166-80.

9. Grady Clay, *Close-up—How to Read the American City* (New York: Praeger, 1973), p. 18.

10. Cf. e.g., Morton and Lucia White, *The Intellectual Versus the City* (Cambridge: Harvard University Press, 1962).

11. John J. McDermott, "Nature Nostalgia and the City: An American Dilemma," *The Family, Communes, and Utopian Societies,* ed. S. Te Selle (New York: Harper Torchbooks, 1972), p. 2. An interesting dimension of American nature nostalgia was mentioned in conversation by Judah Stampfer, who pointed out that, contrary to Europe and most of the rest of the world, American military history took place on the land, rarely and less importantly in and around cities.

12. Theodore Roszak, *The Making of a Counter-Culture* (New York: Anchor Books, 1969), and *Where the Wasteland Ends* (New York: Anchor Books, 1973).

13. Charles Reich, *The Greening of America* (New York: Random House, 1970).

14. Cited in White, *op. cit.,* p. 35.

15. Norman O. Brown, *Life Against Death* (New York: Random House, 1959), p. 283. In response to a question about contemporary American cities, Brown stated that in his judgment an urban Armageddon had already taken place and that he wrote for the fleeing remnant.

16. We ask of metaphor something more than its technical, dictionary meaning. Rather we have in mind the version of George Steiner, for whom "Metaphor ignites a new arc of perceptive energy. It relates hitherto unrelated areas of experience." Cf. "The Language Animal." *Encounter* (August 1969), p. 11 (cited in Clay, *op. cit.,* p. 21).

17. Cf. John J. McDermott, "Nature Nostalgia," pp. 2-11.

18. Cited in Perry Miller, "The Romantic Dilemma in American Nationalism and the Concept of Nature," *Nature's Nation* (Cambridge: Harvard University Press, 1967), p. 201.

19. Eliot Porter, *In Wildness Is the Preservation of the World* (San Francisco: Sierra Club, 1962).

20. Germane to our discussion is the remark of Peter Farb: "If

it were possible to X-ray a patch of soil to a depth of a few feet, it would look very much like a busy intersection in a city, for the soil is a great concourse of throngs which jostle through the particles." *The Living Earth* (New York: Harper Colophon Books, 1968), p. 51.

21. Los Angeles is often cited as an exception to this generalization. Strictly speaking it is not, for Los Angeles has more tall buildings than most other American cities. It is true, however, that Los Angeles conceived itself in radically different terms than other American cities by adopting a horizontal rather than a vertical approach overall, and therefore endowed roads, automobiles, spatial proximity, and distance with entirely different meanings than traditional urban environments. If it is true that nature and open land are the sources of a distinctive American ethos, then Los Angeles is the most distinctive urban rendition of America.

22. Cf. Kevin Lynch, *What Time Is This Place?* (Cambridge: M.I.T. Press, 1972).

23. Perhaps urban buildings share the double meaning of an urban "pad," namely, a place to repose and a place from which one can launch.

24. A city "block" is a miniature world. The best of the recent efforts to capture its peculiar life-rhythms is the photographic essay of Herb Goro, *The Block* (New York: Vintage Books, 1970).

25. Kevin Lynch writes that "a landmark is not necessarily a large object. Its location is crucial: if large or tall, the spatial setting must allow it to be seen; if small, there are certain zones that receive more perpetual attention than others: floor surfaces, or nearby facades at a slightly below eye-level." *The Image of the City* (Cambridge: M.I.T. Press, 1960), p. 101.

26. An earlier generation of New Yorkers was more self-conscious about this need, choosing to meet, quite literally, under the clock at the Biltmore Hotel.

27. Plotinus *redivivus*, stated simply and with regard to our problem, comes to this: as superior is to inferior, so is one to many. *Nous* to body and "body to artifact." It is relevant to think here of the computer as the disembodying of artifact, in much the way mathematics purifies the visible world in a Platonic pedagogy.

28. Herbert Schneider reports John Dewey as having said: "I think this whole problem of understanding should be approached not from the point of view of the eyes, but from the point of view of the hands. It's what we grasp that matters." Cf. Corliss Lamont, ed., *Dialogue on John Dewey* (New York: Horizon Press, 1959), p. 95.

29. Among others, we have in mind here the work of Herbert Marcuse, N.O. Brown, Ronald Laing, and the late lamented Ernest Becker.

30. John Dewey, *Art as Experience* (New York: Capricorn Books, 1958) (1934), p. 3.

31. Cf. Dewey, *Art as Experience*, p. 11.

32. Material in this section is taken from two public lectures, (a) "A Metaphysics of Relations: William James's Anticipation of Contemporary Experience," delivered at the James Seminar held at Winterthur, Switzerland, in 1973 and (b) "Human Existence and Human Violence," delivered at the Fifteenth World Congress of Philosophy held at Varna, Bulgaria, in 1973.

33. *John Dewey and Arthur F. Bentley, A Philosophical Correspondence*, eds. Sidney Ratner and Jules Altman (New Brunswick: Rutgers University Press, 1964), p. 646.

34. William James, *The Principles of Psychology*, vol. I (New York: Henry Holt and Co., 1890), p. 285.

35. James, *Principles*, II, p. 333.

36. William James, "Reflex Action and Theism," *The Will to Believe* (New York: Longmans, Green and Co., 1897), p. 114.

37. For James's statements as to the meaning of radical empiricism and his "radically empirical" version of classic

philosophical problems, cf. John J. McDermott, ed., *The Writings of William James* (New York: Random House, 1967), pp. 134-310.

38. James, "The Stream of Thought," *Writings*, p. 38.

39. Cf. A. J. Ayer, *The Origins of Pragmatism* (San Francisco: Freeman, Cooper and Co., 1968), pp. 288-93.

40. Of an escalating number of efforts to show the aesthetic import of artifacts, cf. Sterling McIlhany, *Art as Design: Design as Art* (New York: Van Nostrand-Reinhold Co., 1970), and the "Vision and Value" series edited by Gyorgy Kepes, especially the volumes entitled *The Man-Made Object* and *Arts of the Environment*. A psychological litmus paper test of artifact sensibility would take this form: When you hear the word "crane," do you think of a pond or of a building?

41. Nature time is not always kind and regenerative, as the Dakota sod-farmers of the nineteenth century and the Okies of the twentieth century discovered. A recent and extraordinarily powerful and original version of the systematic madness often found in nature time is the photographic essay by Michael Lesy, *Wisconsin Death Trip* (New York: Pantheon, 1973). The setting is rural Wisconsin from 1895 to 1900 and the common experience is laced with misery and affliction.

42. Cf. Robert Sommer, *Design Awareness* (San Francisco: Rinehart Press, 1972), p. 66. In his chapter on "Space-Time," Sommer tells us that "a San Francisco radio station announces the exact time 932 times a week."

43. Surveying big city newspapers, one finds that the screeching headlines of the first edition frequently do not merit even a paragraph in the last editions. Are these instances references to pseudo-events, or is it the pace?

44. We refer here not only to the erosion of aesthetic quality in the urban environment, symbolized by the faceless projects of the days of urban renewal, but to the more subtle and equally important fact that we fail to articulate, let alone

sanction, the still existing aesthetically rich experiences of city life. The development of such an articulation is equivalent to an urban pedagogy. For an important step in this direction, cf. Jonathan Freedman, *Crowding and Behavior* (New York: Viking Press, 1975).

45. James, *Writings,* p. 205.

INDEX OF NAMES

About the Author

John J. McDermott is Distinguished Professor of Philosophy, Abell Professor of Liberal Arts and Head of Humanities in Medicine at Texas A&M University. He is the editor of five volumes of scholarly editions of the writings of William James, Josiah Royce and John Dewey, published by the University of Chicago Press. He is the editor of *A Cultural Introduction to Philosophy,* Volume I, *From Antiquity to Descartes,* published by Alfred Knopf and the author of *Streams of Experience: Reflections on the History and Philosophy of American Culture,* published by The University of Massachusetts Press, as well as many essays in the fields of education, medicine, architecture, social politics, and the history of philosophy. Professor McDermott has lectured extensively in America, Europe and the Far East. He has received many teaching awards, including the National E. Harris Harbison Award for Gifted Teaching.